MÉLIÈS BOOTS

Méliès Boots

Footwear and Film Manufacturing in
Second Industrial Revolution Paris

Matthew Solomon

UNIVERSITY OF MICHIGAN PRESS

ANN ARBOR

For questions or permissions, please contact um.press.perms@umich.edu

Published in the United States of America by the University of Michigan Press
Printed and bound by CPI Group (UK) Ltd, Croydon, CR0 4YY
Open access e-book first published April 2022;
Additional formats first published August 2022

A CIP catalog record for this book is available from the British Library.
Library of Congress Cataloging-in-Publication data has been applied for.
ISBN 978-0-472-05558-6 (paper : alk. paper)
ISBN 978-0-472-90295-8 (open access ebook)

DOI: https://doi.org/10.3998/mpub.12196353

The University of Michigan Press's open access publishing program is made possible
thanks to additional funding from the University of Michigan Office of the Provost
and the generous support of contributing libraries.

Cover image: Méliès bottines, Collection of the Bata Shoe Museum,
copyright Bata Shoe Museum, Toronto

for Dorothy

diable aux yeux verts

CONTENTS

Digital materials related to this title can be found on the Fulcrum platform via the following citable URL: https://doi.org/10.3998/mpub.12196353

ACKNOWLEDGMENTS

My most heartfelt thanks and appreciation go to my colleague Richard Abel, whose generosity and celerity in reading draft chapters bolstered and encouraged me in the most important of ways. From the beginning, his feedback has helped immeasurably in keeping the writing of this book on track. *The Ciné Goes to Town*, *The Red Rooster Scare*, and *French Film Theory and Criticism* continue to be the model of thoroughness, accuracy, and fully bilingual engagement to which I have always aspired. What a tremendous privilege it has been to have known Richard since 1994 and to have worked with him since 2011.

I cannot imagine an editor more suited to this book or the disposition of its author than Sara Cohen, who helped *Méliès Boots* become a material reality. She combined unwavering support with perceptive criticism and keen attention to argument and readability. Sara has made working with the University of Michigan Press an absolute dream. If I could somehow obtain a pair of Méliès *bottines*, I hope they would fit her. Additional editorial and publishing support was capably provided by Anna Pohlod, Lisa Stallings, and Sherondra Thedford.

Since we met in 2011, Anne-Marie Malthête-Quévrain has been a phenomenal resource for my research. Conversations in Cerisy, Paris, and Blois, and our many bilingual email exchanges have taught me much about Méliès that cannot be found in print. Her assistance has been tireless, including helping me compile a complete file of *Les Amis de Georges Méliès*, *Cinémathèque Méliès*, and *Cinémathèque Méliès Lettre d'information*, which have been essential sources. Her cousin Marie-Hélène Lehérissey has been similarly supportive and generous. Our conversations in Cerisy and Ann Arbor (with Lawrence Lehérissey) and our lively email exchanges are among my favorite memories of many pleasant recollections of working on this book. Malthête-Quévrain's younger brothers Avraham Malthête and Jacques Malthête both patiently and generously responded to my queries. Speaking with the late Madeleine Malthête-Méliès in Cerisy in 2011 and in Paris in 2015 was inspiring and unforgettable.

The approach I eventually found for this book was belatedly inspired by two late scholars who were profound personal and intellectual influences on me at UCLA during the 1990s: George F. Custen, who introduced me to the study of early cinema and whose research on material culture I assisted, and Peter Wollen, whose graduate seminar on film and fashion I was fortunate to take. Another of my amazing professors at UCLA, Janet Bergstrom, taught me about archival research and showed me how much can be learned from oral histories; she has been an enthusiastic supporter of this and all of my other projects. Yet another favorite UCLA professor, Vivian Sobchack, urged me to think more creatively about historical research and writing and provided me with a model for interrogating objects in film through her own work; she came up with the title for the book during a delightful breakfast in Seattle in 2019. I owe another debt to Clifford E. Clark Jr. of Carleton College, who helped me think like a historian and introduced me to the work of Bill Brown. Jennifer Chapman's still life photographs spurred my first forays into "thing theory," and her weaving has been a continual reminder of cinema's analogies with fiber arts and an ongoing demonstration of what can be fabricated with daily effort. Conversing with her has helped me think differently and her effect on my thoughts is evident throughout this book. I am also grateful for the stimulating and delightful companionship of our three children: Charlie, Margot, and Dorothy. This book is dedicated to Dorothy, the youngest. Often, seeing the twinkle in her eyes was all that I needed to keep writing. Like Margot and me, she loves shoes.

Colleagues who have given me feedback, encouragement, and material assistance of various kinds are many. I am extraordinarily grateful to Phil Hallman, Film Studies field librarian and co-editor *extraordinaire*, who made sure I always had access to the materials I needed to write this book when I needed them. He has gone far "above and beyond the call of duty" as a colleague and as a friend on occasions too numerous to count. Caryl Flinn provided an astute and supportive reading of the manuscript that put me on a path to successful revisions. The manuscript was improved by the careful comments of two incredibly constructive and perceptive anonymous peer reviewers.

Overcoming the challenges of writing during a pandemic would likely not have been possible without sustaining connections with great friends Erich Dietrich, David Gerstner, Murray Pomerance, Timothy Webb, and Matt Yockey. Zoom calls with Joe Culpepper were motivating and thought-provoking. The sincere interest and infectious good humor of Marcus Kreitzer and Joey Pecoraro provided periodic and much-needed boosts to my morale. Others whose supportive words bolstered me in my efforts were Giorgio Bertellini, Hugh Cohen, Kelley Conway, Vincent Longo, and Joshua Schulze. Special thanks to *mes amis dans l'équipe de rêve*, Jean-Pierre Sirois-Trahan and Martin Barnier, and honorary team captain Mireille Berton. Others with whom I recall exchanging ideas and resources relative to this project not previously mentioned include Paolo Cherchi Usai, Roland Cosandey, Nico de Klerk, Victoria Duckett, Mary Francis, Pascal Friaut, Kathryn Fuller-Seeley, Doron Galili, André Gaudreault, Philippe Gauthier, the late Moe Goldy, Emily Goodrich, Laurent Guido, Tom Gunning, the late Paul Hammond, Michèle Hannoosh, Dan Herbert, Antonio Hidalgo, Nathan Holmes, Erkki Huhtamo, Michel Juignet, Frank Kessler, Mark Kligerman, Jean-Marc Larrue, Murray Leeder, Sabine Lenk, Stuart Liebman, Martin Loiperdinger, Laurent Mannoni, David Mayer, Helen Day-Mayer, Didier Moreau, Priska Morrissey, Sheila Murphy, Charles Musser, James Naremore, Matt Noble-Olson, Katy Peplin, James Pepper, Wyatt Phillips, Joey Picciotto, Giusy Pisano, Serge Plantureux, Katharina Rein, Jeff Rosenheim, Brian Selznick, the late Paul Spehr, Drake Stutesman, Antoine Traisnel, Stéphane Tralongo, Yuri Tsivian, Julie Turnock, Frank Uhle, Stephen Waldow, Gwendolyn Waltz, Ya Wen, Tami Williams, Colin Williamson, Cindy Wong, Damon Young, Joshua Yumibe, and Liza Zusman.

At the University of Michigan, I benefited from great research by doctoral students Feroz Hassan and Dimitrios Pavlounis, and countless hours of work by undergraduate researchers Rose Albayat, Olivier Bahizi, Sophia Davidson, Raymond de Simone, Anna Do, Salwa Ibrahim, Claudia Lahr, Jennifer Lipsmeier Guy, Liam Meisner-Driscoll, Alexandra Niforos, Bo Pang, Allison Reck, and Ryan Schaller. Since I met him in 2018, Olivier has consistently inspired me with his resourcefulness as a researcher and his mellifluous French, which both smoothed over many rough patches in the research and writing process. Jennifer Lipsmeier Guy helped prepare the book for publication and directed me to several sources I had not found myself. For their very generous help illustrating the book, I am grateful to Anne-Marie Malthête-Quévrain of the Cinémathèque Méliès; David Pfluger of Basel, Switzerland; Elizabeth Semmelhack and Suzanne Peterson of the Bata Shoe Museum; Myriam Chihab of the Musée du Compagnonnage; and Laurent Mannoni and Véronique Chauvet of the Cinémathèque Française.

This project received generous financial and institutional support from the University of Michigan. The Undergraduate Research Opportunity Program (UROP) funded and supported close to a dozen students who were involved in the "Méliès and the Modern World" project (identified above by name); Sandy Gregerman, Luciana Nemtanu, and Michelle Ferrez helped make this possible. I also benefited from a Michigan Humanities Award, a UMOR Research Award, an LSA Scholarship/Research Grant, a Rackham Spring/Summer Research Grant, and the Associate Professor Support Fund. I am thankful for the endorsements of department chairs Yeidy Rivero and Markus Nornes, and for the generosity of associate deans Alexandra Stern and Derek Collins, and Dean Anne Curzan. A Provost's Fellowship from the College of Staten Island supported me in conducting research on the Incohérents and nineteenth-century French caricature in 2010. Since joining the Michigan faculty in 2011, I have been the continual beneficiary of capable administrative support from Marga Schuhwerk-Hampel, Mary Lou Chlipala, Carrie Moore, and, more recently, Lisa Rohde-Barbeau in the Department of Film, Television, and Media (formerly the Department of Screen Arts and Cultures) and of technological assistance from Keon Ray and his colleagues in LSA Technological Services (formerly LSA IT).

Materializing Méliès

> The past is hidden somewhere outside the realm, beyond the reach
> of the intellect, in some material object (in the sensation which that
> material object will give us) of which we have no inkling. And it
> depends on chance whether or not we come upon this object before
> we ourselves must die.
>
> —Marcel Proust, *In Search of Lost Time*, vol. 1, *Swann's Way*,
> trans. C. K. Scott Moncrieff, 59–60

MARIE-GEORGES-JEAN MÉLIÈS (1861–1938), WHO was called Georges Méliès, was the most accomplished filmmaker of cinema's first decade, and one of its most prolific. (Hereafter, I refer to him by his surname only, unlike other members of the Méliès family.) When I set out to write a book about Méliès, I imagined it as a comprehensive study of the entirety of Méliès' oeuvre: *all* of his films, extant and nonextant (some 520 in all), along with his work as a visual, graphic, and performing artist—the latter spanning a long career directing the Théâtre Robert-Houdin and the Théâtre des Variétés Artistiques. But, I quickly came to the same conclusion Paolo Cherchi Usai had reached in 1991 when he wrote, "despite the imposing number of writings published on Méliès in the last fifteen years—the task of writing a comprehensive ('definitive'?) survey of the life and art of Georges Méliès is, all in all, still a prohibitive one."[1] So, I redirected my research from the "texts" of the numerous films, images, objects, and performances Méliès created to the historical contexts in which they were made. I soon realized the Second Industrial Revolution comprised perhaps the most important historical context of all. The First Industrial Revolution roughly spanned the years from 1760 to 1830, with the advent of steam power, mechanization, and development of the factory system. Some fifty years later, economic and business historians like François Caron and Michael Stephen Smith insist, there was a Second Industrial Revolution, beginning around 1880. The Second Industrial Revolution accelerated industrialization through new technologies powered by electricity and the internal combustion engine along with industrial applications of modern organic chemistry.[2] Just as the First Industrial Revolution depended not only on technologies like the cotton gin and power loom as well as on unremunerated plantation slave labor, so too was the Second Industrial Revolution similarly dependent on a bedrock of exploited labor and rapaciously plundered natural environments, many in colonized settings.

Industrial fashion was one significant category of products that emerged during the Second Industrial Revolution. A number of thinkers have fittingly understood fashion as a crucial harbinger and index of modernity. As summarized by Ulrich Lehmann, "Fashion is the supreme expression of the contemporary spirit. It changes constantly and remains necessarily incomplete; it is transitory, mobile, and fragmentary. This quality ties it in with the pace and rhythm of modern life."[3] Taking cues from Charles Baudelaire, Stéphane Mallarme, and Walter Benjamin, Lehmann adds,

> The view of sartorial fashion as the pacesetter and indicator of stylistic developments within the nineteenth and early twentieth century seemed possible only in Paris. The economic circumstances that created an affluent bourgeois class with its conspicuous consumption [. . .] provided the backdrop for the rise of haute couture. This craft, which soon developed into an industry [. . .] became the paradigm for a society dependent on both industrial production and aestheticized diversion.[4]

This was the story of the Méliès family's successful footwear manufacturing business and the historical context for the beginnings of Méliès' work as a cultural producer, which centered on Paris—the "capital of the nineteenth century" for Benjamin and the "capital of modernity," as David Harvey evocatively puts it.[5]

Méliès described his father Jean-Louis Stanislas Méliès, called Jean-Louis Méliès, as "a large industrial mass manufacturer of de luxe shoes."[6] While Méliès used the word *chaussures* (shoes) to describe the products of the family business, when Méliès worked there during the 1880s (shortly after it was legally incorporated as the Société Méliès), the company in fact manufactured both shoes *and* boots, which comprised an important distinction for nineteenth-century French cobblers, many of whom only made shoes. Along with men's and women's shoes, the Société Méliès produced boots for both men and women in a factory that employed one hundred and fifty workers.[7]

Méliès' direct involvement in the French footwear industry ended during the two years between July 1886, when he sold his share of the Société Méliès to his two older brothers Henri Méliès and Gaston Méliès, and July 1888, when he used some of the funds from this sale to purchase the exhibition rights to the Théâtre Robert-Houdin, one of the most renowned magic theaters in the world, which he directed for close to forty subsequent years.[8] Concurrent with his initial work in magic theater, Méliès launched a short-lived career as a political cartoonist for *La Griffe*, the caricature journal published by his cousin Adolphe Méliès, which ran for six months in 1889–1890. Six years later, Méliès began screening films at the Théâtre Robert-Houdin. From 1896 to 1913, Méliès and his collaborators produced numerous films in two studios constructed early in 1897 and late in 1907, respectively, on family property just outside of Paris in Montreuil-sous-bois (hereafter Montreuil), which Jean-Louis Méliès had purchased in 1860, one year before Méliès' birth. All of this activity was funded by the aggregate proceeds realized from the sales of countless pairs of boots and shoes.

These biographical and economic circumstances should not be underestimated. Indeed, the Méliès family's prosperity and the privilege their youngest child enjoyed were necessary preconditions for his later achievements as a theater director and filmmaker. Readers of Méliès' biography, authored by his granddaughter Madeleine Malthête-Méliès (now finally available in English translation), will realize that had Méliès not liquidated and reinvested his share of his family's footwear manufacturing business—had he instead taken a leadership role in the Société Méliès like his two older brothers—he certainly would not have had either the resources or the time to direct a magic theater or create film production studios.[9] Generational wealth derived from the sale of footwear made Méliès' work in theater and film possible.

Most accounts of Méliès generally gloss over his career in footwear manufacturing in a few sentences, but it was the success of the Méliès brand of boots and shoes that assured Méliès' place in life and made his subsequent career in the performing arts possible. Moreover, I argue, footwear manufacturing actually served as a consequential beginning to Méliès' later work as a filmmaker. This book proposes an affinity between footwear and film manufacturing, showing how the years Méliès spent in the fashion industry were not an unrelated prelude to a subsequent career in theater and film but relevant preparation for a career oriented toward producing de luxe retail commodities. Both footwear and film manufacturing were material practices that relied on industrially produced raw materials, modern systems of infrastructure, and artisanal skills aided by the latest machinery. Films were made to be projected and footwear to be worn, of course, but both types of commodities were manufactured from large quantities of plant and animal matter. Méliès himself wrote very little about the years he spent in footwear manufacturing, but *Méliès Boots* treats fashion as a master metaphor for Méliès' work.[10]

While the juxtaposition of films and footwear might seem counterintuitive (and thus understandably overlooked in previous studies of Méliès), it reminds us of the materiality of cinema and the materiality of the production, distribution, and exhibition of early films. It also suggests new contexts for early cinema while pointing to other kinds of objects and other kinds of practices that have fallen largely outside the purview of previous film and media scholars. Further, *Méliès Boots* argues that the 1880s multimedia avant-garde who called themselves "Incohérents" represent a compelling early modernism that can be used to reframe how we think about Méliès and perhaps early cinema as well. Although dividing historical time into ten-year segments is historiographically suspect, I use that shorthand throughout the book, as did one of the most important chroniclers of the Paris cultural milieu that formed around the Incohérents, Émile Goudeau, who titled his book *Dix ans de bohème*.[11] The title *Méliès Boots* is itself an homage to the Incohérents, whose artworks were deliberately ephemeral and often titled to disrupt expectations and create verbal riddles through wordplay. In England in 1884 (when Méliès was working in fashion in London), Méliès footwear was advertised in English with the possessive as "Méliès' Boots."[12] But, here I omit the apostrophe to emphasize the brand name.

Incohérent Modernity

Several artworks by the Incohérents involved footwear, including the 1882 *Le Facteur rural*, credited to Ferdinandus, in which a well-worn clog was affixed to a painted canvas depicting a rural mail carrier, and the 1884 *Essai de Peinture Mouvementiste*, signed by Bridet, which showed the sole of a boot upturned in midstride.[13] Although a drawing of the latter work, published in an Incohérent exposition catalogue, approximates the appearance of the actual artwork, in many other cases, the titles printed in the catalogues of the Incohérent expositions are all that remains of the art. The same fate befell more than half of Méliès' films, for which not much more than the titles remain. Méliès brand footwear has had a far higher attrition rate, and the title *Méliès Boots* is ironic inasmuch as I have been unable to locate even a single pair of Méliès men's boots during the several decades I have been researching Méliès. Indeed, a photograph of a pair of Méliès bottines adorns the cover of this book. Méliès boots are known mainly

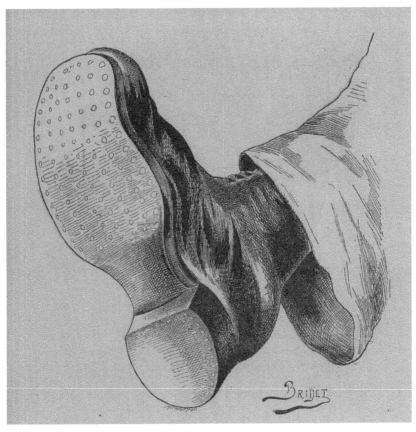

FIGURE I.I. Bridet, "Essai de Peinture Mouvementiste," *Catalogue Illustré de l'Exposition des Arts Incohérents* (Paris: E. Bernard et Cie, 1884), 51, Bibliothèque nationale de France.

from engravings printed in the only extant Méliès footwear catalogue and in fashion plates rather than from actual articles of footwear.[14]

Until relatively recently, the Incohérents were effectively a lost avant-garde. Critically rediscovered during the 1990s, the Incohérents have generally been treated in art historical terms as a modern art movement, albeit a minor art movement, which anticipated features of Dada and Surrealism.[15] The characteristics of Incohérence as it has generally been understood are most clearly manifest in Méliès' caricatures for *La Griffe*, as I argue elsewhere.[16] But, I have come to agree with Daniel Grojnowski and Denys Riout, who insist the Incohérents comprised neither a "movement" nor a "school." They contend that the Incohérents were an "informal group" that was numerous and unstable and

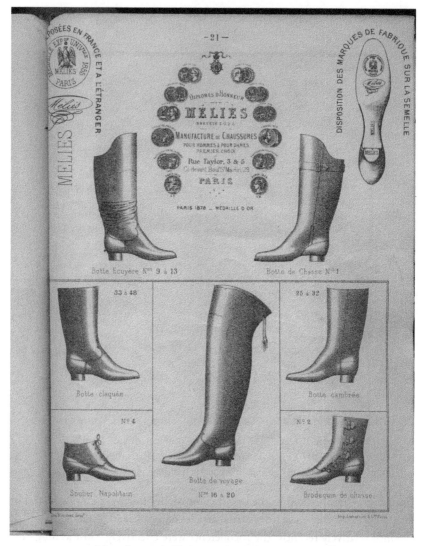

FIGURE I.2. *Manufacture de Chaussures Pour Hommes et Pour Dames: Prix Courant des Chaussures d'Hommes*, 21, Cinémathèque Française.

overlapped with even more obscure avant-garde circles like the hydropathes, hirsutes, zutistes, jemenfoutistes, fumistes, and Chatnoiristes.[17] Thus, here I define Incohérence not as an art movement but more expansively as a creative response to modern life being redefined—made troubling, unstable, and uncertain—by the Second Industrial Revolution. This larger sense of Incohérence is latent in existing accounts of the Incohérents, but in my view constitutes nothing less than a vernacular theory of modernity. Its expressions are found not only in caricatures but also—quite unexpectedly—in the margins of other professions, including the French footwear industry, which bears traces of the bohemian sensibility that is consistent with Incohérence.

A return to Incohérence as an alternative modernism offers new possibilities for film history. Modernism, according to Peter Wollen, represented a "critical semiotic shift, a changed concept of sign and signification" often involving "the play of allusion within and between texts" as well as "attempts to extend the scope of painting, to move outside the confines of the canvas" that conceived "the work of art [...] in terms of objecthood, pure presence [...] and its physical, material support."[18] Wollen, like many others, located "the beginning of modernism" during "the twenties," but these same characteristics were manifest in the work of the Incohérents some four decades earlier. Indeed, the Incohérents share many traits Wollen ascribed to the first of what he described as "the two avant-gardes."[19]

Film history has focused overwhelmingly on the second of these "two avant-gardes," which was constituted primarily by "Russian directors, whose films were clearly avant-garde, but in a different sense."[20] Film historiography has similarly been skewed to the second of Wollen's two avant-gardes. Indeed, the influential "cinema of attractions" paradigm depended on a concept of "attractions" derived from the 1920s writings of Sergei M. Eisenstein, who claimed the concept emphatically as "*my* invention."[21] Insightfully repurposed for film historiography by Tom Gunning and André Gaudreault, "attractions" have proven richly productive for film history in general as well as for studies of Méliès in particular.[22] Although I turn to Dziga Vertov and to Eisenstein's posthumously published writings on Disney and the history of cinema later in the book, the earlier Incohérent avant-garde of the 1880s is its driving inspiration. I believe it offers productive revisions to early film historiography as well as new methods for studies of early film authorship.

During the past forty years, scholars who privilege direct examination of primary-source documents while casting a wider net for relevant evidence have focused their attention on early cinema (before 1915 or thereabouts). One important strand of this scholarship has interrogated early cinema as an expression of historical modernity. Another important strand has documented early cinema's relationships to other media—"intermediality." This book responds to and builds on both of these strands while aligning itself with recent work concerned with media archaeology and the materiality of media. Cinema may well have been a medium defined by modernity, but film form and content were circumscribed by the modern material and technological possibilities available at the time. Grappling with the film medium's relationship to modernity requires attending to the palpable and phenomenological character of cinema and the film production, distribution, and exhibition processes. Numerous early films, including many of Méliès' films, were no doubt defined in part by intermediality, but transfers of content between media were neither seamless nor abstract. Intermediality was enabled by actions and interactions involving physical bodies, objects, machines, and the natural and built environment. Outstanding studies have done much to help us understand the tremendous diversity of early cinema's sights and sounds, but we have just begun to examine its material character.

When cinema emerged during the 1890s, films were appropriated by a variety of existing institutions and the new medium was put to different uses in different contexts. Cinema lacked a single consistent and stable identity. In 1896, Méliès immediately adapted moving pictures to the characteristics of conjuring, caricature, and scenic postcard views, respectively, with films like *Séance de prestidigitation*, *Dessinateur express (M. Thiers)* [lost], and *Place de l'Opéra* [lost]. This diversity, which characterized the work of most nineteenth-century filmmakers, was such that film historian André Gaudreault goes so far as to contend, "Cinema did not come into the world in the nineteenth century. [. . .] Cinema came into the world in the 1910s."[23] Gaudreault supports this seemingly counterfactual claim by reminding readers how little "so-called early cinema really has in common with institutional cinema," concluding, "it is completely pointless to connect the terra incognita known as 'early cinema' to the immense continent that is cinema itself."[24] The diversity and indeterminacy of early cinema extended to the very ontology of film, which was contested in resolutely material ways even as cinema was being institutionalized as a medium of entertainment centered on storytelling. Lee Grieveson points out that in the United States during the 1910s, "Legal definitions [. . .] differentiat[ed] cinema from the press (and from literature and art) [. . .] bringing it together with lumber, cheese, diseased cattle, and turpentine."[25] The hodgepodge of diverse commodities with which films were grouped and regulated suggests the extent to which the material identity of early cinema, despite being stabilized in the form of long perforated strips of celluloid with a width of 35mm, remained fundamentally incoherent.[26]

The material substrate of cinema was constituted from vegetable matter (cotton, wood) that was chemically treated to yield sheets of celluloid that were cut into strips and emulsified with gelatin made of pulverized animal bones to which crystallized silver was added. "In this sense," as Cherchi Usai notes, "cinema was fundamentally at odds with environmental concerns and animal rights."[27] "By the late 1920s," when Mélès was selling candy and toys at the Gare Montparnasse train station, "the amount of celluloid film was spoken of in terms of 'trillions of miles.'"[28] In 1927, it was noted "that films use more silver than the US mint."[29]

An expanding body of research has focused primarily on Mélès' place in film history, but this book is a material culture study that emphasizes his place in broader histories. Like other books about Mélès, mine treats him as a creative and innovative author, but I strive to embed his authorship in specific material contexts. My approach centers on materiality, loosely defined as "the substantial quality of things: their presence, function, and performative volume; in relation to manufacture modes."[30] Drawing on methods of material culture analysis, I acknowledge that the "study of objects and that of materiality itself is [...] never an isolated process but one that contextualizes other phenomena of culture to redefine one another in relation to their real-life [...] interactions."[31] Like other scholars of cinema and media studies who have taken up issues of materiality, I emphasize "just how much film and media studies has to gain from the materialist turn in infrastructure studies and media archaeology, as well as from the broader emphasis on 'new materialism' across humanities disciplines."[32] While heeding Caetlin Benson-Allott's point that "the material culture around film and television is much more heterogeneous than one might assume," *Mélès Boots* (as its title indicates) moves well beyond "objects that viewers carry"—much less *wear*—"into screenings as well as substances they ingest there."[33]

Attention to materiality marks a significant departure from previous studies of Mélès, which—like film studies more generally—have "focused on visual form, textual analysis, and aesthetic lineages—the formations of style—more than the conditions from which texts arise," Brian R. Jacobson points out, "a focus that, although it shifted with the New Historicist tradition and related New Film History, remains rooted in analyses of textual forms."[34] My attention to material culture encompasses the space of Mélès' studio, which was Jacobson's focus, and to a lesser extent, the Théâtre Robert-Houdin as a space of exhibition.[35] But, it transcends the diverse architectural environments of early cinema production and exhibition to encompass a much more diverse set of objects. I let Mélès' beginnings in footwear manufacture guide my research from the ground up, while looking askance at the material traces that Mélès and his various activities in fashion, the graphic arts, theater, and film left in their wake. Inspired by what "stuff" had actually survived from the period, I was impelled to consider the materiality of the cinematic and documentary evidence with which I was conducting the research.

I studied French caricature journals at the Library of Congress and the New York Public Library and I explored the paper record of the late nineteenth-century French avant-garde at the Zimmerli Art Museum. Perhaps most fortuitously, thanks to Elizabeth Semmelhack at the Bata Shoe Museum, I had the opportunity to examine a pair of embroidered bottines imprinted with the Méliès brand on the soles. Might this pair of bottines have been made when Méliès was working at the Société Méliès? More importantly: What could these bottines and the French footwear industry where Méliès got his start professionally tell us about the subsequent (and much better-known) films of Méliès? Eager to learn more about this particular historical context, I explored the history of French shoemaking and bootmaking at the Bibliothèque nationale de France, totally fascinated by what I found in the pages of trade journals like *Le Moniteur de la Cordonnerie* and *Le Franc Parleur Parisien*, which both detailed the activities of the Maison Méliès and the Société Méliès and their places in an evolving industry. (Although both of these designations appear in the trade press, I use "Maison Méliès" to refer to the Méliès family's bootmaking and shoemaking operations before the company was incorporated in 1878 as the Société Méliès.)

Méliès, Manufacturer

Many who have written about Méliès have attributed significant elements of his film aesthetic to his work as a stage magician. Indeed, most accounts of Méliès (including a number of my own) inevitably discuss magic and invoke magic in their titles.[36] While I continue to recognize the ways Méliès' trick films are related to some of the theatrical illusions he staged previously and concurrently in the magic theater, this correlation does not really account for the material character of filmmaking, which involved the production of commodities. Films Méliès made always involved performances (often backdrops and props as well), but these "artificially arranged scenes" (as they were described in Méliès' American catalogues) took the form of material commodities.[37] Méliès was not only a magician but also a manufacturer who produced films in a studio that resembled the iron-and-glass construction of the Société Méliès factory. I contend that Méliès' filmmaking studios of the early 1900s were comparable to the footwear manufacturing facility where he worked during the early 1880s, although the former housed technologies of late nineteenth-century stagecraft rather than band saws and other specialized footwear manufacturing machinery.

As a film manufacturer, Méliès adopted a commercial paradigm that in many ways resembled fabricating footwear more than managing a schedule of performances for which tickets were sold. Unlike directing the Théâtre Robert-Houdin, footwear manufacturing produced tangible commodities for sale to retailers and consumers. Pairs of boots and shoes were produced in multiples, with variations between models, styles, sizes, finishes, and colors. By contrast, performances at the Théâtre Robert-Houdin were inherently transitory live events that yielded relatively few material traces apart from seasonal programs and printed tickets. What spectators saw and heard on any given afternoon or evening at the Théâtre Robert-Houdin was unique and unrepeatable, including films regularly screened as part of the theater's programs beginning in 1896. Even in cases where the exact same film prints were programmed from show to show, variations in projection speeds, disparities in sound accompaniment (including live music and verbal *boniments*), and progressive wear and tear on the prints made every screening a singular audiovisual event, however subtle were the visible and auditory differences.

Films projected at the Théâtre Robert-Houdin were an integral part of countless live performances, but these same film titles—if not some of the same individual prints—became commodities once they were offered for sale, which Méliès did almost immediately. Just a few months after first screening films at the Théâtre Robert-Houdin in April 1896, Méliès began using it as a part-time retail space to sell film prints and filmmaking apparatus in partnership with Lucien Reulos in August 1896. Notices in *L'Industriel Forain*, the weekly trade journal of French fairground shows, invited prospective buyers to view films at the Théâtre Robert-Houdin between 2 and 6 o'clock in the afternoon, or at evening magic shows. By mid-October 1896, buyers had about fifty different film titles from which to choose, each approximately twenty meters in length.[38]

"The sewing machine became the most widely used invention of the second industrial revolution," making the ready-to-wear garment industry possible.[39] French bootmakers and shoemakers appear to have begun using sewing machines widely during the 1850s.[40] The action of intermittent transit sewing machines use to stitch fabric is analogous to the mechanism in motion-picture cameras and projectors that advances the strip of film incrementally, pausing before the aperture to expose or illuminate it many times per second.[41] The analogy with sewing machines was manifest in the Kinétographe (sometimes spelled "Kinétograph") Méliès and Reulos marketed briefly, in which "the film fell freely into a basket after passing through the apparatus."[42] The very first uses to which Méliès and Reulos put the Kinétographe appear to have been confined to the garden of the Montreuil property. This soon extended to shooting staged films shot outdoors against fabric backdrops such as *Une nuit terrible*, and scenic actualities filmed on location (all of the latter of which are believed lost).[43]

FIGURE I.3. Georges Brunel, *La Photographie et la projection du
mouvement: Historique — Dispositifs, Appareils, Cinématographiques*
(Paris: Charles Mendel Éditeur, 1897), 94.

The earliest of Méliès' film promotional materials dates from 1896. It is a flyer
consisting of a single sheet of paper enumerating forty-five film titles. For prospective buyers who were unfamiliar with the category of products listed, several frames of film were attached to the paper like a fabric swatch—a material
sample physically present with the printed advertisement. Although only one
example of this type of Méliès film flyer is known to survive, there were presumably multiple examples, each with different film frames attached. Each flyer
was thus a mass-produced item—one iteration among multiples—*and* a singular
one-of-a-kind artifact, like each Méliès film print, no two of which were ever
exactly identical. Just as significantly, only four of the films listed on the flyer are
presently known to survive, and the film from which this snippet was excised
appears to be lost apart from these three frames.

Méliès assigned successive catalogue numbers to each twenty-meter length
of negative completed.[44] The first seventy-seven catalogue numbers each correspond to individual film titles, but starting with *Le Manoir du diable*, produced
in the winter of 1896–1897, a number of longer subsequent film titles spanned
two or more catalogue numbers, though individual film titles were sold only in
their entirety. Similar to other film producers at the time, Méliès priced motion
pictures by the foot or meter, like so much fabric or ribbon. Surcharges and dis-
counts to this pricing scheme were likewise based on the material characteristics

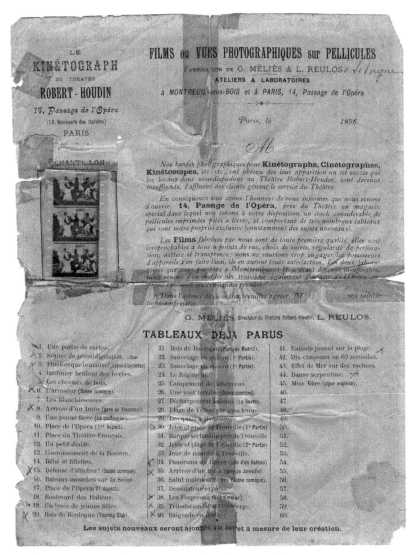

FIGURE I.4. Méliès film flyer, 1896, private collection, rights reserved.

of the individual film print, including the addition of hand-coloring and the print generation. Consistent with this material emphasis, Méliès' American catalogues offered the following endorsement to prospective purchasers: "We guarantee our 'Star' Films as being first-class in every respect, not only in regard to material but also concerning workmanship."[45]

Variable Commodities

Throughout this book, I have used the original French titles to designate specific Méliès films, except where a French title is unknown or perhaps never existed in the first place.[46] Film titles for which no copies are currently known to exist are indicated as "lost" in square brackets. Film titles that are currently known to exist only in fragmentary or substantially incomplete copies are indicated as such in square brackets. I have not noted parenthetical release years after film titles (as per the standard convention) partly to recognize that a number of the films Méliès produced during the winter cannot be reliably dated as having been produced at the end of one year or the beginning of the following year. Although release dates for a number of Méliès films can be reliably specified from copyright dates and trade press listings, release dates could vary between national, regional, or local contexts depending on the many different factors that played a role in the complex landscape of early film distribution.[47] In any case, specifying even a single year fails to take into account how Méliès films in particular could often remain in circulation for years after their initial release. *Le Petit Chaperon rouge* [lost], for example, was produced in 1900/1901, but was still featured on programs at the Théâtre Robert-Houdin during the summer of 1902 in a hand-colored print that was billed as a "new" attraction.[48] Fairground exhibitors especially, who were one of Méliès' major constituencies, showed films years after they had been released, as did department stores like the Magasin Dufayel in Paris, which screened films to entertain children while their parents shopped.[49] There was also a fairly robust market for secondhand films that kept films in circulation after their initial release.[50]

Because individual film prints and indeed individual screenings could vary considerably, even the use of a title is perhaps not sufficient, though obviously unavoidable. Méliès' American catalogues indicate that in some cases, different versions of the same title were offered. Buyers could choose the option of shorter or longer versions of films like *Le Barbier de Séville* [lost], *Voyage à travers l'impossible*, and *Le Palais des Mille et Une Nuits*. In at least one other case, two different versions of the same title and the same catalogue number exist, corresponding to two different negatives: *L'Illusionniste fin de siècle*. Méliès appears in both versions as the eponymous illusionist, along with the same unidentified dancer. Although the same table, chair, stool, oversized cone, mannequin, and large piece of fabric appear in both versions, the illusions in the film and the order in which they occur are different, as are the respective backdrops.[51] Whether or not Méliès ever "remade" any other film titles in this way is unknown.

Méliès' film catalogues indicate that hand-colored and/or extended versions of a number of Méliès titles could be purchased for an additional charge. Hand-coloring was subcontracted to colorists like Elisabeth Thuillier in Paris, whose hundreds of female workers meticulously applied multiple colors of aniline dye to countless translucent images of countless film prints—frame by painstaking frame.[52] Exhibitors and audiences alike generally preferred hand-colored film prints, especially for *féeries* (an early fairy tale film genre with which Méliès was closely associated), even though hand-colored prints were typically more than twice the price of black-and-white prints of the same titles.[53] *Damnation du docteur Faust* was one of a number of titles listed for sale in both black-and-white and hand-colored versions (no two of which were ever exactly the same of course). Méliès' American catalogues also occasionally suggested combining films, noting, for example, that *Damnation du docteur Faust* "forms a natural beginning to" *Faust aux enfers*.[54] Such possible conjunctions of films sold separately are evidence that early films were what Thomas Elsaesser described as "semi-finished products" that could be variably configured by exhibitors in juxtaposition with other films, projected magic lantern slides, recorded music, and countless modes of live performance—musical, spoken, and otherwise.[55] Méliès' American catalogues even listed "Specially arranged Music for piano" to accompany *Damnation du docteur Faust*.[56]

In France, a *résumé* of *La Légende de Rip Van Vinckle* [incomplete] was printed that was meant to be "read to the audience during the projection, sentence by sentence, at the exact moment the corresponding parts of the film are projected," asserting, "the cinematographic pantomime takes on twice as much interest for the viewing audience" when what was visible onscreen was also accompanied by this spoken narration.[57] This résumé is quite unlike the highly descriptive catalogue description of the film printed in Méliès' American catalogues, which differs from the French-language brochure printed to advertise the film.[58] This résumé avoids duplicating what is visible onscreen and instead mainly concerns information that would be more difficult for the viewer to glean solely from the mise-en-scène. It suggests that catalogue descriptions were promotional documents that were not necessarily intended to be read alongside the films they advertised (although a number of modern DVD editions have used the texts of Méliès' American catalogue descriptions as scripts for voice-over narration).[59]

Another source of variations in how Méliès' films were seen was introduced through differences in projection speed, which varied greatly during the silent period when projectors were generally hand-cranked.[60] Every silent film screening was unique—individual film prints of specific titles often diverged, and projection speeds between individual venues and between (and within) individual screenings varied. Additionally, "A distinction must be made at the outset between the running speed of the negative film stock within the camera and that of the positive film in the projection equipment. In the silent film era, the two did not necessarily coincide."[61] Méliès wrote about varying camera speeds in his 1907 essay "Les Vues Cinématographiques."[62] Recommended projection speeds can be calculated from indications of the "Length" in feet and the "Duration of exhibit" for a number of the film titles listed in Méliès' American catalogues. Occasional programs for the Théâtre Robert-Houdin published in the daily *L'Orchestre* that include specific film titles also provide indications. For example, the September 28, 1902, issue of *L'Orchestre* advertised a screening of a hand-colored version of *Voyage dans la Lune*, noting that the "duration of the projection" was "seventeen minutes."[63] If the guidelines in Méliès' American catalogues were followed, "Duration of exhibit" of a complete version of *La Légende de Rip Van Vinckle* was "about 22 minutes."[64] At a length of 1086 feet, this duration is consistent with the film being projected at thirteen frames per second.[65]

A number of Méliès' film titles survive in multiple versions, both authorized and unauthorized. Méliès' film *Voyage dans la Lune*, for example, "was so hugely successful that we have no idea of how many prints were made over the years" from the original negative.[66] Asked in 1930, Méliès replied, "As soon as the first positives were forwarded to U.S.A. [. . .] they were copied (countertyped) and sold in large number," adding, "the number of copies sold in America was enormous relatively [*sic*] to the number printed in my laboratory."[67] Insofar as provenance of individual film prints can be traced, only one complete first-generation nitrate positive print of *Voyage dans la Lune* (presumably dating back to 1902 or thereabouts) is presently known to survive.[68] Some surviving versions are truncated, like the version circulated in 16mm prints by the Museum of Modern Art Film Library for many years.[69] Other versions include added titles, like the German intertitles added to the version that bears the title *Eine phantastastische Reise nach dem Monde*, which is also truncated.[70] Most Méliès films had several different release titles and those that survive exist in different versions. The film known as *Voyage dans la Lune* and *Le Voyage Fantastique dans la lune* in France, for example, was released as *A Trip to the Moon* in the United States, and as *Viaje fantástico á la luna* in Spain.[71] In a disintegrating nitrate print of the latter title rediscovered in Catalunya, the flag saluted is Spanish with red and yellow stripes, but in the hand-colored prints sold in France the flag was presumably the tricolored French blue, white, and red. Each individual version and indeed each individual print in fact constitutes a singular object. Cherchi Usai emphasizes just how much different copies of the same film title can vary: "Each of these prints has a story to tell. Every copy of a film appearing on a screen—as a print or in digital form—has a story too. It is not an abstract entity brought to the present after a logical path designed by history on behalf of posterity. It is the survivor of a complex, often random process of selection."[72]

Méliès was committed to a regular schedule of new film releases, but he protested the adoption of the rental system, whereby film prints were rented temporarily for a fixed period of time, rather than sold outright, to exhibitors. Méliès' competitors at Pathé-Frères spearheaded film rentals, and as part of this process as it was originally conceived in 1907, film prints were chemically stripped of their images after making their way through the rental cycle and then re-emulsioned for reuse: "As of 1909, half of the projection prints distributed by Pathé had been obtained from recycled material."[73] Although the practice of cannibalizing prints was discontinued after Pathé constructed a factory to manufacture raw celluloid (thus achieving horizontal integration to complement the vertical integration the company had achieved through regional distribution and exhibition subsidiaries), the life cycle of Pathé's positive prints continued to conclude with their compulsory destruction.[74] The very structure of the rental system dictated planned obsolescence. Méliès, however, may have concurred with one 1909 commentator, who ridiculed the film rental system by comparing its premise to a tailor who demanded a suit back after four months, a milliner who requested the return of a hat after fifteen days, or a seller who expected a pair of bottines to be returned after they had been worn.[75]

Méliès' peak year of productivity as a filmmaker was in 1908, when both of his studios were operating at near full capacity. But, Méliès' film productions diminished considerably the following year, when his films were distributed by Gaumont, halting completely in 1910 while he was occupied with the production of a traveling stage show.[76] Méliès managed to finance the production of six more films with the benefit of a sizable loan from Pathé, which distributed four of the six, but profits were minimal.[77] In 1914, reeling from financial losses, Méliès attempted to sell some of the Théâtre Robert-Houdin's most precious artifacts in order to raise money and remain solvent, but he was unsuccessful and ended up subleasing the Théâtre Robert-Houdin for the duration of the war. In 1917, Méliès converted his second studio into a live performance venue, the Théâtre des Variétés Artistiques, where a stock company that included Méliès, his daughter Georgette Méliès, son André Méliès, and both of their respective spouses (fellow actors Amand Fontaine and Raymonde Matho) performed opera, operetta, and comic opera—a musical theater venture that merits a book all its own.[78]

A Fateful Bonfire

Proceeds from the Théâtre des Variétés Artistiques and the Théâtre Robert-Houdin were not enough to pay back Pathé's loan. Méliès later wrote he was "overwhelmed by enormous losses of money during the War" and was obliged to sell the Montreuil property.[79] "I had so many debts," Méliès later recalled, "that I was unable to prevent the sale of all my goods."[80]

The year 1923 turned out to be what Malthête-Méliès called "the year of catastrophes": the land in Montreuil the Méliès family had owned since 1860 was sold. The Théâtre Robert-Houdin, which Méliès had directed since 1888, was demolished as part of a public works project to extend the Boulevard Haussmann.[81] Méliès' office and film laboratory in the Passage de l'Opéra was also razed, along with several bookstores, bars, a shoeshine parlor, and an Italian restaurant, according to one account of the time.[82] This is when all of the documentation of the Théâtre Robert-Houdin, including the financial records (receipts, cash-books, payroll)—"in a word, everything written," according to Méliès—perished.[83] Comparable records of Méliès' filmmaking seem to have met the same fate.[84] One of the only things that survived is a fragment of the interior decoration of the Théâtre Robert-Houdin, several painted roses, which Méliès' daughter-in-law Raymonde Matho plucked from the rubble.[85]

Much of the vast amount of material Méliès had accumulated from a long career in theater and cinema was discarded or destroyed in 1923. When the Montreuil property was divided into several parcels and sold, the buildings on the property had to be emptied. These structures included his original filmmaking studio, an adjoining scene shop, costume shop, and dressing rooms, along with the Théâtre des Variétés Artistiques, which was itself adjoined by dressing rooms, office space, and a film laboratory.[86] What accumulated there was the material remains of Méliès' prolific output as a producer of films and theatrical spectacle over a period of thirty-five years. In addition to the scenery and props used to make numerous films, Méliès had also held onto the many settings he had painted himself for the Théâtre des Variétés Artistiques, storing much of it in a rented shed across the street from his Montreuil property—one of the first structures emptied. The scenery was sold to a theatrical impresario, as were the costumes.[87] A large attic was jam-packed with "all the props from the films [...] heads and bodies of Selenites from *Voyage dans la Lune* piled up haphazardly in one corner."[88] Some of this was sold to a junk dealer, but "the sets, the theater seats, and the equipment from the world's first film studio had to be abandoned on site."[89]

FIGURE 1.5. Painted roses from the interior decoration of the
Théâtre Robert-Houdin, private collection, rights reserved.

Film canisters were not as unwieldy as scenery and some of the larger props,
but they nevertheless took up storage space at a time when Méliès and his extended family (which now included Méliès' granddaughter Madeleine Fontaine,
born in 1923, later Madeleine Malthête-Méliès) was squatting in a small apartment above the Théâtre des Variétés Artistiques. But, nitrate films were a serious
fire hazard and could not be stored there nor in any of the homes or shops where
Méliès had squirreled away other smaller, less flammable items for safekeeping.
Malthête-Méliès writes that in 1923 Méliès "burned most of his films in the garden to which he had temporary access" on the Montreuil property.[90] The conflagration must have been difficult to extinguish given how flammable nitrate film
is: "There is absolutely no way to douse the flames, as the cellulose nitrate gives
off the oxygen that feeds the fire even if submerged under water, covered in sand,
or sprayed with extinguishers of any kind, whether using carbonic acid or other
substances. [. . .] The real danger comes from the deadly smoke emitted by the
burning nitrocellulose: if inhaled, its toxic cloud can kill humans and animals
within minutes."[91]

Méliès also disposed of the negatives. According to Malthête-Méliès, "the complete collection of five hundred negatives that Georges Méliès had filmed [...] was given to a salvager who planned to extract the celluloid and silver salts. This was an irrevocable loss."[92] Méliès knew just how irreplaceable negatives were. In May 1907, the New York branch office had been burglarized. The most devastating loss was some fifty negatives that were never recovered and were likely used to produce counterfeits nearly identical to authorized prints of these same titles.[93] In Paris, Méliès kept a second set of negatives in his laboratory in the Passage de l'Opéra, where he took great precautions to secure them. Indeed, André Méliès recalled that his father kept the negatives locked in iron boxes affixed with handles so that he could throw them to safety in case of a fire.[94] In 1923, however, the imminent destruction of the Passage de l'Opéra left Méliès no place to store them and so he sold his remaining negatives as scrap, but they had relatively little value. Legend has it that some of the celluloid from Méliès' negatives was recycled to make shoe heels, thus effecting a highly circuitous material return to Méliès' beginnings in footwear manufacturing, but this is impossible to verify.[95] (Shoe heels and eyelets were frequently made of celluloid, and Jean-Louis Méliès held a patent for a method of affixing shoe heels.[96]) The sale of nearly a ton of lead from the sinks and plumbing in the film laboratory was somewhat more profitable, although it took three people a week to remove it all and their skin turned temporarily blue in the process from toxic levels of lead exposure.[97]

In a 1930 letter, Méliès wrote, "I have destroyed in 1923 all my negatives and positive films. I had all of them since the N° One, (la partie de Cartes), untill [sic] the last number."[98] By destroying all of his negatives and positive prints, Méliès went on, "I recognize that I have been quite stupid. But I could not think that I could require, one day, these films."[99] Why continue storing hundreds of highly flammable canisters of celluloid nitrate films? How could he have known that old films would have any future value? Once outdated or physically worn out, as they generally were within a few years, films had limited value and were therefore typically disposed of like other kinds of objects bought and sold through catalogue and retail sales around the turn of the century.

To date, some three hundred of Méliès' films are still considered lost: no physical copies are known to exist or have yet been identified. Lost films are a structuring absence in Méliès' oeuvre—a glaring absence that is often mentioned but is difficult to address since what remains of these films are texts, unpublished and published, as well as images, photographed and drawn, that have survived despite the loss of the corresponding film prints.[100] In a number of cases, only titles survive, and in other cases, like Méliès' "Star" Films catalogue numbers 280, 1467–1475, 1486–1494—made in 1900, 1908, and 1909, respectively—not even the titles are known.[101] As Allyson Nadia Field points out, "Film history is a history of survivors, and scholarly writing is consequently disproportionally weighted toward extant films."[102] *Méliès Boots* takes up part of Field's charge to "apply the same scholarly curiosity and inquiry to so-called lost films that we do with extant film artifacts" and to "go beyond accumulating filmographic data to ask the same questions of nonextant films, with adapted methodologies, as we would ask of film history's survivors."[103]

Celluloid, Paper, and Posterity

For many lost Méliès films, the celluloid has vanished, leaving only paper. No print or fragment of *L'Armoire des frères Davenport* [lost] is known to survive, for example; what has survived is a drawing, a production still, and a six-sentence catalogue description.[104] For thirty-six films Méliès produced in 1903–1904, however, surviving paper prints were later transmuted into celluloid. Since Gaston Méliès (who managed the New York branch office of Méliès "Star" Films) deposited long strips of paper contact printed from the negatives with the Library of Congress to secure copyright protection in the United States for these titles, during the 1950s, these paper prints were painstakingly re-photographed during the 1950s to produce 16mm projection prints of a number of titles.[05] But, Gaston Méliès used production stills to make subsequent U.S. copyright deposits and the still photographs of backdrops he deposited with the Library of Congress between 1904 and 1909 (some fifty-five of which have survived) cannot readily be used to reconstitute the corresponding films.

Other kinds of paper documents must suffice for film titles for which celluloid copies, paper prints, or photographs do not survive. "Scholarly research has identified some materials as being especially relevant to a better knowledge of silent cinema (they are often referred to as 'ephemera': not by any means to diminish their importance, but to simply indicate that—like the films themselves— most of these artefacts were intended for use over a very short timespan)."[106] This part of the film historical record includes "the vast galaxy of surviving papers: production lists, photographs, actors' memoirs, account books, legal documents, telegrams, reviews, posters, music scores, copyrights and minutes of meetings."[107] The catalogues used to market Méliès' films to buyers constitute some of the most important material traces apart from the films themselves. Like the films advertised within them, these film catalogues are mechanically reproduced artifacts that survive in small numbers of copies with respect to the number that were presumably originally printed.

Catalogues, like other forms of printed matter, are "subgenres of the document," Lisa Gitelman points out, "but they are also familiar material objects to be handled—to be shown and saved, saved and shown—in different ways."[108] Catalogues, promotional materials, and letterhead were produced by "so-called job printing," which Gitelman describes as "a porous category used to designate commercial printing on contract—often small jobs—standing in habitual distinction from the periodical press and 'book work,' in the nineteenth-century printers' argot."[109] Gitelman writes, "this sector of the economy has gone missing from media history, encountered if at all in that most unglamorous and miscellaneous of bibliographical and archival designations, ephemera," adding, "Books are for keeps, but job printing—if it survives—tends to reside in collections of ephemera."[110] Michael Twyman notes, "whereas books have been preserved in libraries from ancient times, and in more recent centuries have been joined there by newspapers and periodicals, most printed ephemera have survived only by chance. Some libraries accept them, others do not; most regard them as of only marginal concern, and they are not normally included in arrangements for legal deposit."[111]

These ephemera include Méliès' film catalogues and the four-page *feuilles spéciales* (special sheets) Méliès used to advertise a number of the films he produced, including *Jeanne d'Arc* and the series of films (all lost) he made in conjunction with the 1900 Exposition Universelle in Paris.[112] Méliès also had one-page two-sided flyers printed to advertise *Le Petit Chaperon rouge* [lost], *Le Cake-Walk infernal*, *Voyage dans la Lune*, and other films.[113] How many such so-called feuilles spéciales may have been printed in these or other formats are unknown because "most ephemera produced throughout history has been lost. [. . .] It has simply been discarded, having outlived its immediate purpose."[114]

Often uncredited, job printers produced a great many "documents that [had] relevance only for a short time, normally the day or days of the event or situation they relate[d] to."[115] Many documents Méliès had printed were meant to remain in circulation for at least a few months and at most a few years, including thirty surviving issues of Méliès' American catalogue supplements variously dated 1903, 1904, 1905, and 1906, which were printed regularly to promote the latest releases and vary in length from one to ten pages. Some supplements contain several successive catalogue numbers, along with short printed descriptions of

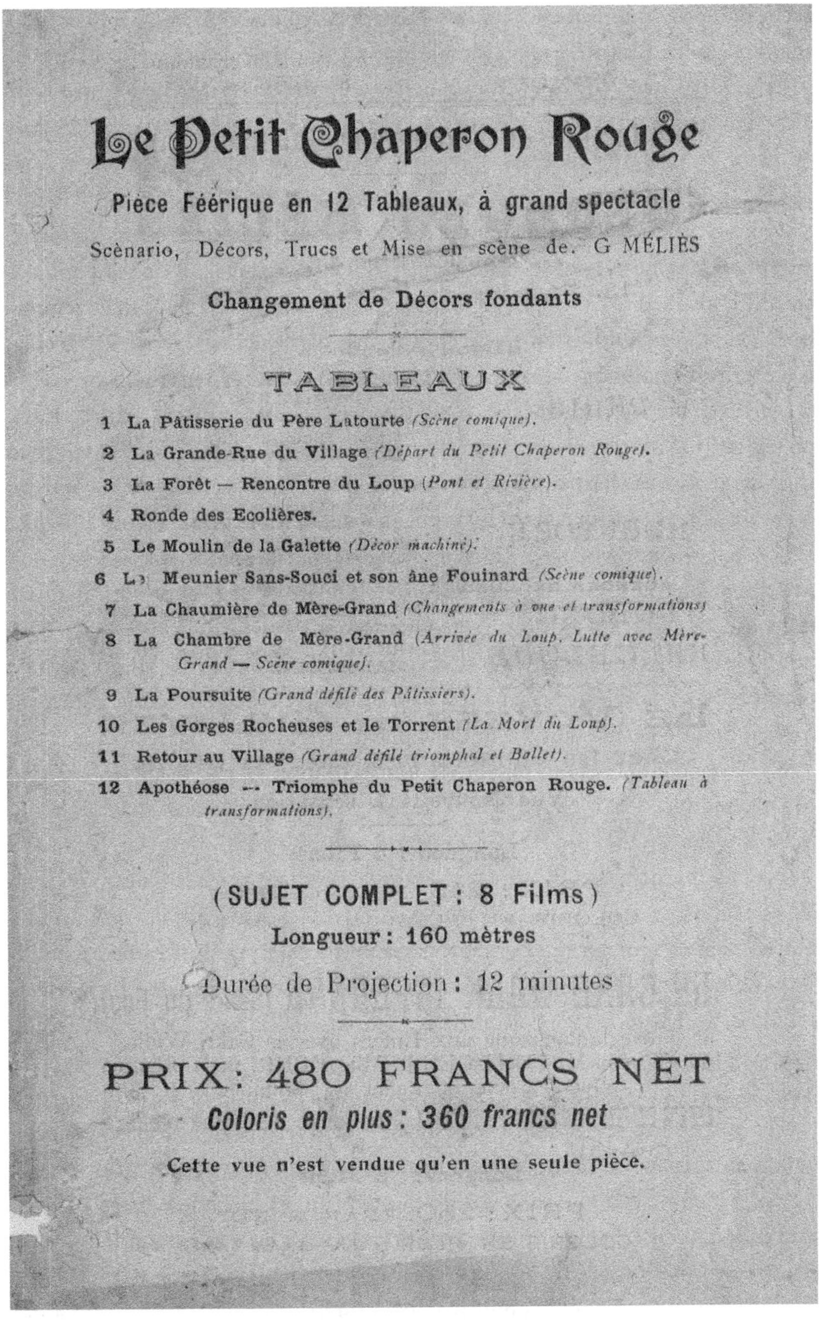

Le Petit Chaperon Rouge

Pièce Féérique en 12 Tableaux, à grand spectacle

Scénario, Décors, Trucs et Mise en scène de. G MÉLIÈS

Changement de Décors fondants

TABLEAUX

1 La Pâtisserie du Père Latourte *(Scène comique)*.

2 La Grande-Rue du Village *(Départ du Petit Chaperon Rouge)*.

3 La Forêt — Rencontre du Loup *(Pont et Rivière)*.

4 Ronde des Ecolières.

5 Le Moulin de la Galette *(Décor machiné)*.

6 Le Meunier Sans-Souci et son âne Fouinard *(Scène comique)*.

7 La Chaumière de Mère-Grand *(Changements à vue et transformations)*

8 La Chambre de Mère-Grand *(Arrivée du Loup, Lutte avec Mère-Grand — Scène comique)*.

9 La Poursuite *(Grand défilé des Pâtissiers)*.

10 Les Gorges Rocheuses et le Torrent *(La Mort du Loup)*.

11 Retour au Village *(Grand défilé triomphal et Ballet)*.

12 Apothéose — Triomphe du Petit Chaperon Rouge. *(Tableau à transformations)*.

(SUJET COMPLET : 8 Films)

Longueur : 160 mètres

Durée de Projection : 12 minutes

PRIX: 480 FRANCS NET

Coloris en plus : 360 francs net

Cette vue n'est vendue qu'en une seule pièce.

FIGURE I.6. *Le Petit Chaperon rouge* flyer, private collection, rights reserved.

each film; other supplements contain more detailed descriptions of longer films that are divided into numbered tableaus and illustrated with photographs.[116] (The "tableau" was Méliès' preferred designation for a segment of a longer film, although segues from one tableau to the next are not necessarily marked by cuts or dissolves, the latter generally serving as Méliès' method of transitioning from one location to another.[117])

Film catalogues are what literary theorist Gérard Genette terms "epitexts," part of his larger category of "paratexts": "The epitext is any [. . .] element not materially appended to the text [. . .] but circulating, as it were, freely, in a virtually limitless physical and social space."[118] The title of a work, in Genette's schema, is a "peritext" (another subset of the paratext) since it is "materially appended to the text," but for many Méliès films that were not issued with a title printed on the strip of film, even the title is an epitext that circulated independently of the film and would have differed depending upon the national context. Genette notes, "paratexts without texts do exist. [. . .] [T]here are certainly works—lost or aborted—about which we know nothing except their titles. [. . .] These titles, standing alone, certainly provide food for thought."[119] It is worth adding that there are also epitexts without texts—for lost works—although Genette does not mention this specifically. In such cases, the epitexts assume far greater importance, especially when the epitexts are discursive enough to constitute texts in their own right, like some film catalogue descriptions.

Méliès knowingly exaggerated the number of films he had made by claiming to have produced four thousand.[120] Jacques Malthête estimates that the more than 520 films Méliès did make totaled around thirty-five kilometers, outtakes and copies not included.[121] Efforts to compile the complete Méliès filmography are one set of attempts to grapple with Méliès' voluminous output, and it seems noteworthy how much filmographic research has been part of Méliès scholarship. Filmographies work to itemize for posterity what circulated formerly as celluloid. Although very incomplete lists of Méliès' films were compiled earlier, more comprehensive filmographic research on Méliès began with the work of film historian Georges Sadoul. The first version of Sadoul's Méliès filmography was published in 1947 as "An Index to the Creative Work of Georges Méliès," which enumerated all of the Méliès film titles that Sadoul was able to document, fifty of which he had also managed to locate prints of in film archives and private collections.[122] For the hundreds of titles he could not locate, Sadoul found crucial information in Méliès' 1908 American catalogue in particular.[123] While working concurrently on his multivolume *Histoire générale du cinéma*, Sadoul noted in a 1942 letter to a fellow film historian that film catalogues were "often the only contemporaneous documents" available given the absence of so many of the films, and "studying them carefully allows one to learn almost all of the essentials. But one is practically lost without them."[124]

Crazyloff's Journey; Or, Méliès and Material Culture

Méliès Boots aims to restore the vital connections between Méliès' cinema and a range of relevant material practices and material culture artifacts, including Méliès' film catalogues and other kinds of more or less ephemeral documents. It is a work of film history that borrows from studies of visual culture, which "can include anything from painting, [and] sculpture, [. . .] to photography, film, [. . .] fashion, medical and scientific imaging, the graphic and print culture of newspapers, magazines[,] and advertising, the architectural and social spaces of museums, galleries, exhibitions, and other private and public environments of the everyday."[125] In their multivolume compendium *Visual Culture*, Joanne Morra and Marquard Smith insist that visual culture studies must "continue engendering new objects or mobilizing more established things in new ways."[126] This impetus to discover new *objects* dovetails with Elsaesser's appropriation of the methods of media archaeology for film historiography: "Media archaeology would then be something like a revision of (as well as an extension to) classical film history, with a wider scope of pertinent phenomena and more inclusive in its understanding of the visual and material culture that is relevant to a historical analysis of cinema."[127] Media archaeology largely concerns "the non-visual," Jussi Parikka writes, "transporting it from investigation of texts to material culture as well."[128]

Approaching Méliès through material culture should dislodge two binaries that have long been promulgated by film theorists as well as film historians. The first binary opposes Méliès and Lumière, contrasting Méliès' studio-produced fiction films with the Lumières' nonfiction films shot on location.[129] This opposition is complicated by a closer look at Méliès' filmography, which contains a number of actualities and reconstructed actualities.[130] Consistent with his work as a caricaturist, I would add that Méliès was a cultural producer who consistently—although almost always humorously—responded to the realities of the modern world. Like the caricatures he drew, in which real individuals and objects were represented, even though their particulars were grotesquely distorted, Méliès' cinema was often both reality-based and completely fantastic. The second binary opposes Méliès and Pathé, contrasting Méliès' ostensibly artisanal methods with the industrial model pursued by his competitors at Pathé, sometimes yoking this opposition to a story of the industrialization of cinema that bypassed Méliès during the first decade of the twentieth century.[131] While this perspective has validity, its underlying conception of industrialization is insufficiently nuanced. Indeed, Méliès pursued aspects of the industrial system that emerged in the wake of the Second Industrial Revolution, some derived from prior experiences in footwear manufacturing. Méliès' mode of film production made widespread use of Second Industrial Revolution technologies and newly formulated materials produced through modern organic chemistry.

The proliferation of objects that came with the Second Industrial Revolution's surge in production capabilities is indexed by the sheer density of Méliès' mise-en-scène, which often shows profilmic spaces replete with objects. Specific objects recur, like the bust of the namesake of Méliès' magic theater, Jean Eugène Robert-Houdin, which is a more or less incidental prop in *Robert Macaire et Bertrand, les rois des cambroleurs, The Mischances of a Photographer, Les Illusions fantaisistes,* and *Hydrothérapie fantastique.*[132] Similarly, the sumptuously embroidered robe Méliès wore in the first two tableaus of *Voyage dans la Lune* (which survives at the Cinémathèque Française) can also be seen in *L'Alchimiste Parafaragaramus ou la Cornue infernale* as well as in *Hallucinations pharmaceutiques ou le Truc du potard.*[133]

Consistent with Méliès' early experience in fashion, some of the most consequential objects in his films are articles of clothing or accessories. Sometimes fashion accessories have fantastical and marvelous properties like the eponymous hat, umbrella, and fan, respectively, in *Le Chapeau à surprises, Le Parapluie fantastique,* and *Le Merveilleux Éventail vivant.* Each of these films endows a French-produced fashion good prized by consumers of the late-nineteenth and early twentieth centuries with magical qualities. Other times, less individually distinct items of clothing are the locus of illusionism, as in Méliès' films that feature instantaneous changes of clothing as in *Dix chapeaux en soixante secondes* [lost], *L'Homme protée* [lost], *Le Réveil d'un monsieur pressé, Les Costumes animés* [lost], *La Chaise à porteurs enchantée,* and others.[134] Boots and shoes specifically are foregrounded at various points in the mise-en-scène of Méliès films like *L'Auberge ensorcelée, Le Réveil d'un monsieur pressé, Cendrillon, Barbe-Bleue, Le Repas fantastique, La Guirlande merveilleuse, Les Mousquetaires de la reine* [lost], *L'Auberge du bon repos, Le Système du docteur Souflamort* [lost], *Les Quat' Cents Farces du diable, La Nouvelle Peine de mort* [lost], *La Cuisine de l'ogre, Why That Actor Was Late, The Woes of Roller Skaters, Tribulation or the Misfortunes of a Cobbler, La Gigue merveilleuse* [lost], and *Cendrillon ou la Pantoufle merveilleuse,* among others.[135]

But, the trajectory of *Méliès Boots* is organized not as a catalogue of objects seen in Méliès' films, but as a series of historical encounters with selected materials and material practices that surrounded Méliès' work as a footwear and film manufacturer. If a "stability of film historical methodologies" has meant that historical research has proceeded in some sense in "a straight and steady line" (as one commentator puts it), this book offers a very different tack.[136] It takes inspiration from the most conspicuous use of the term "Incohérent" in Méliès' oeuvre. Publicity materials circulated for the film *Voyage à travers l'impossible* indicate that the first tableau of the film takes place at "L'Institut de Geographie Incohérente," which corresponds to the location "The Institute of Incoherent Geography" in Méliès' American catalogue, where the film was titled *An Impossible Voyage*.[137] Prospective purchasers in the United States could choose a 1233-foot version of the film with "Duration of exhibit about 25 minutes" or a version of the same length with "Coloring," as well as a version "with new finish" that added 181 feet, which was also available with "Coloring."[138]

A hand-colored version of *Voyage à travers l'impossible* is extant, but no copies are known to exist of the "Supplementary Section," which consisted of three additional tableaus. In these lost supplemental tableaus, the travelers, according to a surviving catalogue description, "in spite of their fortunate return, bitterly reproach the wretched man for having lost in the course of the voyage more than half of the material which had cost them so much to construct."[139] After the travelers vent their frustrations on the leader of the expedition, the engineer Crazyloff (Méliès), this lost "Supplementary Section" depicted a magical recovery of all that had been materially dispersed during the preceding expedition:

> Crazyloff is suddenly seized with an idea [for] something marvelous. [. . .] He leads the savants to the top of the tower of the Institute and orders brought up an electro-magnet of enormous size. By passing a current of 20,000 volts through the magnet he makes it strong enough to draw and pull back the automobile lost in Switzerland, the train lost in the sun, and the submarine lost in the sea. [. . .] Crazyloff turns on the current, and suddenly the train, the auto, the balloon and the submarine come back from the four corners of space and fix themselves upon the arms of the electro-magnet.[140]

Like many lost Méliès films that will probably never be "found," we will likely never see this stunning supplement to *Voyage à travers l'impossible*, but its material emphasis is clear.[141]

The spectacle of a complete and immediate reclamation of all that was "lost"—or at least everything made of metal—during the film's admittedly impossible journey would have served as an even more impossible coda to *Voyage à travers l'impossible*. The transposition of this film scenario to the material culture Méliès generated in his long career has served me as a historian's fantasy, although no archival electromagnet—no matter how powerful—could ever possibly have done the trick. The full accumulation would no doubt have proven far more unwieldy than the rich collection of material that Malthête-Méliès and the Cinémathèque Méliès have managed to gather in more than sixty years.[142] It will forever remain a fantasy more fantastic than the comprehensive survey of Méliès' work to which Cherchi Usai alluded or the complete Méliès filmography to which Sadoul and Malthête have aspired.

Recognizing both the magnitude of the material loss and the inherent impossibility of comprehensiveness, *Méliès Boots* instead offers a more selective and thoroughly Incohérent geography that corresponds less to actual locations within and beyond Paris than to a series of discontinuous sites selected from an assemblage of industries and practices. The arrangement of the chapters is loosely chronological, beginning with the work of Méliès and his family in shoe manufacturing and proceeding through a series of examples of materials and material practices that relate to his work as a caricaturist, magic theater director, and *cinéaste*. Like *Voyage à travers l'impossible*, which careens from Switzerland to the Sun and then under the sea, the trajectory of the journey is not a straight line, but rather a zig-zag—one of the quintessential graphic motifs of Incohérent art.

Chapter 1, "Artisanal Manufacturing," historicizes the Méliès family footwear business, which was founded by Jean-Louis Méliès during the 1840s. It traces the growth of the Maison Méliès and the formation of the Société Méliès at the start of the Second Industrial Revolution. Comparing the de luxe footwear and films produced, respectively, by Méliès *père* and *fils*, reveals several unexpected homologies. Both were "artisan manufacturers" who relied on factories in which industrial materials, methods, and machinery were combined with more artisanal handiwork.

Chapter 2, "Incohérent Infrastructure, Incohérent Fashion" reframes existing accounts of the Incohérents by recalling that the very first Incohérent art exposition was a direct response to a modern urban tragedy, the rue François-Miron catastrophe, a horrific 1882 Paris gas explosion that resulted from flawed infrastructure. The Incohérents responded to the dysfunction and disconnections that characterized modern life with a series of absurd and entirely ephemeral creations, and this sensibility even found a footing in the margins of the French footwear industry, where the Incohérents and the distinctive "pointy shoes" with which they were associated incited contemporaneous comment.

Chapter 3, "Stretching the Caricatural Aesthetic," takes stock of the importance of drawing for Méliès' aesthetic, examining the series of caricatures he published pseudonymously. Rather than reading these caricatures symbolically, this chapter looks closely at the iconography of Méliès' published drawings along with unpublished drawings made in preparation for films and theater productions and ex post facto drawings made decades later. Drawing was the foundation of Méliès' scenography and mise-en-scène because it allowed for erasure, "plasmaticness," and radical changes of scale and disproportionality.

Chapter 4, "Modern Laughter and the Genre Méliès," considers what Méliès and others termed the "genre Méliès." Méliès has long been associated with trick films and special effects, but this chapter focuses on the absurd juxtapositions and unexpected transformations Méliès mobilized to provoke "modern laughter." It argues that the genre Méliès had a foundational material relationship to Second Industrial Revolution materials like celluloid, acetone, and other products of modern organic chemistry, which Méliès used to make people and things appear to disappear.

Chapter 5, "The New Profession of the Cinéaste," examines the methods and some of the individuals that animated film manufacturing at Méliès' Montreuil studios. Like the factory that was operated by the Société Méliès, Méliès' filmmaking studios combined Second Industrial Revolution technology with skilled labor. Looking closely at the illustrated version of Méliès' "Les Vues Cinématographiques" alongside Méliès' recollections and those of a number of his collaborators allows us to detail what comprised the new Second Industrial Revolution métier, which Méliès later described as "the new profession of the cinéaste."

The Conclusion, "Toy Stories," uses the years Méliès spent selling toys and candy in the Gare Montparnasse as a point-of-arrival, contending that Méliès' work as a toy retailer during the 1920s and early 1930s was consistent with elements of play in his work as a filmmaker. By looking at some of the toys available in turn-of-the-century Paris, it suggests dimensions of tactility and interactivity that were never fully available to Méliès' audiences, but directly adjacent to them. In doing so, I propose an expanded history of cinema informed by media archaeology that includes hand-held amusements analogous to those that proliferate today.

Contemporary viewers can readily watch versions of many of Méliès' films on hand-held digital devices because his entire body of work entered the public domain in 2009, seventy years after his death as per French law.[143] This has allowed for previously unprecedented opportunities to see surviving Méliès films, albeit at unspecified frame rates with added titles, music, and in some cases newly recorded voice-over narration.[144] The convenience of streaming has given the sheer visibility of Méliès' films a tremendous boost, but it is worth recalling the

machines, materials, and labor that made Méliès' cinematic activities possible in
the first place. Similarly, the digitization of periodicals, books, and other historical documents has facilitated historical research on Méliès and countless other
topics, allowing me remote digital access to many useful primary sources. But, it
was the materiality of the research process that proved most crucial for this book,
even if "writing" it was done entirely with keystrokes on laptop computers—and
one gold-colored 13-inch 2019 MacBook Air in particular, beneath my fingers
at this very moment. Physical encounters with undigitized sources—unwieldy
bound volumes of oversized caricature journals, 35mm films requiring careful
handling and some measure of manual dexterity to manipulate, and countless
archival boxes and folders containing one-of-a-kind documents—provided me
with crucial evidence while crucially inspiring my approach.

CHAPTER I

Artisanal Manufacturing

I N ONE OF THE earliest published accounts of Méliès boots, from 1855, a knowledgeable observer found fault with the cut of a pair of riding boots made by the Maison Méliès, claiming that—although the apparent defect was not visible to the untrained eye—the boots would not fit snugly because of how the leather was cut.[1] This criticism highlights the disjunction between a visual examination of an article of clothing and the wearer's physical encounter with its material construction. It also implicitly suggests the shortcomings of footwear that was mass produced in standard sizes rather than made to measure for the exact size and shape of one individual's feet, ankles, and calves. But, most apposite here, it points to the paramount importance of cutting for footwear manufacture in all of its forms, a quality that was equally important for Méliès' later film practice.

The namesake of the Maison Méliès was Jean-Louis Méliès, who had learned the trade of the *cordonnier-bottier* during seven years as a journeyman on the Tour de France as an initiate of the Compagnons Cordonniers-Bottiers du Devoir. *Cordonnier* designated a craftsman capable of making shoes of all kinds except boots, which were the handiwork of the *bottier*.[2] The Tour de France was the itinerant apprenticeship during which *compagnons* learned all of the aspects of a manual profession from master craftsmen in towns and cities along the route while lodging with fellow compagnons and absorbing the specific quasi-Masonic rituals that were associated with their order of *compagnonnage*.[3] After becoming a full-fledged compagnon, Jean-Louis Méliès settled in Paris, marrying Catherine Schueringh (whom he met while both were working in a shoemaking workshop) in 1843.[4] In 1845, Jean-Louis Méliès was working on the rue Beaubourg as a *cordonnier en chambre* making boots and shoes to order, soon pivoting to making "shoes for commercial sale with mechanical methods."[5] By 1853, the first year "Méliès, bottier" appeared in Paris city directories, Jean-Louis Méliès was the proprietor of two different workshops in the second arrondissement.[6] In 1855, the high quality of Méliès men's footwear (notwithstanding certain critical

31

comments about the cut of Méliès riding boots) was confirmed at the 1855 Exposition Universelle in Paris, where several pairs of Méliès boots were showcased at the Palais de l'Industrie in a massive vitrine in which outstanding examples of French footwear were displayed. The Maison Méliès was awarded a bronze medal.[7] This was the first of a number of commendations the brand would receive during the ensuing decades, when the firm branched out to include women's footwear and was subsequently incorporated as the Société Méliès.[8]

At least two of Méliès' films, *L'Auberge ensorcelée* and *L'Auberge du bon repos*, show Méliès removing tall riding boots. The boots Méliès wears and then takes off in these films are presumably like the pair at the 1855 Exposition Universelle, but it is difficult to discern the fit and impossible even to confirm that the boots were made by Méliès. In *L'Auberge ensorcelée*, Méliès plays a visitor to a haunted inn. Arriving to stay the night, he sets his suitcase and umbrella down on the bed, where they vanish. As he gets undressed, articles of his clothing begin to move and then vanish: his helmet flies off the bureau and slides across the floor; his coat flies onto the wall and then disappears overhead; and his trousers levitate out of the top of the frame. Meanwhile, a candlestick disappears from the bureau and reappears on the nightstand, exploding in a puff of smoke after he lights it. As he sits down in a chair, the chair vanishes, then reappears in another place. After managing to sit down, he removes his boots. But, after the boots are set down on the floor, they slide across the room and out of the frame, eluding his grasp. As he lies down, the bed disappears beneath him, but reappears; both the night stand and the bureau disappear completely. Visibly flummoxed, he flees the room through the door in his stockinged feet.

In the ironically titled *L'Auberge du bon repos*, a restful night's sleep is likewise impossible. Méliès plays a visitor to a larger and more well-appointed inn staffed by two employees that also appears to be haunted. Objects, including what appear to be the same pair of riding boots, similarly move mysteriously on their own. After being shown into the room, Méliès awkwardly kicks off the boots he is wearing while standing, visibly unsteady on his feet. A servant places the boots neatly at the foot of a clothes rack where his clothes have been draped and leaves the room, "The boots become animated and [. . .] began to dance about the room," as the events of the film are described in Méliès' American catalogue, "The poor intoxicated fellow goes after them, but the boots ascend the wall and disappear in the ceiling."[9] Although the riding boots are among a number of different objects that move autonomously in both *L'Auberge du bon repos* and *L'Auberge ensorcelée*, riding boots that move and walk on their own take on special significance in light of the Méliès family footwear business.

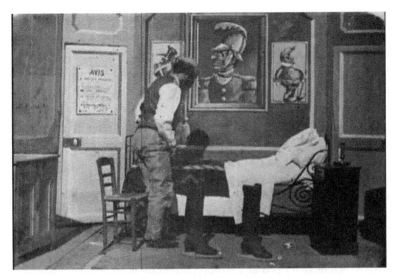

FIGURE I.I. *L'Auberge ensorcelée* digital frame enlargement.

Tom Gunning makes an "analogy between object animation and Marx's description of the commodity fetish," suggestively pointing out, "Firstly, the animation of objects gives them the appearance of having a power of their own; secondly, the occluding of the actual work of human hands creates this illusion through a process in which awareness of the actual producers of the illusion is systematically eliminated."[10] Gunning relates this to Marx's

> discussion of the commodity in the first volume of *Das Kapital* [that] traces the construction of a table from raw material, asserting that its greatest transformation comes not from its construction, but as "soon as it steps forth as a commodity . . . [I]t is changed into something transcendent. It not only stands with its feet on the ground, but, in relation to all other commodities, it stands on its head and evolves out of its wooden brain grotesque ideas, far more wonderful than 'table-turning' ever was."[11]

Marx's allusion here, as Gunning points out, is to "the Spiritualist movement's 'modern manifestations' [. . .] table turnings [. . .] [and] apparently unmotivated movement of objects."[12]

In *L'Auberge ensorcelée* and *L'Auberge du bon repos*, riding boots spring spectacularly into motion as commodities and—more specifically—as fashion articles that prove unruly and ultimately impossible to control. It seems equally significant that the character in the film whose grasp the riding boots elude also happens to be the maker of the film and a former bootmaker. Unlike the animated objects Gunning discusses, which were created through the cinematic trick of exposing the film strip one frame at a time and moving the object incrementally between the exposures, the movements of the boots in Méliès' *L'Auberge ensorcelée* and *L'Auberge du bon repos* appear to be the result of a profilmic trick accomplished in real time in front of the camera. Boots that moved on their own comprised a familiar theatrical effect at the time these films were made.[13] Although Gunning's citation of Marx still seems apposite, I am less interested in the magical qualities that commodification endowed to material objects than in Marx's analysis of the obverse quality of the commodity, described as the "invisible bond uniting the various branches of trade" in the process of manufacture.[14]

To explain the "invisible bond" concealed within the manufactured commodity, Marx's chosen example was the process of "making [. . .] leather into boots," which he described as a prototypical example of how commodity producers, "by adding fresh labour, and therefore more value to the value in hand," created surplus value.[15] By Marx's reckoning, "the value of a commodity" was calculated "not only by the quantity of labour which the labourer directly bestows upon that commodity, but also by the labour contained in the means of production. For instance, the value of a pair of boots depends, not only on the cobbler's labour, but also on the value of the leather, wax, thread, &c."[16] Elsewhere, Marx reverse engineered the material and labor concealed within a pair of boots:

> For instance the cattle-breeder produces hides, the tanner makes the hides into leather, and the shoemaker, the leather into boots. Here the thing produced by each of them is but a step towards the final form, which is the product of all their labours combined. There are, besides, all the various industries that supply the cattle-breeder, the tanner, and the shoemaker with the means of production.[17]

Anatomizing footwear manufacturing reveals the extent to which the French shoe and boot industries depended on the large-scale conversion of animal and vegetable matter into enormous quantities of tanned, treated, and dyed leather for its raw materials.[18]

Examining the material contexts that supported the growth of the Méliès footwear brand while examining how the Méliès family's footwear manufacturing process combined the use of raw materials and labor reveals compelling parallels with Méliès' later mode of film production. Méliès footwear and Méliès films were both manufactured in similar glassed-in enclosures with Second Industrial Revolution technologies. Both also privileged the skilled labor of cutting while outsourcing the handicraft of finishing each individual mass-produced commodity to numerous female outworkers who were paid, respectively, to hand-stitch footwear and hand-color release prints.

Leather Goods and De Luxe French Fashion

Most men's shoes and boots were "entirely made of leather, and this provided resistance to rain, mud and bad weather."[19] Suppliers made leather by treating the "raw hides" (*peaux vert*) of slaughtered cows and, to a lesser extent, sheep, goats, and other animals.[20] The Méliès family was related by marriage to the Saraux families and the Pallardy families, which were both involved in tanning and leather production.[21] Making leather was the work of tanners who soaked animal skins in water and pulverized tree bark for long periods after depillating, washing, bleaching, and drying them. Much leather used for men's footwear was black, which required dyeing. Producers made a distinction between hard leather and soft leather: the former was used to make soles and the latter was used to make other parts of shoes and boots. Soft leather was made pliable, smoother, and more regular in thickness by hammering it with mallets and hydraulic machines, the latter introduced in the 1860s.[22] Around this time, the Maison Méliès sourced leather from Madame Croisier, whose leather was used by several other leading Paris producers.[23]

Leather goods like the boots and shoes manufactured by the Maison Méliès and the Société Méliès were among the luxury items that Thorstein Veblen classed as "items of conspicuous consumption" that were also a wearable "expression of the pecuniary culture" typically worn until they were no longer fashionable rather than until they were worn out.[24] Veblen described this as "conspicuous waste":

> The imperative requirement of dressing in the latest accredited manner, as well as the fact that this accredited fashion constantly changes from season to season, is sufficiently familiar to every one. [. . .] Obviously, if each garment is permitted to serve for but a brief term, and if none of last season's apparel is carried over and made further use of during the present season, the wasteful expenditure on dress is greatly increased.[25]

Many of the shoes and boots sold in Paris, including those produced by Méliès, likely ended up with the city's rag-pickers (*chiffonniers*), who numbered 18,000 workers, approximately half the number of people employed in the Paris footwear industry.[26]

Histories of fashion elevate the work of dressmaker Charles Frederick Worth, who is associated not only with the emergence of modern couture but also with industrialized fashion. Worth, as biographer Diana de Marly describes, was "an artist, but on an industrial scale."[27] His international renown as a fashion designer, de Marly contends, was made possible by a sizable industrial operation and the global sprawl of modern Second Industrial Revolution infrastructure:

> Yet all that artistic taste, all that glamour and glory could only exist because of industry: it was improvements in looms and sewing machines which made Worth gowns possible. It was the construction of an international telegraph system which enabled customers to call him from afar. It was long-distance locomotives and trans-Atlantic steamers which conveyed his goods at unprecedented speed.[28]

De Marly points out that Worth had "1,200 employees" and that "Worth stood at the top of an enormous pyramid of fashion suppliers and producers."[29]

The industrialization of fashion extended to the practices of French shoemaking, Marie-Josèphe Bossan explains:

> The Second Empire also marks a decisive stage in the history of footwear, characterized by advances in mechanisation and large-scale industry. Traditional shoemaking [. . .] was transformed by [. . .] Thimonnier's invention of the sewing machine, patented in 1830. A perfect invention, the sewing machine made it possible to stitch uppers of soft materials and began to spread among shoemakers in 1860. The technique improved their production yields, as machines positioned the heel, stitched the upper, and attached the upper to the sole. [. . .] Industrial development began to overtake hand-made shoes as factories were established and expanded.[30]

This period saw not only the development of new machines but also new materials such as rubber and gutta-percha, the latter which could be molded into solid, lightweight shoe heels.[31] Elizabeth Semmelhack writes,

> The industrialization of shoemaking [. . .] made a wide variety of fashionable footwear available to women at many different price points. Women who could afford fine footwear sought out the exquisite boots made by Jean-Louis François Pinet. As Charles Frederick Worth was the first haute couture fashion designer, Jean-Louis François Pinet was the first celebrated shoemaker of the modern age.[32]

Both Pinet and Jean-Louis Méliès were traditional made-to-measure cordonnier-bottiers who were trained as compagnons before founding leading French shoe brands and successful family businesses.

Like his better-known contemporary Pinet, Jean-Louis Méliès transformed himself from crafting made-to-order footwear *en chambre* and in small workshops to an *industriel* mass producing de luxe boots and shoes in a factory employing more than a hundred workers.[33] French shoe manufacturing was deeply rooted in the traditional practices, personnel, and personal networks of compagnonnage.[34] Pinet and Jean-Louis Méliès were Compagnons Cordonniers-Bottiers du Devoir: both cherished lifelong relationships with fellow compagnons, fortifying these ties at regular meetings of the Chambre Compagnonnique des Cordonniers and Bottiers du Devoir and by the employment of their fellow compagnons throughout the industry.[35]

Pinet and Jean-Louis Méliès were also "entrepreneurs du luxe" who prospered in Paris during the Second Empire catering to a new class of French and international consumers who could afford higher-priced, high-quality "de luxe" products.[36] Luxury items had formerly been made for royalty, the aristocracy, and the very wealthy. But, during the second half of the nineteenth century, these products became more readily available to other segments of the population who were now able to afford premium goods, achieving a "democratization" of luxury.[37] Jean-Louis Méliès' father-in-law Henricus Schueringh had been a bootmaker to the Dutch royal court at La Haye, but Jean-Louis Méliès produced quality goods for a new class of consumers. As Bossan points out, "the Second Empire's taste for magnificent clothing was matched with opulence in the art of the shoe. Examples of these styles, worn by [. . .] the increasingly wealthy bourgeoisie, [. . .] they are proof of the traditional expertise handed down from one generation to the next, revealing the individuality and the craftsmanship of their creators."[38] Like other "entrepreneurs du luxe," Jean-Louis Méliès won awards, medals, diplomas, and other recognition at various international competitions and trade fairs. An image of these laurels was printed on the ephemera that comprise surviving traces of the business.[39]

According to oral histories of the Méliès family, the sale of Méliès footwear was oriented primarily to the export market.[40] At the 1862 International Exposition in London, Jean-Louis Méliès won an Honorable Mention and was lauded as "one of the glories" of the French export business, with a reputation for "good fabrication known in France and America."[41] Subsequent indications in the trade press confirm that the Méliès brand was especially successful abroad.[42] French shoe manufacturers like Méliès took special pride in the marketability of French taste, which made French footwear a prized class of export commodities.

FIGURE I.2. Header used in printed materials distributed by
the Société Méliès, private collection, rights reserved.

French footwear manufacturing was concentrated in and around Paris, but
other French cities supported factories as well.[43] Auguste Frétin produced "de
luxe" men's footwear "sewn by hand" in a factory located next to the railroad
station in Auxi-le-Château. Frétin published a catalogue, shipped mail orders,
and stocked several retail stores in Paris.[44] Frétin's operations were depicted in
a series of engravings showing "industrial progress in the fabrication of French
shoes" published during the 1880s in the trade press. These illustrations show
the steam-powered Frétin factory, including its shipping and accounting de-
partments, and one of Frétin's several Paris stores, bustling with well-dressed
shoppers among hundreds of pairs of shoes displayed pyramidally on tables and
in illuminated vitrines.[45]

By the 1880s, French footwear manufacturers—including de luxe Paris producers like the Société Méliès—were inextricably tied to the global economy.[46]
French producers were reliant on foreign markets and on machinery and raw materials made outside of France. Regular columns in the French footwear industry
trade press reported international developments in Europe, North America, and
South America, along with less frequent dispatches from Asia, Australia, and
Africa.[47] Developments in the United States, especially in connection with mass
production of low-priced footwear, were of particular interest. Trains and steamships dispatched French footwear to markets around the world, but these modes
of transportation also brought imported products into France. Commentators

within the French footwear industry were especially critical of Paris department stores that stocked imported knockoffs of higher-quality French-made footwear.[48]

Artisanal Manufacturing

Jean-Louis Méliès transitioned from making shoes and boots individually on a made-to-measure basis to supervising workshops and later a factory where boots and shoes were mass produced. Between 1855 and 1870, Jean-Louis Méliès' workforce grew from ten to seventy employees.[49] In 1878, after more than forty years as a cordonnier-bottier and around twenty-five years of running his own business, Jean-Louis Méliès incorporated as the Société Méliès.[50] That same year it was reported that Jean-Louis Méliès "employs workers who are always among the most skilled in the capital."[51]

Jean-Louis Méliès and his three sons, who were third-generation shoemakers on their mother's side, are exemplars of what business historian Philip Scranton describes as "artisan-manufacturers."[52] Scranton emphasizes that "the mainstream story of the Second Industrial Revolution" tends to focus on the largest firms that were incorporated and financed through the sale of shares of stock, but "the industrial past is rich with examples of variety and versatility," including many "big businesses [that] remained under family control, rather than having dispersed, anonymous shareholders."[53] Scranton explains,

> specialty manufacturing [w]as an industrial and institutional dynamic that paralleled, complemented, and at times conflicted with the achievements of [. . .] celebrated mass production corporations. Specialty sectors [. . .] initiated technological and organizational transformations distinct from, but comparably significant to, the creation of routinized assembly, bureaucratic management, and oligopolistic competition. This "other side" of the Second Industrial Revolution is complex and diffuse, neither tidy nor reducible to formulas.[54]

The "custom and specialty goods" that the Société Méliès produced were not throughput commodities that made their way from one end of an assembly line to the other while being worked on by relatively unskilled laborers along the way. These were products that took shape in the hands of skilled laborers working with both hand tools and larger machines on a factory floor more loosely organized by specific phases of the footwear production process, working together on

Figure 1.3. Méliès' drawing of the Société Méliès factory, Cinémathèque Française.

a more flexible basis to fill orders for specific models and sizes rather than large quantities of identical commodities.

Paris had long been the undisputed capital of international fashion. The 1880s saw the introduction of economies of scale that helped to make footwear the fourth-largest industry in Paris, where some 36,000 people were employed in the business of making and selling footwear, which was also the fourth-largest industry in France.[55] In 1881, the Société Méliès and the entire extended Méliès family relocated to a building at 3 and 5, rue Taylor in the tenth arrondissement. Jean-Louis Méliès' several earlier locations appear to have been workshops, but this was a full-fledged factory that employed one hundred and fifty workers; it was adjoined by a retail store and the company's business offices.[56]

Méliès made a drawing of the factory interior, dated "c.1880," which shows an expansive space with a high ceiling. Tall windows stand along the left side of a vast factory floor. Taller pillars hold up a vast glass ceiling that allows additional light onto the factory floor. A long workbench runs the length of the factory floor beneath the windows where workers, both male and female, are working; gas lamps beneath the windows provide additional illumination, and allowed work to be done even when it was dark outside. Square pieces of leather are stacked nearby and workers standing at tables on the factory floor are working with different sized pieces. Along the right side of the factory floor a row of large machines are arrayed.[57]

The filmmaking studio Méliès put into operation in Montreuil was a similar kind of structure. The similarities between Méliès' studio and the Méliès shoe factory underscore the fact that both were manufacturing facilities within which artisanal labor coexisted more or less symbiotically with the use of machines. Writing about early filmmaking studios, Brian R. Jacobson explains that structures like these were only possible because "new building materials including reinforced concrete, steel, and prismatic glass allowed architects to increase solar illumination (much as they did in modern factories)."[58] Jacobson explains,

> Closely following the developments of the Industrial Revolution, architects and engineers used new materials to fill increasingly large spaces with natural light, while also sheltering them from rain, snow, and, with the addition of ventilation and cooling systems, heat. Historians of technology have argued that these changes marked the climax of the greatest technological revolution in history. [. . .] Iron-and-glass architecture and glass house film studios were quintessential products of that revolution. [. . .] By the mid-nineteenth century, a period of large-scale and increasingly complex building led to new spatial designs and structural techniques, the mass production of iron, and, after 1870, the availability of cheap steel.[59]

Iron-and-glass construction provided the built infrastructure for the modern industrial world. At the same time as the streets of Paris were being widened and reconfigured under the direction of Baron Haussmann during the Second Empire, large buildings were being constructed as sites for manufacturing goods of various types. Even larger structures of similar construction were being built as nodal points in the built infrastructure of the city. These included the Gare Montparnasse train station, constructed in 1852, where Méliès worked more than seventy years later; the central food market, Les Halles, constructed in 1853; and the leather market, the Nouvelle Halle aux Cuirs, constructed in 1867.[60]

With industrialization, "The division of labor in boot and shoemaking followed the same general pattern as in the clothing trade," Sean Wilentz explains, "Work [. . .] in the shops of [. . .] shoemakers and [. . .] bootmakers was divided into the very few skilled cutting chores [. . .] and the simpler, more repetitive tasks of the crimpers, fitters, and bottomers."[61] Cutting multiples from the same pattern rather than cutting out each and every piece individually was a crucial element

FIGURE 1.4. Advertisement, *Moniteur de la Cordonnerie*
(December 16, 1884), Bibliothèque nationale de France.

of emerging modes of mass production. For shoemaking, as for other garment trades, this was done with band saws, which were widely used to "cut leather for boots and shoes."[62] A band saw is visible in the foreground of the drawing of the Société Méliès factory. Machines like those depicted on the right side of the drawing likewise made construction of shoes considerably more efficient. An advertisement published in many issues of *Le Moniteur de la Cordonnerie* during the 1880s illustrated the exponential increases in productivity that could be achieved with mechanization: the advertisement shows a man seated on a bench, hunched over a shoe pulling a stitch tight to attach the sole of a shoe—right next to that, the same man is shown standing beside a rotary machine doing the same job; beneath the illustration on the left the caption reads "3 pairs per day" and beneath the illustration on the right the caption reads "300 pairs per day."

The importance of "cutters" (*coupeurs*) in the shoemaking and bootmaking process was of such great importance that this category of workers had their own organization within the industry, the Société Dite Réunion des Coupeurs.[63] The paragon of the métier of the cordonnier-bottier was the ability to make a shoe that did not need a separate sole—so skillfully designed and cut that it required only a single piece of leather; thus, a separate sole was not needed, nor was any sewing, gluing, nailing, screwing, or fastening required. Indeed, in 1878, Jean-Louis Méliès created something of a sensation in the industry by producing a Molière slipper made with "a single piece of leather" that required no sewing whatsoever. Years later, it was recalled by industry insiders as nothing short of a *"tour de force."*[64]

In 1885, "When he [Méliès] came back from England his father made him work [. . .] cutting shoes all day long."[65] Later, as a filmmaker, Méliès treated celluloid like a shoemaker treated leather—he was loathe to waste any, and he placed similar emphasis on cutting, even though his cuts were made straight across strips of celluloid negative film between individual 35mm film frames rather than around patterns on pieces of leather.[66] The process of assembling an article of footwear was known as "confection" or "montage"—the latter term would later be used to describe what became known as film editing. Individual pieces were most often sewn together, although parts of some types of footwear were sometimes joined with nails, screws, and/or glue.

By the 1880s, factory-made shoes and boots constituted the lion's share of the market, and footwear manufactured by Jean-Louis Méliès and Pinet epitomized the high-quality fashion goods that could be produced in Paris through the factory system. Mass production of French footwear ramped up significantly as large firms increased mechanization and division of labor. But, even as Jean-Louis Méliès and Pinet constructed factories and staffed them with numerous workers to increase the volume of their output, they retained handicraft as an adjunct to methods of mass production. Handicraft was one of the hallmarks of French shoemaking and bootmaking that conferred international prestige on high-end French footwear, helping to make its products distinctive from lower-priced goods produced in the United States and elsewhere.[67]

One distinctive feature of "first-class shoes" manufactured by the Société Méliès was that they were "sewn by hand" (*cousues à la main*).[68] Unlike footwear that was "machine-sewn" (*cousu machine*), hand-sewn footwear relied to a far greater extent on skilled human labor, conferring international distinction and prestige (and higher prices) on French shoes and boots.[69] But sewn by hand and machine-sewn were not mutually exclusive because the production practices employed by the Société Méliès—like Pinet and other de luxe manufacturers—relied on combining and conflating individual human handwork with machinery-assisted methods of mass production.

Much of the handcraft that was marketed to buyers of de luxe French footwear appears to have been done by specialized—and exclusively female—outworkers called *piqueuses*, whose work was done "entirely by hand" in their homes, and who were employed by the day (working ten-to eleven-hour days) or on a piecework basis making the uppers for bottines. The handiwork of piqueuses was further subdivided into successive phases that involved varying levels of skill, experience, and training, each of which was assigned to different categories of

female workers—*bâtisseuses, mécaniciennes,* and *finisseuses.*[70] Piqueuses constituted a comparatively large outwork workforce generally paid on a piecework
basis that complemented factory labor involving machines and a much greater
proportion of more stably employed male workers.

Female outworkers appear to have greatly outnumbered their factory counterparts. In 1881, Pinet employed one hundred and fifty workers in his factory
and between seven and eight hundred more outworkers.[71] Like Pinet, Jean-Louis
Méliès manufactured footwear with a mode of production that was both industrial and artisanal. Although some part of the work done by some piqueuses might
be replaced by machines, the most visibly distinctive and highest-paid handiwork
was impossible to accomplish with machines. It was done by a specific subset of
piqueuses: female workers called *brodeuses mécaniciennes* who were, as one 1886
account explained, nothing short of "worker-artists" (*ouvrière-artistes*). Their
"pretty embroideries ornament the finest and most elegant shoes with capricious
arabesques and charming designs that so beautifully decorate the *bottines* and *sou-
liers* destined for our elegant Parisiennes."[72] These embroidered patterns can be
seen on the pair of Méliès bottines that was chosen as the cover image for this book
and on many of the bottines manufactured by Pinet.[73] High-heeled bottines were
recognized around the world during the late nineteenth century as a distinctively
French contribution to the sartorial arts and embroidered finishes helped make
some styles of Méliès brand women's footwear prized international luxury items.

Peter McNeil and Giorgio Riello note that men have long been quite "concerned with how they are shod,"

> Yet the shoe museums and the extant objects prioritize women. [. . .]
> Apart from a few striking examples, men might almost not exist in the
> shoe museum. The ordinary nature—or perhaps better to say the norma-
> tive nature—of men's shoes makes them unremarkable objects to collect.
> Women's shoes, on the other hand, have all the right features to become
> collectors' items. Although we have insisted on designer wear and the im-
> portance of the shoe with provenance (the "unique" piece), women's shoes
> are collected for other reasons. They are often tokens of memory and are
> left by mothers to daughters. Nineteenth-century wedding slippers survive
> in their thousands and are carefully preserved in old chests for generations
> to come. Other shoes are kept because of their inherent beauty or because
> of their decoration.[74]

One of the best examples of Méliès brand footwear is the pair of wedding shoes
worn by Eugénie Génin when she and Méliès were married in 1885.

FIGURE 1.5. Eugénie Méliès' wedding shoes, Musée du compagnonnage.

Footwear/Film

Marshall McLuhan treats clothing as "media" because they are "extensions of man [*sic*]." While television and radio extend the senses of sight and hearing across great distances beyond the body, clothing provides individuals with an "extended skin" that is a "direct extension of the outer surface of the body."[75] Clothing provides the individual protection from the elements and an ability to survive and thrive in different climates while serving "as a means of defining the self socially."[76] Shoes and boots allow the wearer to transit surfaces more smoothly and safely while helping cushion the impacts of countless footsteps. Historically, footwear furnished the perambulatory baseline that developments of the Second Industrial Revolution extended with faster and more efficient modes of locomotion and transportation as well as more direct, more seamless, and more extensive road, rail, and water networks on which vehicles drawn by horses and driven by steam and internal combustion engines traveled. Many of these modes of locomotion relied on leather straps, as did conveying the motive power of rotating steam and internal combustion engines.[77]

Here, however, I understand clothing, and shoes specifically, less as actual media, than as material commodities that were analogous to motion pictures. Film director Josef von Sternberg used the comparison pejoratively, "I work on assignment; namely, to order. And this order is exactly the same as those

the [. . .] shoemaker commissioned to do a particular job receive[s]."[78] Despite
the ostensible self-deprecation of Sternberg's comparison between shoemaking and filmmaking, by the time of these comments, the very idea of ordering
made-to-measure shoes was a privilege available only to the extremely wealthy.
Indeed, during the 1920s, Salvatore Ferragamo was producing custom shoes for
a wealthy clientele of Hollywood stars for whom he crafted individual wooden
lasts that yielded an exact fit.[79]

While no film could ever provide the sheer utility of a good pair of boots,
Soviet filmmaker Dziga Vertov welcomed the comparison after "a certain filmmaker" tried to denigrate an installment of the state newsreel *Kino-Pravda* by
saying that the films were made by "shoemakers not filmmakers." Intended as
an insult, Vertov retorted that he and his collaborators, the Kinoks "were the
first to make *film-objects* with our bare hands," and like shoes, these films were
"necessary objects, vital objects, aimed at life and needed in life."[80] Vertov thus
claimed that he was "very flattered by such unconditional recognition as the *first
shoemaker of Russian cinema*," a title he said was much preferable to either "artist
of Russian cinema" or "artistic film director," adding for emphasis, "To hell with
shoe wax. To hell with boots that are nothing but shine. Give us boots made of
leather."[81] Acknowledging the material character of leather footwear and what
is translated as "film-objects," Vertov contrasted shoemakers with "shoe shiners,"
accusing other filmmakers of "polish[ing] someone's literary shoes (they have
high French heels, if the film's a hit) with cinematic wax."[82]

Vertov used the analogy between cinema and shoes (which had their own specific literary and artistic connotations in Russian culture) to strike a rhetorical
blow in a debate within Soviet circles about cinematic specificity and adaptation,
but his acknowledgment of the material basis of cinema and boots is apposite
here. Although Vertov does not seem to have pushed the analogy further himself,
the work of filmmaking—especially as it was practiced by Soviet filmmakers—
shared with shoemaking an emphasis on cutting. Despite their relatively modest
size, a typical pair of shoes might have been made up of a dozen individual pieces
of leather inside and out.[83] Cutting these pieces was perhaps the most skilled part
of the shoemaking process. It was vitally important because it determined the fit
of the finished product and because mistakes resulted in wasted material.[84]

In *The Fashion System*, Roland Barthes makes a pertinent distinction between the "photographed or drawn" garment, which he calls "image-clothing"
and "the same garment, but described, transformed into language, [. . .] this is
a written garment. In principle these two garments refer to the same reality
[. . .], and yet they do not have the same structure, because they are not made

of the same substances."[85] Barthes emphasizes that "image-clothing" and the "written garment" are distinct from "the real garment [that] forms a third structure, different from the first two, even if it serves them as model."[86] Examples of Méliès brand boots and shoes have survived less as real garments than as "image-clothing"—black-and-white engravings in the single Méliès shoe catalogue known to survive—and "written clothing"—scattered descriptions in the industry trade press. Images of many styles of Méliès footwear are quite scarce because many of the color fashion plates that were published with *Le Moniteur de la Cordonnerie* and *Le Franc Parleur Parisien* have gotten separated from the surviving bound issues of the journals, which can seemingly only be found in single copies at the Bibliothèque nationale de France (acquired because French law dictated mandatory deposit of all publications).[87]

Unlike "image-clothing" or "written clothing," examining surviving material objects presents challenges, which Barthes describes,

> "Seeing" a real garment, even under privileged conditions of presentation, cannot exhaust its reality, still less its structure: we never see more than part of a garment, a personal and circumstantial usage, a particular way of wearing it; in order to analyze the real garment in systematic terms, i.e. in terms sufficiently formal to account for all analogous garments, we should no doubt have to work our way back to the actions which governed its manufacture. In other words, given the plastic structure of image-clothing and the verbal structure of written clothing, the structure of real clothing can only be technological. The units of this structure can only be the various traces of the actions of manufacture, their materialized and accomplished goals: a seam is what has been sewn, the cut of a coat is what has been cut; there is then a structure which is constituted at the level of substance and its transformations, not of its representations or significations.[88]

Physical examination of the pair of Méliès bottines shown on the cover of this book revealed "traces of the actions of manufacture" not visible on the exterior of the article of clothing: the conjunction of individual pieces of fabric (including the cotton and silk with which this pair was lined) and leather that were cut, sewn, and nailed together in three dimensions to fit the contours of human feet. The trained eye could discern that the uppers of this pair of bottines were machine stitched, although the eyelets were indeed "sewn by hand" (as the epithet of the Société Méliès promised) by a piqueuse.[89] Even an untrained eye could appreciate the precise needlework of the unknown *brodeuse mécanicienne* (or *brodeuses mécaniciennes*) who embroidered the autumnal wheat motif with which these bottines were so beautifully embellished.

Surviving 35mm prints of Méliès films reward this same kind of hands-on scrutiny. A closer look at individual frames of a viewing copy of a hand-colored print of *La Légende de Rip Van Vinckle* [incomplete] on a flatbed viewer at the Motion Picture Study Center at the George Eastman House Museum of Photography and Film showed traces of the brushstrokes applied by hand-colorists who finished Méliès' release prints like the piqueuses who embroidered bottines that had been manufactured by the Société Méliès. Direct examination of a print of *Le Chevalier mystère* revealed, surprisingly, that "Méliès accomplished some of his photographic tricks not only by manipulating the negative but also by cutting and splicing parts of each positive print. [. . .] Méliès [. . .] in some cases 'edited' the visual effect on *all* distribution copies, certainly a time-consuming job for his collaborators."[90]

Wendy Haslem notes, "Celluloid materiality privileges contact, touch, physical connection."[91] While the manipulations involved in watching digital media may constitute "an alternative form of tactility," Haslem suggests, the element of materiality is in any case much diminished although "traces of cinematic specificity" do visibly persist after "the transformation of celluloid material to virtual images."[92] Digital technology can of course be used to eradicate these traces and to approximate inherently analog aspects of the silent film experience like hand-coloring, as the version of *Voyage dans la Lune* screened at the Cannes Film Festival in 2011 and subsequently marketed on digital video disc demonstrates. Such are the hazards of what I would describe as an "over-restoration" that effaced the material traces left by splice marks, regularized some of the inherent irregularities of hand-coloring, and inserted digitally colorized black-and-white footage to offset sequences missing from a brittle, disintegrating, hand-colored print.[93]

Paolo Cherchi Usai emphasizes that "silent films have morphed over the years. [. . .] Every time a silent film is duplicated, some of its material history becomes hidden from sight, adding or subtracting a new layer to it (a digital reproduction makes it disappear altogether into an eternal present, one for each new migration; no further stratification is allowed)." Digital copies of these same titles tend to obscure "the constant change of film as an artefact and as a creative work," traces of which are so often visibly and palpably present in physical prints.[94]

CHAPTER 2

Incohérent Infrastructure, Incohérent Fashion

I
N HIS SWEEPING HISTORY of technology, Bertrand Gille insists, "An industrial revolution must be dealt with in global terms, not in terms of isolated disparate elements."[1] For Gille, industrial revolutions occur not as the consequence of a progressive series of technological improvements but are fundamentally relational, produced by an "interlocking of techniques and the establishment of a satisfactory equilibrium," yielding "the formation of a new technical system."[2] Gille describes this state of technical equilibrium between multiple systems, subsystems, and techniques as a "coherent ensemble of compatible structures," while stressing the interdependence of technical systems. "This means therefore, that, in general, all techniques are dependent upon the others, and this necessity requires a certain coherence: the coherence within the structures, ensembles, and series constitute what could be called a technical system."[3] Thus, for Gille, an industrial revolution is characterized by a "mise en cohérence" of previously disconnected or ill-connected technologies and systems—not by a rupture or a caesura.[4]

In France, according to François Caron, this mise en cohérence began around 1880 at the onset of the Second Industrial Revolution with more effective linkage between technological systems and systems of infrastructure that intensified the Industrial Revolution through increased access to energy sources and new modes of transportation.[5] Like other French de luxe footwear manufacturers, the Société Méliès relied on new technologies (as well as skilled human labor). The Société Méliès was also embedded within stable, coherent Second Industrial Revolution networks of infrastructure that provided its factory with energy to power machinery and for interior illumination, raw materials with which to manufacture footwear, and the transportation systems required to supply domestic and export markets. Once achieved, however, the coherent equilibrium state of technical systems often proved remarkably fragile. Indeed, in Caron's historical schema, dysfunction was almost inevitable.[6] Interconnected systems almost always became misaligned, and the consequences were economic as well as material, resulting in financial calamities and catastrophic accidents, which were sometimes—but not always—rectified through subsequent systemic adjustments.

The beginning of the Second Industrial Revolution was a period of systemic adjustments when interconnected systems were aligned to achieve a more sustainable coherence. The initial incoherence of these systems caused a sustained economic depression that affected much of the world economy. Roger Price explains,

> The period, c. 1880– [. . .] [w]as one of crisis [. . .] during which the industrial economy gained its maturity and technical development accelerated, in particular through the introduction of new products especially by the chemical, engineering, [and] electricity [. . .] industries [. . .] [which] prepared the way for a "second industrialization." [. . .] By c. 1880, the basic structure of an industrial economy had been established. There followed a difficult period of adaptation to the more competitive conditions of relatively integrated national and international markets created by improved communications and free trade. [. . .] Along with other industrialising countries, France experienced a long period of economic depression and crisis.[7]

The depression was particularly hard on rural areas. Price notes, "The period between 1874 and 1895, that of the 'great depression' in agriculture, was to be particularly difficult because of the decline in the prices of most farm products [. . .] [which] also affected, although far less severely, the producers of meat."[8] Caron likewise refers to this as "the great agricultural depression of the late nineteenth century," which resulted in "a general and marked drop in prices."[9] These falling prices were noted with alarm in the trade press of the French footwear industry.[10] The great agricultural depression in France helped consolidate the shift from local made-to-measure shoemaking to mass production of ready-to-wear footwear in standard sizes. As Caron puts it, "The fall in industrial prices permitted a transfer of activity from peasant production of articles for peasant use toward industrial production of the same goods."[11] Some mass production also shifted from Paris to provincial localities as a response to the 1882 strike of cordonniers.[12]

Until the 1880s, the majority of France's national product had come from agriculture. Unlike artisanal made-to-measure (*au détail*) shoemaking, which persisted mainly at the local level through the work of numerous cordonniers and bottiers who combined making and selling footwear in a single location and sometimes a single individual, shoe manufacturing was part of the increasingly significant industrial sector. The footwear industry, however, was totally reliant on farm-raised animals for its primary raw material. Various substitutes for leather were tried, but none replaced cowhide. Nor was an acceptable alternative to the time-consuming "tanning" process used to make durable high-quality leather devised.[13]

Despite falling cattle prices, tanners and shoemakers alike were caught in the downward spiral of lower prices for raw leather and the declining value of leather goods that exacerbated what was consistently described during the 1880s as a "commercial crisis" for the French footwear industry.[14] Because meat prices were relatively unaffected by the depression, only butchers profited from lower prices for cattle, according to Arthur Taire, the publisher of *Le Franc Parleur Parisien*.[15] Although it seemed counterintuitive that falling cattle prices would not result in lower leather prices, this was one of numerous examples of how a disruption in one part of the economy could have unexpected and damaging repercussions for other parts of the economy.

The commercial crises that affected the French leathermaking and footwear industries (along with countless other international industries) during the 1880s were tragic demonstrations of the degree to which different parts of the French economy were linked not only to one another but also to markets and supply chains that extended far beyond France's borders. Ironically, French footwear manufacturers were unable to benefit from lower prices for slaughtered cattle because the footwear industry was subject to the actions of the leather industry, where tanners were loath to invest their scarce capital in animal skins, however discounted. Leather producers were reticent to stockpile animal hides offered for sale at reduced prices because consumer demand for leather products (including footwear) had decreased and because the availability of lower-priced fake leather (much of it imported) was further stunting demand for high-quality leather produced in the traditional way.[16] Some so-called fake leathers (*cuirs fraudés*) were made from cowhides but involved an accelerated chemical process rather than the time-intensive tanning process, compromising quality and durability. The difference between "fake" and properly tanned leather was not necessarily visible to the untrained eye, and so consumers generally only discovered that the shoes or boots they had purchased at lower prices were made from fake leather when their footwear wore out more quickly than previous pairs and needed to be replaced sooner than expected.[17]

The effects of imported fake leather on the French footwear industry were but one example of the kinds of deleterious disconnections that were endemic to modern global capitalism. The Société Méliès was dependent on a number of different domestic suppliers and international markets and the transportation and communication networks that linked them all together (along with several hundred employees who were split between factory labor and outwork). The viability of numerous Second Industrial Revolution enterprises like the Société Méliès entirely depended on the vagaries of interconnected suppliers, markets, and intermediaries, as did the livelihoods of millions of French citizens. While the refusal to speculate on leather commodity futures had contributed to the stagnation of the footwear industry during the 1880s, a more speculative approach doomed what remained of the Méliès family business in 1895 when a disruption to the supply chain, "a sharp increase in the price of leather ruined Gaston" Méliès, who had previously secured a remunerative "contract to supply boots to the military" that was canceled when Gaston Méliès et Cie, the company which Gaston Méliès had formed to supersede the Société Méliès, was no longer able to supply the contracted boots at the agreed-upon price because of the unexpected increase in the cost of a primary raw material.[18]

The Rue François-Miron Catastrophe

Just as market misalignments in the modern world economy could have damaging consequences, so too were material disconnections in the modern urban built environment liable to cause disastrous results. The 1882 rue François-Miron catastrophe was one damaging example that stemmed from a tiny flaw in the interconnected infrastructure for distributing gas throughout Paris. Initially, construction of gas mains in France had lagged behind other European countries, but by the 1880s Paris had become the "city of light" through gaslight illumination.[19] Consolidation occurred when Paris's six separate gas suppliers merged to form the Paris Compagnie du Gaz, which supplied the city with more than 244 million cubic meters of gas in 1880.[20] One consequence of this infrastructure was what Wolfgang Schivelbusch aptly calls the "industrialization of light" through which individual unconnected light sources were progressively replaced by an interconnected network of illumination: "While the individual oil lantern with its fuel reservoir was a self-contained, autonomous apparatus, the individual gaslight was part of a big industrial complex."[21] Schivelbusch adds, "Gaslight, like the railway, reigned supreme as a symbol of human and industrial progress."[22] Along with fueling numerous street lamps, gaslight also provided interior lighting for countless businesses and factories, including the Société

Méliès. Gaslight was more of a means of extending the working day than it was a domestic convenience.[23]

Functionally, gaslight was brighter than light produced by burning oil, paraffin, or wax; it was also omnidirectional because gas flames did not have to be upright and were adjustable, since the intensity of gas flames could be dimmed or brightened with the turn of a knob. Because no wicks were involved, gaslight did not produce smoke or soot. Perhaps most convenient was its self-renewing supply, which meant consumers were not responsible for refueling individual lights because each flame was supplied with gas through built infrastructure. But, gas was costly and gas flames burned very hot, consumed lots of oxygen, and released noxious ammonia, sulfur, and carbon dioxide vapors that could blacken ceilings and were hazardous to inhale so needed to be properly ventilated.[24]

With the convenience of getting gas from a central supply (and all the construction that made this convenience possible) came environmental consequences. Gas mains were notoriously leaky and foul smelling and could poison the soil and the water supply.[25] The effects of natural gas on the water supply were particularly problematic because placement of gas lines typically paralleled water infrastructure and—if not properly sealed—could contaminate drinking water. Gas explosions occurred with some frequency and were often extremely violent and destructive. The explosions that devastated part of the rue François-Miron in the fourth arrondissement of Paris on the morning of July 12, 1882, were the direct results of the proximity of gas and water pipelines. Water from a leaky pipe had seeped into an adjacent gas line, causing gas to leak and accumulate underground.[26] Once ignited, the burning gas spread beneath streets, where it was difficult to extinguish, resulting in subsequent explosions.

The rue François-Miron catastrophe destroyed several buildings and caused numerous casualties. London's *Journal of Gas Lighting, Water Supply, and Sanitary Improvement* called it a "terrible disaster, involving instant death to five persons and grievous injury to about forty more." After the odor of gas was smelled and an explosion was heard, firefighters were brought to the scene, but the fire had already begun spreading underground, with "flames issuing from an open sewer-pipe. [...] These excited the curiosity of the passers by who, unfortunately, gathered round in a large crowd, little dreaming of the peril to which they were exposing themselves. [...] [A] deafening explosion took place, accompanied by a dense cloud of dust. As soon as the dust cleared, the pavement was seen to be covered with bleeding and unconscious forms."[27] Streets were barricaded for days while the cleanup and the search for bodies continued. The carnage was horrific, with a number of survivors suffering serious injury. Clearing the debris took a week.[28] When the street lights were eventually put back on, traumatized area residents panicked, fearing more explosions.[29]

Tragedies like the rue François-Miron catastrophe revealed the horrifying damage that could ensue from a small imperfection in the interlocking systems of the modern city. The violence and destructiveness of gas explosions was well known—indeed a gas explosion had rocked the rue Béranger only a few months earlier—but the inaccessible location of the gas leak and its underlying cause were especially troubling. In effect, the physical proximity of two forms of vital infrastructure (engineered as separate but parallel systems) had compromised both, with devastating consequences.

Also troubling was the failure of other forms of infrastructure leading up to the fatal explosions and ensuing conflagration. What was sometimes omitted from the reporting on the rue François-Miron catastrophe (including the account quoted above) was that several people in the area had smelled gas and reported it sometime before the first explosion, but local authorities had failed to respond in time. As investigators worked to identify the cause of the catastrophe, they discovered that the gas leak had in fact been reported to the police department, the fire department, and the gas company relatively quickly, but confusion over who was responsible to respond had slowed and ultimately thwarted a timely response. Duchêne, the proprietor of the Café des Entrepreneurs, which was obliterated by the blast, had smelled a strong odor of gas coming from the cellar early in the morning and had gone immediately to the nearest post office to notify authorities, "But, since there was no one in the office at that time, he had to wait until the proper employee arrived."[30] The proprietor of another restaurant in the area had also smelled gas and had informed the gas company. But, by the time the gas company and firefighters arrived on the scene, the first explosion at Chaland's hairdresser shop had already occurred, followed soon thereafter by a second, larger explosion across the street at the Café des Entrepreneurs.[31]

Gas explosions and the resulting fires were a continual source of concern in Paris at the time. Just a few months earlier, the Opéra-Comique caught fire after a gas line in the theater exploded, but luckily a group of workmen working nearby averted catastrophe by shutting off the gas despite the imminent danger: "But for the gallantry of a gas-fitter, who braved almost certain death to turn off the metre, the whole building and the adjoining houses would have been blown to atoms."[32]

In the aftermath of the rue François-Miron catastrophe, local authorities took action to try to prevent further accidents like it. In addition to the commission charged with investigating its cause and the municipal response to the disaster, charitable efforts were organized to help the victims and their families.[33] One such charitable effort was the very first Incohérent exposition, an August 2, 1882, benefit held in a fairground booth on the Champs-Élysées. Scholars of the Incohérents have paid relatively scant attention to this first Incohérent exposition or the event to which it responded. But, by taking stock of this earlier exposition, we can understand the art of the Incohérents in direct relationship to a specifically modern Second Industrial Revolution urban tragedy.

The 1881 edition of the *Dictionnaire de la langue française* defined "incohérent" negatively as a "lack of coherence" while citing its figurative meaning as the incomprehensible use of language—"ideas, words, or phrases that do not follow, that do not form a whole or a well-connected combination," including "incoherent metaphors that combine two incompatible images."[34] This definition accords with most existing accounts of the Incohérents inasmuch as the group relished wordplay and created art based on visual metaphors, but the rue François-Miron catastrophe resonates with more literal and material definitions like the physical state of incoherence exemplified by water, a substance that was fluid because its constituent elements did not cohere.[35] Gas was an even more incoherent substance, one that was so fluid and subject to dispersal that it was typically invisible and often perceptible only with the sense of smell. This part of the definition accords with Prudence Boissière's definition of "incohérent" as a state of discord in which parts were poorly linked together.[36]

The First Incohérent Exposition

In a modern world that did not cohere—in which the material incoherence of water and gas could prove corrosive and even explosive—the Incohérents responded with absurd aesthetic inconsistencies.[37] The artists who called themselves "Incohérents" highlighted the inevitable frictions that remained despite the mise en cohérence that occurred in the 1880s with the Second Industrial Revolution and its increasing coordination of interconnected systems and technologies. Some at the time who would not necessarily have called themselves Incohérents—much less artists, perhaps—shared certain aspects of this Incohérent sensibility.

Among extremely few documents of the first Incohérent exposition on Wednesday, August 2, 1882, was a report by Paul Fresnay published in the daily newspaper *Le Voltaire*.[38] It was part of a show to benefit victims and survivors of the rue François-Miron catastrophe and their families. The benefit consisted of several booths staffed by more than a dozen known Parisian actresses selling flowers, cigarettes, fans, and trinkets who together raised several thousand francs. The actresses also worked as barkers trying to attract visitors into several sideshows, which visitors were charged to enter. Rodolphe Salis, founder of Montmartre's Chat Noir cabaret, was shilling a booth that he called the "musée du Chat Noir," loudly claiming that what was inside was superior to Paris's famous wax museum, the Musée Grévin. The highlight of the benefit, according to Fresnay, was "l'exposition des incohérents" Jules Lévy offered as a preview of the large exposition he was organizing for October. Lévy, "the inventor of the whole thing," Paul Bilhaut, Henri Gray, "the caricaturist," and others organized a traditional fairground parade in front of the Incohérents' booth.[39] Fresnay described it as "a parody of a Salon" and "a very amusing caricature of a Salon" that included a painting on a silk top hat; a painting on a broom explained verbally as *peinture à poil*, a phrase that literalized the colloquial phrase *à poil*, meaning nude, with a painting *on a brush* (*à poil*); and "some microscopic watercolors" of which no further description was given other than the farcical claim that they were the work "of Téniers and Meissonier the Younger." Also on display was a parody of Alfred-Philippe Roll's 1882 realist painting "La Fête du 14 Juillet" made abstract by Gray, in which only the nocturnal fireworks of France's first Bastille Day celebration (adopted as a national holiday just two years earlier) were visible as spots of different colors on an otherwise entirely black canvas. The painting was signed "D'roll," a pseudonym that humorously conflated the prepositional phrase "d'Roll" ("by Roll") with its homonym "drôle" (funny). Fresnay declared the event a great success despite how hot the day was and despite how many Parisians had left the city on summer vacations.

Most accounts of the Incohérents focus on the widely reported and well-attended Incohérent art exposition Lévy held at his Paris apartment several months later on October 1, 1882. Lévy described it as an "exposition of drawings by people who do not know how to draw."[40] Two thousand visitors were reported to have seen the show in only four hours, which was as long as the art remained on display—an appropriately evanescent public opening for what would be a highly ephemeral series of art exhibitions. This and the first Incohérent exposition were a deliberate affront to standards of artistic training and measures of artistic accomplishment that rejected established venues for exhibiting art and traditional materials used to create art. The Incohérents flouted artistic norms while creating works that were often conspicuously unaccomplished.

The catalogue for the 1884 Incohérent exposition contained an entry for a work entitled "Le gaz à vingt-cinq centimes du litre" (Gas at twenty-five centimes per liter) followed by a description, "Offered by the Compagnie du Gaz for the decoration of the new Hôtel-de-Ville."[41] This presumably immaterial Incohérent artwork made a joke of the high prices charged by the municipal gas supplier for Paris, which had a monopoly on the utility and sold gas at prices that were too expensive for most residential consumers. What the artwork might have consisted of—if it consisted of anything material whatsoever—is entirely unclear.

The March 12, 1885, issue of *Le Courrier français* was devoted to "Les Incohérents." *Le Courrier français* had begun publication in 1884 as a weekly illustrated journal of literature, fine arts, and theater—as well as medicine and finance, according to its facetious masthead. Edited by Jules Roques, it was more or less the official organ of the Incohérents during their heyday.[42] Its front page featured an engraved image of a man and a woman wearing variegated costumes and unusual hats making their entry to an Incohérent ball, drawn by Henri Gray. Peeking around the edge of the image is another costumed figure wielding a stick. Below the image, the caption reads, "The Entrance to the Ball and the Flight of Formal Dress." Seven miniature men wearing black tailcoats striking unusual physical poses arrayed around the edge of the image correspond to the second part of the caption. In this drawing, the Incohérent ball is depicted as a festive happening that visibly discombobulated existing codes of formal dress. Masquerade balls, Incohérent and otherwise, provided regular opportunities to upend conventional dress codes. Méliès reveled in a variety of costumes as a stage and screen actor, but outside of the theater and the studio, he typically wore a dark suit in photographs—with the exception of one notable example, dated 1879, in which Méliès was photographed in costume as "l'Incroyable."

Gray's engraving suggests how Incohérent costume balls offered a temporary reprieve from monochromatic male dress, leaving formality dwarfed and in disarray in its wake. Fashion historian John Harvey writes, by "choosing to wear certain clothes, one may be [. . .] conjuring a new persona for oneself," because with clothing, "a kind of magic is involved, as if, by arraying oneself in their colours, one were inviting the genius or daemon of fun [. . .] to possess one body and soul."[43] Shortly after the 1887 Incohérent ball, Lévy declared that Incohérence was dead, but his proclamation hardly put an end to either Incohérent expositions or balls, which continued for nearly a decade.[44]

Mary Gluck includes the Incohérents as part of the historical and geographical category of "popular bohemia," which centered on late nineteenth-century Paris.[45] Gluck's focus on the inherently popular character of bohemia is generative and yields a version of Incohérence that is a bit more inclusive and vernacular than strictly art-historical accounts. The version of Incohérence proposed here designates an even wider and more widely shared response to possibilities, precarities, fragmentation, and disconnection produced by the Second

FIGURE 2.1. H. Gray, "L'Entrée du Bal et la Fuite des Habits noirs," *Le Courrier français* (March 12, 1885): 1, Bibliothèque nationale de France.

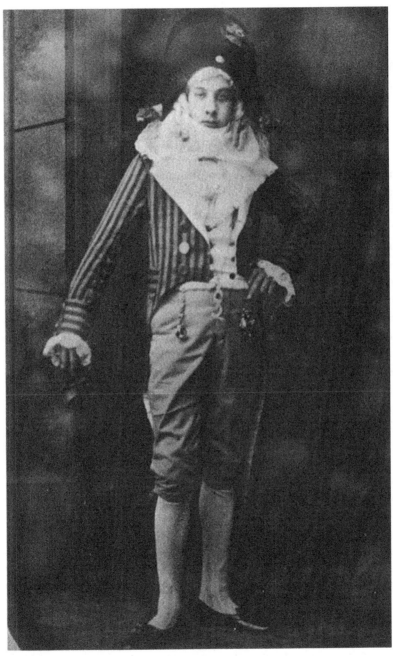

FIGURE 2.2. Méliès in costume as l'Incroyable, c.1879,

Industrial Revolution. It was a flippant para-literary and quasi-aesthetic response to the increasingly industrialized, impersonal, bureaucratic, mediated, and mass-produced character of modern life that flourished in Paris during the 1880s. Although I suspect its impertinent spirit can likely be found in other professions, my focus is on the French footwear industry and the professionals who worked in its administrative, managerial, and journalistic ranks.

Incohérent Transportation

Late nineteenth-century France was physically linked domestically and internationally through transportation systems involving steam-driven locomotives, horse-drawn conveyances, and later by vehicles powered by internal combustion engines. Transportation systems facilitated the circulation of people and objects (including employees of the Société Méliès and its wares), but these very systems were subject to frustrating failures. Several of Méliès' earliest films were filmed on location at Paris railway stations: *Arrivée d'un train (gare de Vincennes)* [lost] and *Arrivée d'un train (gare de Joinville)* [lost] showed trains arriving at the Vincennes and Joinville stations, while a third film, *La Gare Saint-Lazare* [lost] showed another even larger Paris train station. Railroad lines served a commercial function while facilitating access to new sites for leisure, as seen in *Le Voyage de la famille Bourrichon*, one of Méliès' last films. The Ligne du Nord allowed Méliès and his family to vacation annually at the seashore in Mers-les-Bains near Le Tréport in Brittany, departing and returning from Paris by way of the Gare Montparnasse, where Méliès later worked as a toy and candy merchant.[46]

But, transportation did not always proceed smoothly and without incident. Recurring railroad accidents were recognized in the nineteenth century as a feature of modern life that, according to Schivelbusch, actually served as "a negative indicator of technological progress" despite—or perhaps because of—the horrible accidents that could result: "One might also say that the more civilized the schedule and the more efficient the technology, the more catastrophic its destruction when it collapses. There is an exact ratio between the level of the technology with which nature is controlled, and the degree of severity of its accidents."[47] Méliès staged railroad accidents on a small scale in his studio for films like *Le Voyage à travers l'impossible* and *Le Tunnel sous la Manche ou le Cauchemar anglo-français*, but he was personally subject to less catastrophic—though nevertheless unpleasant—effects of railway journeys as a regular railroad passenger. A year before making his first films, after taking no less than eight round trips from Paris to Tréport on the Ligne du Nord between Paris and Brittany (where the tracks were in disrepair) during the summer of 1895, Méliès wrote a letter to the newspaper complaining about how badly he and his fellow passengers had been knocked around during the three-hour-and-ten-minute express train trip. Méliès wrote that some people on the train experienced violent motion sickness and feared the train would derail at any moment, causing an accident (which had recently happened along that route). In his letter, Méliès mentioned that he had complained during a stop in Beauvais, to which the station employee had responded laconically, "Yes, I know, everyone complains."[48]

Méliès' films often show us a world beset by accidents, mishaps, and disconnections, which Méliès found ways to make entertaining. According to an often-repeated anecdote that has become legendary, one of the foundational principles of Méliès' filmmaking aesthetic was an accidental discovery that purportedly occurred while Méliès was filming a Madeleine-Bastille horse trolley along the Place de l'Opéra:

> the camera I used in the early days (a primitive thing in which the film tore or frequently caught and refused to advance) jammed and produced an unexpected result. It took a minute to disengage the film and to start the camera up again. In the meantime, the passersby, horse trolleys, and other vehicles had, of course, changed positions. When I projected the strip of film, which I had stuck back together at the point of the break, I suddenly saw a Madeleine-Bastille horse trolley change into a hearse and men become women. The substitution or stop-camera trick had been discovered. Two days later, I carried out the first metamorphoses of men into women and the first sudden disappearances that, in the beginning, had such great success.[49]

This anecdote is telling because of the way Méliès describes a fundamental principle of trick cinematography as a constructive response to an accidental technological malfunction (though the discontinuity was orders of magnitude less damaging than the discontinuity that had caused the rue François-Miron catastrophe). This anecdote is doubly interesting because, as recounted by Méliès, the micro-level incoherence within the mechanism of the Kinétographe occurred while he was using it to film a moving demonstration of macro-level coherence: the smooth functioning of the Paris transportation infrastructure in the form of a street scene of circulating urban traffic.

Although it has many of the hallmarks of fiction, Méliès does specify that "the strip of film" was "stuck back together at the point of the break," indicating that the "so-called stop-camera trick" was not simply the result of a camera

stoppage and is more accurately described by the phrase "substitution splice." As
Jacques Malthête noted:

> This effect [stop camera] is always associated with a splice. [. . .] I know of
> no exception to this rule. Every appearance, disappearance or substitution
> was of course done in the camera but was always re-cut in the laboratory on
> the negative and for a very simple reason: this trick effect [. . .] will not work
> if the rhythm is broken. But the inertia of the camera was such that it was
> impossible to stop on the last frame of the "shot" before the "trick," change
> the background or the characters, and start up again on the first frame of
> the "shot" after the "trick" without having a noticeable variation in speed.[50]

The substitution splice was the basis for nearly all of the cinematic disappearances and appearances Méliès created. It is the sine qua non of his cinematic
aesthetic—a nearly ubiquitous technique across his entire career as a filmmaker.
In his own revealing account, the substitution splice trick was a creative transformation of one of the inevitable chance material discontinuities of modern technology into a bona fide cinematic technique—one which Méliès incorporated
into countless subsequent films.

By systematizing what was essentially a method of repairing broken films as
an aesthetic strategy, Méliès found a productive response to a micro-level incoherence. Modern life was fraught with the unintended consequences of seemingly minor misalignments, some of which could prove to be catastrophic rather
than entertaining. When a tiny fissure developed in a gas line that served the rue
François-Miron, a large quantity of leaking gas accumulated invisibly beneath
the street and was accidentally detonated, causing several violent explosions.
When a mismatch between the price of leather and the market for footwear
went unresolved, the entire industry was affected.

In the Margins of the French Footwear Industry Trade Press

During the second half of the nineteenth century, there was a fairly strong connection between shoemaking and the creative arts that left unmistakable traces
in the emerging trade press of the French footwear industry. The earliest of these
specialized publications was L'Innovateur: Journal des Cordonniers-Bottiers,
which became L'Innovateur: Le Moniteur de la Cordonnerie around the time
the first notices for the Maison Méliès appeared in 1855.[51] From the beginning,
the trade press of the shoe industry was closely linked to the leather industry.
Charles Vincent published both Le Moniteur de la Cordonnerie and La Halle
aux Cuirs, trade publications, respectively, for footwear and leather, but during

the 1850s, he was also a dramaturge who co-authored the play *L'Enfant du Tour de France*, set in the milieu of compagnonnage and a songwriter whose many published songs included "Un Chantier de Bohème," set in bohemia.[52]

In the pages of *Le Moniteur de la Cordonnerie*, Vincent's bohemian artistic sensibility coexisted with more straightforward and practical reporting on professional issues that directly related to the work of shoemakers and bootmakers. This dual emphasis on material productivity and creative expression was also characteristic of another important French footwear industry journal, *Le Franc Parleur Parisien*, which began publication in the wake of the 1882 cordonniers strike.[53] Along with help wanted advertisements, issues of *Le Franc Parleur Parisien* listed recent shoemaking patents, newly incorporated French shoemaking and leather businesses, mergers, separations, and bankruptcies. Several pages in each issue advertised selected French shoe manufacturers, makers of shoemaking machinery, producers of leathers and fabrics, pattern cutters, last makers, sellers of varnishes, waxes, and other products for treating leather, and vendors of shoe components and shoemaking supplies like heels, uppers, laces, eyelets, buttons, thread, and glue. Both journals reported on the professional activities of the Méliès family, including their participation in the trade organization formed by French footwear manufacturers, the Chambre Syndicale de la Chaussure en Gros de Paris (which Jean-Louis Méliès served as vice-president), gave marginal notices to the family firm, and occasionally discussed specific styles of Méliès shoes and boots.[54]

Both *Le Moniteur de la Cordonnerie* and *Le Franc Parleur Parisien* had varying subtitles that indicate the extent to which these trade publications were not exclusively or solely oriented to issues that had direct impact on the business or the practice of shoemaking. *Le Moniteur de la Cordonnerie* bore the subtitle *Journal Professionel, Artistique et Littéraire*, which indicates how "artistic" and "literary" matters were understood as complementary to the "professional" issues of shoemakers, who were especially interested in their own history, which dated back to the very beginnings of human civilization. Vincent himself published a magnum opus on the history of footwear and its most accomplished practitioners.[55] For its part, *Le Franc Parleur Parisien* carried the subtitle *Politique, Historique et Professionel Organe de la Cordonnerie et des Professions qui s'y rattachant*, indicating how "political" and "historical" matters were implicated in its contents. As both *Le Moniteur de la Cordonnerie* and *Le Franc Parleur Parisien* were published for the next several decades, these publications included fiction, poetry, songs, historical articles, and theatrical listings and reviews.

Storytelling was a part of compagnonnage that made its way into oral histories of the Méliès family, some of which were captured in Madeleine Malthête-Méliès' biography of her grandfather. There she recounted stories from long before her birth, tall tales which her great-grandfather Jean-Louis Méliès presumably told his family from his compagnon days: stopping a runaway freight train car with his bare hands, knocking six rival compagnons to the ground in a fistfight.[56] Stories like these connected individual compagnons to the storied past of fellow and former compagnons. A similar narrative impulse appeared in the print culture of the French shoe industry. *Le Moniteur de la Cordonnerie* included a *feuilleton* in every issue. These feuilletons were serialized stories about shoemaker characters that continued across consecutive issues with narratives that ranged from domestic melodramas to fairy tales. (Footwear, it bears noting, has long played a disproportionately important role in the fairy tale genre, as examples like *Le Chat Botté* [Puss in Boots] and *Cendrillon* [Cinderella], the latter which Méliès twice adapted for the screen, suggest.) Along with fictional content through these regular feuilletons, the report from Niort of the death at age seventy-eight of a cordonnier known as Père Vivier in an 1885 issue of *Le Franc Parleur Parisien* reads like a tall tale or a fairy tale: During his lifetime, Vivier had sired some forty-seven children (the youngest of whom was three at the time of his death) by four different wives and had successfully petitioned for the creation of a law that granted the fortieth child of a sexagenarian a special exception from mandatory military service.[57]

Songs were perhaps as important as stories to compagnons who had bonded along the Tour de France. Regular reunions of the Compagnons Cordonniers-Bottiers du Devoir in Paris often involved singing as well as verse recitations. The oral tradition of songs and poetry left its imprint on the trade press of the late nineteenth-century French footwear industry, in which it was not unusual to see a poem on the same page as quantities of leather imports and exports or on the same page as a discussion of a new fabric used in shoemaking.[58] The narrative and lyrical impulse found in *Le Moniteur de la Cordonnerie* and *Le Franc Parleur Parisien* appears to be largely absent from trade publications connected with other contemporaneous French industries and professions.

Gluck looks to this same historical period and this same geographic context to excavate "an alternative vision of modernism, capable of incorporating within it popular and everyday forms of culture."[59] Gluck proffers a "culture of everyday modernity" that is derived from "a historical archeology of [. . .] forms of popular culture [. . .] which [. . .] have fallen into oblivion."[60] Through the category of "popular bohemia," Gluck works "to uncover a hidden world of aesthetic discourse that has been swept aside by more familiar models of modernism formulated in the early twentieth century."[61] Her account of "everyday modernity" glosses "discussions [. . .] [that] took place outside established artistic circles or academic culture."[62] Along with Gluck's archaeological method, my work shares her conviction that "the origins of modernism [. . .] [are] an inseparable part of the humble and neglected regions of popular culture and everyday experience that found increasingly commercial articulation by the middle of the nineteenth century."[63] If, as Gluck suggests, popular bohemia can be excavated from "the debris of all professions," then footwear manufacturing in Paris during this period is no exception.[64]

Gluck is primarily concerned with late nineteenth-century "ironic bohemians" who helped promulgate "a myth about the artist's life invented by artists and mediated, perpetuated, and reinvented by popular culture [. . .] 'ironic bohemia' [. . .] aimed to differentiate the artist of modernity from his middle-class counterparts."[65] This vision of the bohemian was "one of the most enduring stereotypes of nineteenth-century culture," a popular mythology in which "the artist's life [w]as an alternative to bourgeois norms of respectability and conformism; and the artist's calling [w]as a counterpart to modern commercial and professional identities."[66] But, unlike "true bohemians [who] were artistic professionals whose products were recognizable in the market and able to command a price comparable to other commodities," so-called popular bohemians were less interested in identifying themselves as artists and relatively unconcerned with issues of monetary value. Indeed, many were involved in producing, marketing, or selling other kinds of commodities that extend beyond the forms of print culture (newspapers, journals, small-print-run books) that are the primary sources for Gluck's discursive archaeology.[67]

What especially interests me is a specific sarcastic strand of professional marginalia that was reasonably widespread and pervasive in 1880s Parisian culture. Being "Incohérent" was not incompatible with having a remunerative job. Indeed, from the start, as Émile Goudeau wrote in an 1887 account of "L'Incohérent,"

> He belongs to all the crafts that draw near to art: a typographer can be Incohérent, a zinc worker, never! So the Incohérent is a painter or a bookseller, a poet or a bureaucrat, or a sculptor, but what distinguishes him is the fact that the moment he surrenders to his incoherence he prefers to pass for what he is not: the bookseller becomes a tenor, the painter writes verses, the architect discusses free trade, all with exuberance.[68]

The "surrender to incoherence," as Goudeau puts it, was not an irrevocable renunciation of remunerative work but rather was perfectly compatible with Goudeau's categorization of "all the crafts that draw near to art." To Goudeau's list of professions, I would add cordonniers and bottiers. Indeed, a humorous, quasi-Incohérent, popular bohemian sensibility is often manifest in what the administration of *Le Franc Parleur Parisien* described as a variety of "humorous morsels" (*morceaux humoristiques*) published in its pages. These "morsels," the journal added, were meant to be enjoyed by an implicitly male readership as well as by the wives and children of subscribers, who presumably "like to read and laugh" (*aiment à lire et à rire*), a phrase that rhymes in French, adding to the playful quality conveyed even in this relatively straightforward description of the changes the journal was making to its contents in 1884.[69]

"Pointy Shoes"

In its July 20, 1885, issue, *Le Franc Parleur Parisien* published an article entitled "Tout À L'Incohérence" [All for Incohérence] by A. Privé (who is identified elsewhere as Clément).[70] By this point, Catherine Charpin points out, Incohérence had already assumed the status of something like a popular culture genre, one that was associated with "unbridled gaiety."[71] Existing accounts of the Incohérents have stressed their relationship to publishing and performing arts, but this article suggests the sensibility of Incohérence was operative in the sartorial arts as well:

> Between Bicêtre and Charenton, there exists a society of young men—spirited folk, in my view—[. . .] The *Cercle des Incohérents* [. . .] is not what shallow people think it is—these sages came together not in order to play charades and paint rebuses like second-rate artists in their workshops. Our Incohérents had a higher purpose. They have dedicated themselves to guiding and leading the aspirations of the current generation by admirably and accurately representing the actions and gestures of this generation in other forms. [. . .] Many of our colleagues had the honor of gaining entry to this circle by virtue of their zeal for encouraging and propagating the fashion for shoes with pointed tips; they were deemed worthy to join when one of the members of this learned group observed that the human foot was broad at the end.[72]

The link with shoemaking was of prime importance for *Le Franc Parleur Parisien*, as it was for the author, who added, "We do not want to boast, or to have our readers believe that our industry is favored over others" among the Incohérents. The article posits no contradiction whatsoever between art and industry, concluding by noting that shoe manufacturing "has an honorable place" in the Incohérents circle, which encompassed such "other industries as commerce, finance, law, and religion."

Noteworthy for readers of *Le Franc Parleur Parisien* was the indication that Incohérent fashion favored "pointy shoes" (*bouts pointus*) for men. The most extreme versions of this style recalled fifteenth-century *poulaines*, which were worn by men and women and were sometimes adorned with bells at the tip of long toes. But, within the French footwear industry of the 1880s, "pointy shoes" were largely dismissed as an impractical and uncomfortable "English" style popularized by department stores. The French fashion for pointy shoes was a continual outrage to industry insiders, who understood square-toed and round-toes as far more sensible choices that did not unnaturally compress one's feet. Pointy shoes were associated with dandies and others like the Incohérents and their ilk who were intent on making a fashion statement even if it meant wearing shoes that protruded well past the ends of their feet. Consumers intent on wearing pointy shoes obliged shoemakers to increase the size of their shoes by as much as five or six *points* (the system of measurement used for French shoe sizes at this time) beyond the actual fit.[73]

The excessive length attained by pointy shoes was a source of consternation for French industry insiders. In 1886, *Le Franc Parleur Parisien* published a letter to the editor ostensibly written by an eighteen-year-old woman who preferred to be known only as "Marguerite" decrying the popularity of this "beastly, absurd, incomprehensible fashion among the French." Although "Marguerite" loved to dance, "Marguerite" claimed she had lost patience dancing with "young men wearing shoes twice as long as their feet; all so as to have *bouts pointus*!" "Marguerite" complained of "continually feeling her partner's shoes roughly pressing down on her own fine, delicate feet," pointing out, "with these overlong shoes, men no longer know how to place their feet and so, with every movement, with each dance step, they ruthlessly crush their female dance partners' feet." As "one of the principal victims" of this incommodious style of footwear, "Marguerite" concluded with a rather desperately worded plea imploring the editor to change the style and thereby end the "torture" and "the indescribable suffering" that resulted in "bloody feet."[74] The editor of *Le Franc Parleur Parisien*, Arthur Taire, responded that he had long opposed the style despite occasionally publishing images of pointy shoes in the journal's fashion plates. Could he change the style with a wave of a magic wand, like the fairy godmother in *Cinderella*, Taire insisted that he would.[75] Given the hyperbolic, and at times hysterical, rhetoric of this letter (as well as the many ways it echoes the journal's own consistently critical stance toward pointy shoes), one senses

one or more of the journal's contributors (including perhaps Taire himself)
behind this waltzing epistolary *gamine*.

This letter from the probably apocryphal "Marguerite" suggests a fascinating
glimpse of creative spaces within and adjacent to the French footwear industry
at this time. An even more Incohérent sensibility appears in "Le Salon Vu Par
les Pieds!" [The Salon Seen from the Feet], reviews of the annual French art salons by Arthur Eriat (a pseudonym that simply reversed the order of the letters
in Taire's surname) published in *Le Franc Parleur Parisien*. "Le Salon Vu Par
les Pieds!" took an irreverent look at the sculptures and paintings on display in
the Salon, focusing on the footwear represented in the artwork exhibited and
critiquing these details from the shoemaker's point of view. Explicitly making a point of saying that he was not an artist and had no aesthetic training
(a familiar Incohérent refrain), the author offered criticism strictly from the
point of view of a knowledgeable cordonnier-bottier, some in humorous verse
couplets. "Le Salon Vu Par les Pieds!" yielded detailed observations about disproportionately large or small shoes in paintings (disparities that were made
manifest by specifying the sizes of the painted shoes as per the points system).
Other commentaries noted material and historical inaccuracies in sculpted and
painted footwear reflecting intimate knowledge of the material construction of
footwear and its history.[76]

"Le Salon Vu Par les Pieds!" was a humorously sarcastic form of art criticism.
One iteration of "Le Salon Vu Par les Pieds!" chided painter James McNeill
Whistler for having spent too much time rendering the exquisitely detailed
mouth and facial expression of the subject of his *Portrait de Lady Archibald
Campbell*, leaving too little time to paint footwear that would have been truly
appropriate for the gown she is wearing. The review found fault with one of
Adolphe Yvon's full-length portraits because his model was wearing shoes that
were sold at the Louvre department store rather than more bespoke footwear.
Another iteration of "Le Salon Vu Par les Pieds!" singled out the paintings of
Madame Coutan for accurately rendering feet and shoes. In 1885, Eriat (Taire)
wrote that he was gratified some artists had sought his advice for footwear in future paintings, but after the press pass for *Le Franc Parleur Parisien* was revoked
the following year, Eriat (Taire) was obliged to view the artwork like everyone
else, but nevertheless continued publishing his "Le Salon Vu Par les Pieds!"[77]

The single surviving shoe catalogue for the Société Méliès dates from this
period and it includes only men's footwear. Clearly cognizant of current styles, it
offered customers a choice of pointy shoes ranging between option number one,

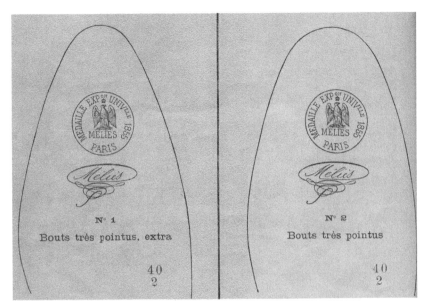

FIGURE 2.3. "No. 1 Bouts très pointus, extra, No. 2 Bouts très pointus," *Manufacture de Chaussures Pour Hommes et Pour Dames: Prix Courant des Chaussures d'Hommes,* unpaginated illustration, Cinémathèque Française.

"extra pointy shoes" (*Bouts très pointus, extra*), option number two, "very pointy shoes" (*Bouts très pointus*), and option number three, "pointed tips" (*Bouts pointus*), along with several options for more traditional box toes.[78] A closer look at a Méliès family picture from around this same period, seemingly taken after a garden party game of croquet, shows Méliès at the edge of the family group. Several in the party are smiling (including Méliès' wife Eugénie Méliès) and some are seated, holding croquet mallets and balls, but many are posed somewhat stiffly with more somber expressions on their faces. Méliès, however, is smiling broadly, head cocked to the side, the handle of a croquet mallet pointed skyward. He is smiling, perhaps laughing, and his left shoe is visible—it is pointy.

Méliès spent most of 1884 in London preparing for a career in the French footwear industry.[79] He appears to have worked first for the boot and shoe shop of Robert Dobbie and subsequently for clothing outfitter Jones and Company.[80] Méliès' memoirs suggest that the most memorable parts of the year he spent in London were learning English and watching magic shows.[81] However, it was the fashion business that took Méliès to London. Thus, it seems likely that Méliès participated in the fashion section of the 1884 London Exposition where

FIGURE 2.4. Méliès family photograph, Cinémathèque Française.

a number of Méliès brand women's shoes were on display. *Le Moniteur de la Cordonnerie* published a glowing report of the Société Méliès display, translated from an issue of the *Leather Trades' Circular*:

> The vitrine of M. Méliès is small, but very full, mainly containing women's shoes that combine comfort and attractiveness and represent the very best of French production. The ornamentation of some of these articles is as attractive as elegant in design and execution. In short, the products of this manufacturer are marked by incontestably superior traits, and they will undoubtedly be carefully examined by English manufacturers.[82]

Just as English manufacturers closely observed developments in French shoe manufacturing, so too did French manufacturers closely observe developments in English shoe manufacturing.[83] No photographs, drawings, or engravings of the Société Méliès 1884 London display are known to exist, but the description of the vitrine, dense with ornamented objects arranged for the view of a consumer, is highly suggestive of Méliès' later work in the graphic and performing arts, in which caricatures, stages, and screens are crowded with (represented) objects and individuals.

CHAPTER 3

Stretching the Caricatural Aesthetic

FOOTWEAR MANUFACTURERS TRAFFICKED IN three-dimensional wares mostly made of leather, but the circulation of footwear was mediated by ephemeral two-dimensional textual and pictorial documents like catalogues, price lists, invoices, receipts, patterns, and fashion plates printed on paper. Fashion plates regularly published with issues of *Le Moniteur de la Cordonnerie* and *Le Franc Parleur Parisien* represented an array of various women's and men's models in profile in a visually legible matrix of footwear styles labeled by name. It was sometimes acknowledged, however, that even a skilled drawing could not capture the nuances of an especially well-made shoe and the materials that had been combined to make it.[1] Subscribers were encouraged to make footwear in the latest styles that were depicted in fashion plates and offer these items for sale to their customers. Patterns were also published regularly in the trade press that subscribers could unfold, cut out, and use as templates to make component parts of specific models of footwear.[2] In each case, two-dimensional plates and patterns printed on paper anticipated the construction of wearable three-dimensional footwear fabricated from leather and other materials.

The homology between two-dimensional drawn representations and the corresponding three-dimensional objects helped to animate the international circulation of footwear. A similar correspondence animated Méliès' film practice, which relied on two-dimensional drawings as the basis of many of the key components of the three-dimensional worlds he created in his studio, which were then remediated as two-dimensional films and photographs.[3] Méliès' "artificially arranged scenes" were dense with action and objects, like many of the caricatures Méliès drew for weekly issues of *La Griffe* in 1889–1890 using the pseudonym "Géo. Smile," which were lithographed in several colors similar to the way fashion plates were printed. Just as fashion plates mediated footwear, Méliès' caricatures for *La Griffe* mediated scores of different objects, albeit in a considerably less verisimilar fashion.

This chapter explores the productive tension between two-dimensional drawings and three-dimensional objects, beginning with Méliès' caricatures for *La
Griffe* and continuing with the importance of drawing for Méliès' film production process. Méliès made many preparatory drawings for his films on paper with
pencil and/or ink, which mediated the material objects that Méliès had modeled
them on and/or had imagined. He sketched designs for scenery, costumes, and
props that were then fabricated on a larger scale as physical objects from wood,
fabric, paint, and other materials. Integrated into the mise-en-scène of his film
productions, the backdrops, scenery, props, and costumes were juxtaposed in
the studio with performers playing their roles. The film production process then
transformed these three-dimensional bodies and objects into mostly two-dimensional strips of negative film, which took on more palpable volume when rolled
and stored on reels and inside of canisters. After the negatives were developed,
edited, printed on lengths of positive film stock, and sometimes hand-colored,
Méliès' film titles were then sold, purchased, and projected onto flat screens.
Together with the illumination of the light source, the intermittent mechanism
of the projector endowed these flat translucent strips of celluloid with illusory
movement and depth, the screened scenes seeming to transpire in three-dimensional space. The visual paradox of cinema's deceptive dimensionality was explicitly thematized in a number of Méliès' films that show the transformation of
two-dimensional representations into moving three-dimensional figures.[4]

Some of the drawings Méliès made in preparation for specific films were on
the backs of sheets of letterhead for the Manufacture de Films pour Cinématographes G. Méliès, and some were drawn in color. As a surface for the inscription
of text, letterhead, as Lisa Gitelman points out, blurs the distinction "between
a blank and (blank) paper" inasmuch as it combined clearly demarcated spaces
to be filled in with an entirely blank slate of sorts.[5] Like most letterhead, Méliès'
"official letterhead work[ed] like filling in a blank form" with spaces in which
the date could be specified (within the decade) and an expansive empty space on
the sheet for the body of the missive itself.[6] Letterhead that was not drawn upon
was used to correspond with others in the film business, both in France and
internationally.[7] By drawing on the verso side of his letterhead, Méliès creatively
misused the work of job printers intended for official textual correspondence
with individuals and entities outside his organization. He also sometimes extended the material limits of the letterhead itself to better suit his purposes. A
long horizontal sketch made for *Le Raid Paris—Monte-Carlo en automobile* was
drawn on the backs of multiple sheets of letterhead that were trimmed, laid end
to end, and taped together.[8]

For Méliès, drawing was an integral part of the production process. In enumerating the arts that were employed in filmmaking, Méliès placed drawing just after the dramatic arts at the head of the list.[9] Méliès did not compose written film scenarios, claiming that the way he worked "consisted of inventing the details before the whole thing" and that whatever story there was in his films served as "only the thread intended to link 'effects' without much of a relationship to each other."[10] Thus, Méliès emphasized, "the script was without any importance because my only aim was to use it as an excuse for mise-en-scène."[11] The survival of a number of drawings made in preparation for specific films confirms that drawing—not writing—was the most crucial component of Méliès' preproduction process.[12] Long after Méliès stopped making films, when he believed most of his films no longer existed, Méliès made numerous ex post facto drawings of scenes he could remember from his films, often recalling the mise-en-scène with remarkable accuracy, and he sometimes captioned them too.[13] Drawings not only provided the basis of Méliès' mise-en-scène and functioned as *aides de mémoire* for films he believed to be lost, they also modeled the very studios in which he produced many of his films. Although Méliès' first film studio was abandoned in 1923 after the Montreuil property on which it was built was sold, falling into disrepair before being demolished in 1948, detailed drawings made of it do survive.[14]

Studies of Méliès typically mention his pseudonymous caricatures for *La Griffe*, but the drawings themselves have rarely been examined. For Georges Sadoul, who reproduced one of Méliès' caricatures from *La Griffe* in his Méliès monograph, Méliès' political cartoons were evidence that despite being "shut up in his studio," Méliès had not "forgotten the reality of the contemporary world."[15] Sadoul pointed to the series of films Méliès made in 1899 detailing the Dreyfus Affair as further evidence, while acknowledging that few of Méliès' films were quite as politicized as *Affaire Dreyfus*.[16] Looking closely at Méliès' films, however, one can sometimes find the kinds of critique that caricature makes visible: notice the air pollution that besmirches the skyline in the painted backdrop of the fourth tableau of *Voyage dans la Lune*, the massive cannon and projectile that visually dominate the film's next few tableaus, and the highly ironic take on the self-satisfaction of colonialism with which the film concludes, the latter resonating with one of Méliès' caricatures, "La Raison du Plus Fort..." (*La Griffe*, January 23, 1890).[17]

More often, however, Méliès' films offer what Donald Crafton, in his excellent book on Émile Cohl, Méliès' contemporary and fellow caricaturist, describes as "*satire de moeurs* (satire of manners), or essentially nonpolitical comments on French social life."[18] For example, Méliès took satirical aim at contemporaneous fads like the Cakewalk dance, which he quite literally demon-ized in *Le Cake-Walk infernal*, and roller skating, which he made comedic in *The Woes of Roller Skaters*.[19] But, for Sadoul, it was drawing—more than caricature specifically—that was of decisive importance for Méliès' overall aesthetic.[20] Like photography and cinema, drawing is a two-dimensional medium, but unlike photographs or films, drawings have an entirely arbitrary relationship to the three-dimensional world that they may or may not represent, more or less faith-fully, in two dimensions on paper. Indeed, drawing is infinitely malleable, and in many ways, it was Méliès' preferred medium.

A Caricatural Aesthetic

Throughout his life, Méliès was a "compulsive draughtsman," as Paul Hammond and Paolo Cherchi Usai both put it.[21] In his memoirs, Méliès wrote he had be-come possessed by the "demon of drawing" as a schoolboy and recalled that his notebooks and even his textbooks were "copiously illustrated" with count-less sketches; he declared that he would continue drawing until his dying day, and indeed he did.[22] The drawings Méliès made in profusion throughout his life subtended his overlapping careers as a footwear manufacturer, caricaturist, illusionist, filmmaker, musical theater actor-director-manager, and toy retailer.[23] Drawings Méliès made during every phase of his life survive, but with the excep-tion of the twenty-six caricatures he drew for *La Griffe*, most were unpublished during his lifetime.[24] Many more were dispersed, discarded, destroyed, or other-wise lost. Although a number of Méliès drawings were published posthumously, researchers have paid them relatively little attention in their own right.

Several of Méliès' earliest films, *Dessinateur express (M. Thiers)* [lost], *Dessi-nateur (Chamberlain)* [lost], *Dessinateur (reine Victoria)* [lost], and *Dessinateur (von Bismarck)* [lost], directly incorporated the act of drawing. Although the films are lost, the titles indicate that each was a "quick-sketch" or "lightning sketch" film in which a performer—likely Méliès himself—drew a likeness of the named celebrity in real time on a chalk board or a large tablet.[25] Before an-imated films, quick-sketch films flourished as a genre—and some of the ear-liest animated films, including Cohl's *Fantasmagorie*, combined animation created by successive single frame exposures with filmed quick-sketch perfor-mances, segueing between the respective modes.[26] Méliès subsequently embed-ded quick-sketch performances with chalk on a chalkboard in *La Lune à un mètre, Le Chevalier mystère, Voyage dans la Lune*, and *Le Roi du maquillage*.[27]

Quick-sketch films thematized their own evanescence: as soon as the drawings were wiped from the chalkboard, the celluloid on which the quick-sketch performances were recorded was the only tangible record of the respective drawings. Similarly, the lithographed covers of a handful of surviving copies of *La Griffe* are all that remains of the corresponding drawings made by Méliès. A similar evanescence defined the art of the Incohérents. In most cases, the engravings published in Incohérent exposition catalogues (which were themselves made from drawings) are often the only visual records of the utterly ephemeral artworks themselves, which have perished or were discarded. So too for examples of footwear manufactured by the Maison Méliès and the Société Méliès, which have mostly vanished: what survives are engraved images printed in catalogues and fashion plates.

Elsewhere, I have examined how a number of Méliès' caricatures for *La Griffe* mocked the political movement of Boulangism and its namesake, the former general Georges Boulanger, whom Méliès and other contributors to *La Griffe* had nicknamed "Barbenzingue" (Zinc-Beard).[28] These caricatures were consumed privately and individually as well as publicly and collectively. In 1880, one French elected official pointed out fearfully about caricatures that were posted in booksellers' windows and elsewhere, "drawing strikes the sight of passersby, addresses itself to all ages and both sexes, startles not only the mind but the eyes. It is a means of speaking even to the illiterate, of stirring up passions, without reasoning, without discourse."[29]

Instead of interpreting the symbolic meanings caricatures impute to nearly everything in an enframed image, my approach here is more straightforwardly iconographic. Art historian (and classical film theorist) Erwin Panofsky defined iconography as "a description or classification of images [...] which [...] furnishes the necessary basis for all further interpretation" but requires historians "to familiarize ourselves with what the authors of those representations [...] knew."[30] Rather than interpreting these images or identifying the caricatured individuals, I consider the range of bodies and objects that make up the mise-en-cadre of Méliès' caricatures for *La Griffe*. The individuals in these caricatures are overwhelmingly male, which is at least partly a function of the journal's focus on historically male-dominated activities like politics, international relations, and military and judicial matters, constituting a remarkably homosocial drawn universe. Of the twenty-six caricatures Méliès drew for *La Griffe*, only two contain recognizably female figures, "1890" (January 2, 1890) and "L'Influenza" (December 26, 1889). A third, "Adam et Eve" (August 29, 1889), inverts costume as a denotation

FIGURE 3.1. Géo. Smile, "Le Mannequin," *La Griffe*
(September 5, 1889), Harvard University Libraries.

of gender by depicting a man with a mustache and a beard cross-dressed in a
corset and bustle alongside a hirsute naked man wearing only riding boots and
spurs.[31] Similarly, "1890" depicts a woman as an object of display, unveiled by a
mustachioed face peeking from behind a curtain.[32] Women in numerous Méliès
films are often posed statically like "1890," sometimes atop literal pedestals, fragmented with individual body parts isolated onscreen, and/or choreographed in
ornamental dancing formations.[33]

One major category of objects in Méliès' caricatures for *La Griffe* are fashion items. Fashion is explicitly invoked in the caricature "Le Mannequin" (September 5, 1889), which foregrounds the torso of a mannequin on a stand, on which a hollow fake head is perched. "Le Mannequin" also explicitly thematizes the difference between three-dimensional representations like the mannequin and a bust perched on a shelf, and the two-dimensional signage on the wall. Clothing itself flexes between two and three dimensionality in both its making and its daily use. Indeed, articles of clothing are typically constructed from pieces of fabric and often stored flat by being hung or folded, fully taking shape only when worn or draped. Footwear is constructed likewise from flat pieces of leather. During the late-nineteenth century, this sometimes involved using paper patterns published with footwear industry journals or available for purchase, all of which were flat and could easily be sent through the mail.

Caricatures necessarily represent footwear and clothing in two dimensions. Items of clothing, especially pants and coats that vary in drawn color, cut, and condition, are important primary elements of Méliès' *La Griffe* caricatures. Clothing serves as an indicator of status and social class. Boots, including riding boots, a Méliès specialty, most of which are colored black like much of the men's footwear manufactured by the Société Méliès, some accessorized with spurs or spats, recur in these caricatures. In Méliès' caricatures for *La Griffe*, footwear is disproportionately small and often clustered near the bottom of the frame, proximate to the captions.

Headgear, by contrast, is emphasized, and is often disproportionately large relative to other objects. Different styles, shapes, and sizes of hats appear in each and every one of Méliès' caricatures for *La Griffe*. Hats were an especially expressive part of the semantic vocabulary of fashion and could indicate a wearer's profession and identify the individual with specific national and/or historical contexts. (This in fact comprises the entirety of Cohl's film *Histoire de chapeaux* in which a succession of historical periods are conveyed entirely through a series of different hats.) In Méliès' caricatures, hats drawn as two-dimensional shapes serve a similar function to communicate the profession and the social status of various individuals. Hats were so expressive (and so recognizable at a glance) that the morphology of headgear supported its own subcategory of performance, chapeaugraphy, which flourished during the late nineteenth century, often in the hands of magicians, including Méliès' contemporary Félicien Trewey, a renowned chapeaugrapher. Chapeaugraphy was a mode of manual dexterity premised on manipulating a ring of felt to form approximations of different forms of headgear.[34]

FIGURE 3.2. Géo. Smile, "Le Roi Carotte," *La Griffe*
(September 12, 1889), Harvard University Libraries.

In her study of Charles Baudelaire's essays on caricature, Michèle Hannoosh
describes the "caricatural aesthetic" as being "as impermanent as the events it
chronicled."[35] Caricatures, Hannoosh concludes via Baudelaire, "provide a historical record, a collection of anecdotes and facts, and constitute part of the
national archives; they are comparable to pages of a newspaper, short-lived and
fleeting, wholly subject to the winds of time."[36] Hannoosh argues, "Maintaining
a likeness while simultaneously deforming it, preserving in its distortion the very
object it attacks, caricature occupies a special place in the vanguard of artistic

change."[37] The maintenance of likenesses makes individual objects and people in caricatures recognizable, but as Hannoosh suggests, the "caricatural aesthetic" also entails deformations.

The "caricatural aesthetic" relishes nonverisimilar representational strategies, including pronounced distortions of scale. One of the most dramatic examples in Méliès' caricatures for *La Griffe* is the massive carrot Barbenzingue straddles in "Le Roi Carotte" (September 12, 1889). Fully the size of a steed, the giant carrot is instantly recognizable as such, even without reference to the title of the caricature or a look at the other carrots—several of which are freakishly large—that trail behind Barbenzingue in the field.[38] The caricatural aesthetic represents size in relative, rather than verisimilar, terms. Thus, one of the five individuals in Méliès' caricature "La Triple Alliance" (*La Griffe*, January 9, 1890), the balding, spike-headed figure in the middle ground, is considerably larger than the others, two of whom are leashed like playthings by lengths of chain. The other two individuals, both in military uniforms, are the relative size of toy soldiers.[39]

Scale can be similarly variable in Méliès' films. Sometimes, a single object is somewhat out of proportion with other parts of the mise-en-scène, allowing a relevant profilmic detail to be clearly seen in a long shot. These include the four-leaf clover the witch gives to the wandering troubadour in *La Fée Carabosse ou le Poignard fatal* and the key to the forbidden chamber Bluebeard's seventh wife finds in *Barbe-Bleue*. Props like these are disproportionately large and unduly flat, as are the facsimiles of a series of food and drink items carried by a procession of servants for the wedding feast in *Barbe-Bleue*.[40] In films like *Le Chapeau à surprises* and *Le Merveilleux Éventail vivant*, the objects themselves, a top hat that is the size of a child and a fan that is taller than a person, respectively, are resolutely three-dimensional, but caricaturally oversized, like the root vegetable in "Le Roi Carotte."

One of the largest figures in Méliès' caricatures for *La Griffe* is the homunculus he drew to represent the "Russian flu" pandemic of 1889 in "L'Influenza" (December 26, 1889). Wearing a cowl labeled with the words "Dengue Fever," the sallow-colored fiend with pointed ears, sharp teeth, long thin fingers, and long sharp fingernails and toenails towers over buildings and people in the streets below. It steps over a long line of people, at least two of whom are women, queued up outside of a pharmacy door.[41] The size differential between the homunculus and the humans in the street, two of whom are in the throes of physical distress caused by the virus, is like the difference between the snow giant and the polar explorers in Méliès' later film *À la conquête du Pôle*. The towering homunculus

FIGURE 3.3. Géo. Smile, "La Triple Alliance," *La Griffe*
(January 9, 1890), Harvard University Libraries.

in "L'Influenza" looks as if it could easily pick up several people, which is just
what the snow giant does in *À la conquête du Pôle*, taking several humans in his
hand before gobbling them up in his gaping maw—an effect Méliès created with
a giant marionette.[42]

The staggering scale of the pandemic meant the homunculus that represents
it fills nearly the entire frame of "L'Influenza." Indeed, it killed more than a
million people worldwide before eventually dissipating in 1892.[43] Epidemiolo-
gists believe the pandemic may have been caused by cattle—the source of the

FIGURE 3.4: Géo. Smile, "L'Influenza," *La Griffe* (December 26, 1889), Harvard University Libraries.

leather supply—infecting humans with a strain of the coronavirus. The spread of the virus during the fall of 1889 was undoubtedly accelerated and extended by modern transportation:

In October 1889 the pandemic spread rapidly out of Russia heading west, east, and south. Mapping the movement of the pandemic [. . .] revealed the railroad's role in rapidly spreading the disease. Influenza traveled with infected passengers, and the stops on the rail line served as the epicenters of spread into different regions. [. . .] Larger cities served as nodes of spread, with the infection then moving to smaller cities and towns and then into the rural communities. [. . .] The data showed that steamships, too, played a role in transmitting the disease. The steamships were larger than their sail-powered predecessors, giving them larger populations for sustaining chains of infection; they were also faster, allowing them to deliver people still actively contagious. As a result, they brought the pandemic to every port [. . .] and from them the infection rapidly penetrated the interior via rail and river lines.[44]

The transportation networks that made the Société Méliès a successful international business also spread the virus. These same networks underpinned the international mail systems that facilitated the traffic in raw materials, footwear, and styles of footwear, along with dozens of international footwear industry trade periodicals and caricature journals.

Writing in 1893, John Grand-Carteret, an early historian of caricature, emphasized the transnationalism of caricature, noting that "the wide circulation of the press"—and the illustrated press specifically—made caricature a mode of international exchange.[45] Exchange was made possible by mail systems that facilitated the circulation of flat and folded documents in envelopes of various sizes. Copies of La Griffe circulated intracontinentally on railroad trains that also carried parcels containing shoes and boots manufactured by the Société Méliès.[46]

Elasticity

Comparing the caricatures Méliès drew for successive issues of La Griffe, the nose and ears of Barbenzingue become larger and more misshapen. In his caricature for the first issue of La Griffe, "Trop de Pression!!!" (August 8, 1889), Méliès drew Barbenzingue's nose and ears in a relatively naturalistic way, but Barbenzingue's nose becomes more bulbous and the ears more enormous in Méliès' caricatures for subsequent issues. Barbenzingue's countenance thus has the quality of "plasmaticness," which film theorist Sergei Eisenstein used to describe the elasticity of Disney films.[47] Paging through successive issues of La Griffe, Barbenzingue's ears become larger than his head in "Le Roi Carotte" (September 12, 1889) and Barbenzingue's nose extends, culminating with "Pauvre Exilé sur la Terre Étrangere!!!" (October 24, 1889), in which his disproportionately small finger is inserted into the nostril of his oversized proboscis. One recurring figure in a number of Méliès' caricatures for La Griffe inexplicably grows a hump in "Le Mannequin" (September 5, 1889), which continues to bulge in "Un Enterrement de Première Classe" (October 10, 1889), in which a coffin is perched atop the hump; "Le Coup de Balai des Invalidations" (November 7, 1889), in which the curved-back figure has peg legs and is being swept down the stairs by a broom; "Les Députés Boulangistes en Route pour Jersey" (November 14, 1889), in which the figure's bulging hump is ringed by several inflated bladders serving as flotation devices to aid swimming; and "La Grande Manifestation Boulangiste" (November 21, 1889), in which the humpbacked figure is inexplicably costumed like a frog while leaping into a fountain.[48] Like Disney films, within the representational world of Méliès' caricatures, sometimes "beasts [. . .] have a habit of stretching and shrinking."[49] A surviving preparatory sketch for an unidentified Méliès film shows the limbs and neck of a traditional French Pierrot clown figure extending in phases: first its legs, then its neck, and finally its arms attenuate to snake-like lengths while another Pierrot figure seated in a chair looks on surprised.[50] How Méliès might have planned on accomplishing this effect cinematically—or perhaps succeeded in a film that is no longer extant—is entirely unclear.

In "Trop de Pression!" the quality of stretching is implicitly ascribed to the materiality of rubber. This caricature includes a number of objects one imagines are made of rubber, including an oversized balloon-Barbenzingue in colorful military regalia floating overhead and multiple hoses through which it has been over-inflated to bursting.[51] Rubber came into widespread use in the mid-nineteenth century. As the French footwear industry sought viable substitutes for leather and wood, flexible resilient substances derived from tree sap—rubber and gutta-per-cha—were widely used for making footwear and molding heels. Vulcanized rubber was waterproof and it could also be painted, making it an especially versatile material for shoes and boots.[52] During the 1850s, American manufacturers began producing footwear entirely made out of rubber, and this development was closely followed by the French footwear industry.[53] Rubber, of course, had many other applications, including bicycle tires, represented on the high-wheel bicycle in the caricature "Le Char de l'État" (*La Griffe*, November 28, 1889).[54]

Rubber was a quintessentially incoherent modern material inasmuch as it refused definitive form when superheated to liquidity and remained flexible as a vulcanized solid. In Méliès' aesthetic, the flexibility of rubber was homologous with the representational flexibility of drawing as a medium. The *portrait-charge*, a genre of caricature that was widely used by caricaturists associated with the Incohérents, was based on conjoining a disproportionately large head on a disproportionately small body, "the practice of drawing a large caricatural head on a squat comic torso."[55] The periodical *Les Hommes d'aujourd'hui*, with which *La*

Griffe seems to have been loosely affiliated, published a portrait-charge on the cover of each of its issues.[56] Méliès drew portrait-charges, including a self-portrait and a drawing of his father in this format, both of which were hand-colored.[57]

Méliès' film *L'homme à la tête en caoutchouc* makes the oversized head of the portrait-charge into a spectacular effect by showing a "chemist in his laboratory" (according to Méliès' American catalogue) inflating his own head with a "rubber hose."[58] However, his assistant over-inflates the head with a bellows, causing it to explode. The film recalls Méliès' caricature "Trop de Pression!!!" as Paul Hammond and Anne-Marie Quévrain have noted.[59] But, unlike drawing the head of a figure larger than the body, or photographing frame by frame incremental drawn changes of scale to make the head of a figure appear to grow larger or smaller, as Cohl did in *Fantasmagorie*, *Le Binetoscope*, and other animated films for Gaumont, Méliès had himself filmed against a black background on a dolly that moved his head closer to the camera to visually simulate its expansion. This was double exposed with a shot of Méliès and his assistant in long shot in front of a backdrop with a black field painted in its center.[60] The title of the film Méliès made immediately before *L'homme à la tête en caoutchouc* was *Le Bataillon élastique* [lost], which suggests that it likewise dealt with elasticity, perhaps in a military context, but nothing is known of the film apart from its title.

A Méliès drawing that he made later depicts the explosion of his over-inflated head in *L'homme à la tête en caoutchouc*—the point at which (as the American catalogue description explains), "The head swells until it bursts with a crash, knocking over the two experimenters."[61] Méliès recalled the setting with a fair degree of accuracy, including the central black field that facilitated the double exposure in the film and much of the other detail painted on the backdrop: the laboratory sign that hangs over the doorway frame right, the table and the platform atop it, the bellows, and even the stools, which appear in a number of different Méliès films.[62] But, for this ex post facto drawing, which he signed and titled "L'homme à la tête en caoutchouc: Trop de Pression!! . . . Catastrophe!!!" Méliès chose a moment that was impossible to show in a live-action film and thus had to be imagined: the moment the head explodes, the directional force of the explosion visibly propelling shards of his skull (and presumably his brain) in a starburst that breaks the glass of the laboratory door. The look on the oversized head registers surprise, and a much smaller Méliès looks up from his bellows with even greater surprise as his assistant's stool tips over from the blast on the other side of the room (one of the few spatial transpositions that does not match the mise-en-scène of the film). In the film, this moment is implied, elided by an

FIGURE 3.5. Méliès' ex post facto drawing of *L'homme à la tête en caoutchouc*, private collection, rights reserved.

abrupt substitution splice that joined a shot of the head appearing to expand to a shot of an explosion and the central table toppling forward as a large cloud of smoke billows and both Méliès and the other performer in the scene are sent sprawling onto the ground; another substitution splice completely clears the smoke instantaneously.[63]

Méliès devised another visual effect to simulate inflatable bodies for the film *Le Raid Paris—Monte-Carlo en automobile*, which was commissioned to be part of a theatrical revue at the Folies Bergère.[64] After more than three hundred performances in which the film was shown, producing "gales of laughter," according to promotional materials, black-and-white and colored versions were offered for sale. The film shows a reckless automobilist careening first through the streets of Paris and then via Dijon on the road to Monte Carlo. The careless automobilist backs over a policeman, "who, by the passage of the automobile over his body, is flattened out as thin as a sheet of paper," explains the American catalogue description; then, the driver "takes his pneumatic pump, adjusts it to the body of the crushed man, and with a few vigorous strokes of the handle he succeeds in starting him to swell," but drives off in a hurry. Several onlookers commandeer three additional pumps from a garage, which they connect to the flattened body with rubber hoses. A crowd gathers while the bystanders are together "pumping up the policeman to his original size," and when the crowd parts, a substitution splice has replaced the flat clothing on the ground with the fully formed body of the police officer moving spasmodically on the ground as the onlookers continue to apply themselves to the pumps. The crowd forms again, concealing a direct view of the police officer's body, but the bystanders at the pumps "become so animated in their efforts that they cause the poor unfortunate to explode" in a puff of smoke that sends everyone running.[65]

Illusions of Dimension and Scale

The transformation from flatness to three-dimensionality is one of the recurring motifs of Méliès' cinema.[66] These transformations thematize the material characteristics that allowed for the kinds of transnational exchange and circulation previously discussed. In the Méliès films *Le Livre magique*, *Les Cartes vivantes*, and *Les Affiches en goguette* transformation occurs when representations—illustrations in books, oversized playing cards, and poster images, respectively—come to life, stepping off of pages, pasteboards, and the apparent surface of a lithographed poster. In *Le Livre magique*, a man (Méliès) brings forth a large book that is taller than he is. He places the thin book, which is bilingually titled "Le Livre Magique" and "The Magical Book," upright on a low table and proceeds to turn its several pages, each of which contains an illustration of a character from a fairy tale or pantomime. Each drawing is signed "Méliès." Méliès the performer reaches a hand up to each illustration in succession, and with a series of substitution splices, individuals costumed to match the illustrations step down from the book in succession, five in all, and move about in front of the table, leaving the corresponding pages of the upright book blank. After the characters gather together momentarily, Méliès returns them one by one to the book: as he ushers each one onto the low table, a substitution splice causes the live performer to vanish in a flash and the corresponding illustration to reappear instantaneously. But the fifth performer, a Pierrot figure, refuses to be returned to motionless two-dimensionality. First it tries to hide, and then when Méliès manages to get it onto the table, it is not transformed into an illustration, and Méliès closes the book, but Pierrot's resolutely three-dimensional body prevents the book from closing and becoming flat again. Instead it reappears in front of the book as if passing magically through the cover, and steps down off of the table. Méliès tries to grab it, but Pierrot eludes his grasp, vanishing and reappearing on the other side of the frame before Méliès manages to get hold of it and put it back on the table in front of the book, whereupon Pierrot vanishes. Méliès opens the book to the page that was formerly blank, and Pierrot is now an illustration once again. Méliès laughs and closes the book. Standing in front of the book, Méliès takes a bow, but the book tumbles down on him, flattening him instantaneously and causing him to vanish. He re-enters the scene through a door in the background, takes another bow, and walks forward, takes the book down off of the table, and carries it out of the frame.

Les Cartes vivantes enacts a similar series of transformations from two-dimensionality to three-dimensionality and back, but combines these transformations with illusions of scale. Playing the role of the magician, Méliès enlarges a playing card through several well-placed substitution splices and then throws it at a huge blank surface atop a stand, "which immediately has outlined upon its surface the face of a huge nine of spades."[67] Through a dissolve, the enormous nine of spades is transformed into a humongous queen of hearts and with another substitution splice and a dissolve, the represented queen becomes a living person dressed like the queen who steps off the oversized pasteboard, leaving a blank expanse on the face of the giant card that now shows only its suit, a heart, in the upper left corner.[68] The living queen steps down from the stand to the ground as Méliès kisses her hand. She turns around and steps back onto the stand, where Méliès positions her carefully and steps away before another substitution splice and another dissolve transforms her back into a two-dimensional representation. Another dissolve transforms the humongous queen of hearts into a humongous king of clubs, and a living person dressed like the king bursts *through* the surface of the giant card, and with a substitution splice, leaves a blank expanse on the face of the giant card that shows only a club in the corner. The king steps down from the stand, Méliès steps out of the frame, and with a substitution splice, throws off his royal raiment, revealing Méliès in a tuxedo who takes a bow and leaps upward, seemingly absorbed *into* the blank card. Méliès then appears behind the card, steps down from the stand, raises his arms, and then exits the frame. The scene is quickly replaced by a full-screen copyright notice for "Geo. Méliès. Paris, New-York."

Other magicians performed versions of expanding playing cards at this time, including Joseffy, who used an elaborate mechanism with which "A queen of hearts, held in the magician's hand, visibly and instantly expands to many times its original size." The apparatus survives and involves a "spring-loaded mechanism" connected to a "giant hand-painted silk card," although the queen of hearts only grew to the size of a sheet of paper rather than the size of a person as in *Les Cartes vivantes*.[69] The inverse illusion, "Cartes diminuées," in which cards diminished some four times in size when pressed between the magician's fingers, was also available from the Paris magic dealer Maison Caroly, whose proprietor Jean Caroly was a member of the Chambre Syndicale de la Prestidigitation of which Méliès was the longtime president, and which held its monthly meetings at the Théâtre Robert-Houdin.[70]

The ending of *Le Menuet lilliputien* [incomplete] offers a cinematic version of Caroly's "Cartes diminuées" in which the size of four oversized playing cards are reduced to normal size in two increments, effectively reversing the action of *Les Cartes vivantes*. But, the film begins with an "art to life" illusion whereby a statue comes to life, although this part is missing from the only known surviving print. According to the American catalogue description, *Le Menuet lilliputien* began as follows:

> A magnificent marble statue is carelessly supported upon an amphora of the same material. Under the passes of a prestidigitateur, the statue becomes animated and serves him as an assistant. The latter takes a pack of ordinary playing cards and places them in a casket of glass. Four cards, the king of spades, the queen of hearts, the queen of clubs, and the king of diamonds, come out of the pack individually and go into the hands of the juggler without any apparent assistance. He places the four cards upright on a small platform, and there the four of them become animated, leave the surface of the cards, advance to the middle of the platform, and dance a minuet gracefully and prettily, the figures preserving the diminutive size of those on the cards.[71]

The surviving fragment of *Le Menuet lilliputien* shows four miniature monarchs dancing on a raised tabletop as four blank playing cards each bearing a different suit, tip upward to a vertical position behind the dancers. This segment of the film emphasizes the visible difference between the flatness of mostly two-dimensional and mostly static pasteboards and the fullness of moving and rotating three-dimensional figures.

In *Le Menuet lilliputien*, the dancing monarchs are moving miniatures, an effect created by superimposing shots of a group of performers filmed from a distant camera position with shots of one or more performers taken from a closer camera position against a backdrop containing a black background, something Méliès also did in the film *Le Voyage de Gulliver à Lilliput et chez les Géants*.[72] In *Le Menuet lilliputien*, this illusion involved shots of four normal-sized performers and four oversized playing cards. (Indeed, the same oversized queen of hearts, king of clubs, blank hearts, and blank clubs cards used in *Les Cartes vivantes* appear to have also been used in making *Le Menuet lilliputien*; the catalogue numbers of the respective films, numbers 678–679 and numbers 690–692, respectively, indicate that *Le Menuet lilliputien* was produced not long after *Les Cartes vivantes*, with only three film titles intervening between these two playing card films.[73]) The shot of the Lilliputians' minuet was double exposed with a shot of Méliès and his assistant in long shot in front of a backdrop with a black field painted in its center.[74]

Although the moment in *Le Menuet lilliputien* when the monarchs depicted on the face cards "leave the surface of the cards" does not appear to be extant, it must have been similar to the corresponding effect in *Les Cartes vivantes* when the queen of hearts and the king of clubs appear to step off the surface of the respective oversized playing cards into three-dimensionality. But, the surviving fragment of *Le Menuet lilliputien* does show what the catalogue description described as follows, "The dance over, each returns to its place before its corresponding playing card, and is mysteriously merged into the card as at first."[75] Touted in the catalogue as "an entirely new trick," it appears to be the same effect used in *Les Cartes vivantes* when the queen of hearts "is at once transformed into a playing card."[76] Lined up next to one another, the cards rise and drop in an alternating rhythm as the magician and his assistant, flanking the table, look on. After a substitution splice ends the double-exposed sequence, the magician gathers up the four cards (perfectly matched in size to the human-sized playing cards miniaturized in double exposure), which are now palpably material as well as visibly flat. Quickly stacked twice against his knee, they diminish in size two times before disappearing altogether as he appears to toss them aside, illusions accomplished with three well-placed substitution splices. Méliès joins hands with his assistant and they take a bow, then exit the frame. *Le Menuet lilliputien* and *Les Cartes vivantes* are illusions of scale as well as dimensional illusions in which two-dimensional representations magically become three-dimensional figures and living people thin out to flat simulacra just as instantaneously.

Méliès made at least one ex post facto drawing of *Le Menuet lilliputien* that survives. It is colored and includes a caption that includes the title of the film, along with the superlative phrase "ultra fantastic magic" at the top of the page.[77] The drawing does not include the assistant depicted in the surviving fragment of the film. Like Méliès' ex post facto drawing of *L'homme à la tête en caoutchouc* discussed above, this drawing depicts one of the film's magical moments that was impossible to accomplish cinematically, an effect that could not be made visible, but could only exist in the imagination of the filmmaker and/or the viewer.

Three of the four miniature monarchs are detached from their respective cards but look like thin cut-outs (which resemble smaller drawn versions of the flattened policeman in *Le Raid Paris—Monte-Carlo en automobile*). The queen of spades in Méliès' ex post facto drawing of *Le Menuet lilliputien* is curtsying with her arm outstretched to the king of clubs, and the king of diamonds stands upright. All three of the respective cards, off of which they have presumably stepped, are tumbled behind them—shadows on the faces of the blank cards indicate the figures' physical separation from the cards. But, the fourth miniature monarch, the queen of spades, appears to be coming detached from the card held above the table by the magician, who resembles a goateed and mustachioed young Méliès. The queen of spades is peeling away from the face of the card: one of her hands reaches out from beyond the edge of the card and touches the hand of the king of diamonds, one of her legs steps down beyond the edge of the card toward the surface of the table, and the bottom of her royal robes are unfurling over the spade on the bottom corner of the card although much of the rest of her body appears to be adhering to the card—if not imprinted on it.

Cinema was an illusion of scale as well as an illusion of movement and an illusion of depth. Looking at an unmagnified strip of 35mm film, individual frames are quite small: the images are visible, but the level of detail that is so crucial for the caricatural aesthetic is difficult to discern with the naked eye.[78] Thus, hand-colorists used optical magnification to apply aniline dyes to different parts of individual film frames. But, when projected onto a screen with a powerful light source, these same images became exponentially larger, a miracle of magnification that later inspired Jean Epstein to rhapsodize about the truly magical potential of cinematic close-up shots.[79] Christian Metz alludes to the remarkable difference in scale between the film strip and the projected image when he describes the film canister like the magician's hat that can produce contents far larger than its apparently limited volume: "a little rolled up perforated strip which 'contains' vast landscapes, fixed battles, the melting of the ice on the River Neva, and whole life-times, and yet can be enclosed in the familiar round metal tin, of modest dimensions, clear proof that it does not 'really' contain all that."[80]

Trademarked Backdrops

Flat painted backdrops were widely used in still photography for studio portraits, for theatrical scenery, and for settings in early cinema. These backdrops mediated three-dimensional spaces with varying degrees of verisimilitude and varying approximations of trompe l'œil. Brian R. Jacobson writes, "filmmakers such as Méliès used painted backdrops to transport viewers into artificial but seemingly natural worlds beyond the screen."[81] The worlds beyond the flat screens on which films were projected were conjured by similarly flat (and similarly fabric) backdrops in Méliès' studio. Méliès put a great deal of care into these backdrops, some of which he re-used for multiple films. Indeed, the American catalogues Gaston Méliès published in New York made a point of stating that the films listed within it were "the personal creations of Mr. Georges Méliès, who himself conceived the ideas, painted the backgrounds, devised the accessories and acted on the stage," a schema in which the "painted backgrounds" were second only to the film's conception, followed closely by "the accessories," all of which were material objects.[82]

Many of the backdrops Méliès used in films were based directly on drawings. A photograph of Méliès at work in his studio shows him painting a backdrop laid across the floor, holding a long-handled brush in one hand and a drawing in the other. A number of other backdrops appear rolled on racks behind him beside the glass wall of the studio.[83] André Méliès recalled his father perched on a ladder, holding a long stick, outlining in charcoal how backdrops were to be painted in black and shades of gray, while the cloth was suspended vertically, as it would be in the films in which these backdrops appeared.[84] The large size of these backdrops made them unwieldy and difficult to store, even after they had been rolled. Méliès added an annex to his Montreuil studio in 1900 for the creation and storage of painted backdrops.[85] The following year, Pathé advertised the film *Plaisir des Sept châteaux du diable* as a costly production consisting of forty tableaus that included "15 décors by master set designer Albert Colas," which were "three meters by four meters, painted in trompe l'œil."[86] The size of these backdrops necessitated additional space and, in 1903, Pathé created a space dedicated to the construction, painting, and storage of scenery that was separate from its main studio facility. This new location supported a greater quantity of film productions and a greater variety of settings within those films.

The materiality of backdrops is the focus of "La Commission des Théâtres" (*La Griffe*, December 12, 1889), which offers a behind-the-scenes view of a Paris theater. A cowed theater director looks on, hands over his head, while one fire inspector applies a torch to a theatrical backdrop to test its flammability and another fire inspector applies fire retardant from a pail labeled "Ignifuge."[87] By showing the obverse side of a theatrical scenery flat in this way, Méliès' "La Commission des Théâtres" highlights the sheer materiality (and inherent flammability) of the represented world painted on the reverse side for the view of an audience. The inspector with a torch kneels beside a stamp that marks the

FIGURE 3.6. Géo. Smile, "La Commission des Théâtres" *La Griffe*
(December 12, 1889), Harvard University Libraries.

approval of the "Commission des Théâtres," which has been applied to the backdrop in several places.[88]

While the Commission des Théâtres stamped its approval on décors that had
been adequately fireproofed, Méliès embedded his trademark on the backdrops
that he used for filmmaking. The first of these trademarks, a black star, was registered by his partner Lucien Reulos on November 20, 1896. Méliès continued to
use different versions of the black five-pointed star trademark, many of which also
included his name and the words "Trade Mark" and "Star."[89] Méliès' "Star" Films
trademark is visible—however incongruously—on the backdrops he used for

many of his films. Trademarking had "the aim of discouraging illegal duplication and plagiarism," Cherchi Usai notes, and often involved the backdrops themselves: "The logo is often visible in the image itself (sometimes as an object in the set direction). [. . .] The logo does not appear systematically in all titles, nor in all scenes."[90]

Footwear manufacturers sought to combat unauthorized knockoffs by trademarking their wares. Copying the design, construction, and external appearance of an article of footwear was permissible, but forging a trademark was illegal. Trademarks made the articles of footwear to which they were applied proprietary, not the patterns used to make these articles or the fashion plates on which they were modeled. Thus, the name "Méliès" was stamped on the sole of shoes, serving as the guarantee the product was authentic and not an inexpensive "counterfeit."[91] The filigreed "G. Méliès" signature that was imprinted along with the trademark star on celluloid prints of Méliès' films is like the filigreed "Méliès" signature stamped on the leather soles of Méliès shoes and boots (along with the name "MELIES" in block letters on the heels and instep). Physically impressing a trademark and/or embossing a signature on products was a practice that the manufacturers of commodities used to prevent their merchandise from being counterfeited. The Société Méliès imprinted its trademark on footwear it manufactured because counterfeiting was rampant in the fashion industry, and French shoe manufacturers like Méliès were trying to protect the international market for authentic French-made de luxe products from inexpensive knockoffs.

Like footwear, early films were initially not intellectual property eligible for copyright protection, but material commodities subject to the protection of trademarking.[92] Méliès applied his trademark black star to the moving pictures, photographs, and painted backdrops he produced, just as he signed many of his drawings. Trademarks were also placed on Méliès' printed sales and promotional materials, including publicity photographs, "probably the earliest film production stills ever distributed."[93] Méliès' letterhead specified, "reproduction of our pictures is strictly *forbidden*."[94] As mentioned in the introduction, Gaston Méliès originally deposited paper prints of entire films with the Library of Congress to secure copyright protection for "Star" Films in the United States, but in 1904 he began depositing only a still photograph of a single backdrop from a film, a telling indicator of the importance of this specific component of Méliès' products. Beginning around 1904, English-language "Star" Films promotional materials were also trademarked and copyrighted in the United States.[95]

Méliès' American catalogues emphasized: "No 'Star' Films are genuine unless marked with a 'Black Star' printed on the second picture, our embossed trade mark on the first one and our embossed signature at the beginning of the film."[96] In some cases, a star-shaped hole was punched in a single frame near the beginning of the film strip. The exact inspiration for Méliès' choice of trademarks is unknown.[97] Stars were not uncommon commercial symbols: during the 1880s, the Vincennes shoe manufacturer Henry Jumelle used a black star in advertisements, as did Brousté. French law acknowledged that the novelty of new trademarks was relative inasmuch as there were a potentially limited number of iconic symbols for manufacturers to choose from; thus, symbols that were part of existing trademarks could be registered as new trademarks provided they were applied to a new class of products.[98] French law did not specify where trademarks were placed, and in fact trademarks did not need to be visible on the surface of the trademarked item or its packaging to be legally protected from infringement.[99]

Just as the Société Méliès tried to deter counterfeits by trademarking the footwear it produced, "Méliès aggressively fought against this practice by inserting the logo of his company (Star-Film) on the main title of his films. [...] [H]e also resorted to applying his signature on the film leader, and to punching and embossing the logo on all positive prints."[100] Richard Abel writes,

> Georges Méliès [...] came up with the brand name "Star" Films, for which he could substitute an easily identifiable logo. When Gaston Méliès set up facilities in New York to print and sell "Star" Films, in May 1903, his [New York] *Clipper* ads promoted the trademark star as much as the Méliès name in order to authorize the company's products. That star appeared in black in all "Star" Films ads, and its "negative" (a white cutout) was punched into, and later embossed on, the opening frames of every film reel the company sold. Méliès adopted this trademark strategy for several reasons. One, of course, was to counteract Edison's and Lubin's extensive practice of duping and selling his films as their own, which reached a crisis point with the phenomenal success of *A Trip to the Moon*. The trademark proved ineffectual for Méliès as a means of asserting ownership (as did copyright), but it did assure the quality of his "original" film subjects in contrast to that of the dupes.[101]

Motion pictures were subject to counterfeiting as unscrupulous entrepreneurs like Siegmund Lubin of Philadelphia attempted to circumvent legal trademark protection by scratching Méliès' logo off each individual frame of a positive print and using that print to make a duplicate negative—as he did with the twenty-sixth tableau of *Voyage dans la Lune*. In 1930, Méliès explained, "As soon as the first positives were forwarded to U.S.A. [. . .] they were copied (countertyped) and sold in large number."[102] Other companies simply sold unauthorized duplicate prints. When nitrate prints of what appeared to be two Méliès films turned up at a French flea market in 1988, the presence of Méliès' engraved signature and the trademark black star, still clearly visible on both film prints, vouchsafed their authenticity.[103] It continues to be one of the most reliable ways of identifying genuine Méliès film prints.[104]

Lost Films, Surviving Drawings

Méliès recalled making numerous drawings backstage at the Théâtre Robert-Houdin during evening performances when he was not needed onstage.[105] Méliès also made many ex post facto drawings of his films while selling toys and candy in two different kiosks operated successively in the Gare Montparnasse by his second wife Stéphanie "Fanny" Méliès from 1925 to 1932.[106] He wrote at the time that he was "never so happy as when" he was on vacation "draw[ing] to his heart's content way up on top of [the] rocks in Brittany."[107] Conditions in the kiosks in the Gare Montparnasse were considerably less blissful, however. In 1930, Méliès complained, "I am in the worst conditions for drawing, with my hands frozen, and such a bad light," later adding, "the cold [. . .] prevents me to be able [*sic*] to make drawings," which "is a very very long work of patience."[108] After retiring in Orly, Madeleine Malthête-Méliès remembered her grandfather sitting by a window in the Orly retirement chateau, reconstituting selected tableaus from his films on paper with ink and colored pencils.[109] According to Stéphanie Méliès, much was burglarized from their rooms in the chateau. "Everything was stolen at Orly," she recounted in 1944, "I had posters, I had photographs."[110]

In 1931, Méliès was still in possession of a number of "original drawings" he had made during the production of his films, including "a few of the original sketches made [. . .] in 1902 for 'Trip to the Moon' [. . .] with ordinary ink and shadowed only with blue pencil."[111] Some of these drawings have survived. As is typical in the fine arts, "frequently drawings relate to works by the same artist in other media [. . .] which [. . .] are usually more familiar."[112] So it is for drawings Méliès made of films like *Voyage dans la Lune*. But, in Méliès' case, a number of the works in other media are not just unfamiliar, but nonexistent. Indeed, for certain lost films for which no production stills survive, including *Le Petit Chaperon rouge* [lost], among others, drawings constitute some of the only extant visual records.[113]

CHAPTER 4

Modern Laughter and the Genre Méliès

ÉLIÈS' LIFELONG INVOLVEMENT IN magic performance was partially mediated by personal connections in the French footwear industry. It was a yearlong apprenticeship in fashion that took Méliès to London in 1884, where "assiduous attendance" at John Nevil Maskelyne and George Albert Cooke's Egyptian Hall magic theater, he writes in his memoirs, inspired him to take up amateur magic and later to frequent performances at the Théâtre Robert-Houdin after returning to Paris.[1] One of Méliès' earliest magic performances that can be confirmed through extant primary sources took place at an 1887 gathering of footwear industry professionals. Not coincidentally, it was through François Pinet, Jean-Louis Méliès' footwear manufacturing contemporary, that Méliès reportedly met Émile Voisin, the magic dealer who helped broker the sale of the exhibition rights of the Théâtre Robert-Houdin to Méliès in 1888.[2] Additionally, Jules-Eugène Legris, the magician who performed much of the magic onstage at the Théâtre Robert-Houdin during Méliès' long tenure as director, was a cordonnier before he became a magician (and occasional film performer) for Méliès.[3]

A number of Méliès' earliest productions for the Théâtre Robert-Houdin were reported in *Le Moniteur de la Cordonnerie*, which published a biweekly column on Paris theater. Among the reviews pseudonymously authored by Arthur Taire (using the pseudonymous palindrome "A. Eriat" with which he undersigned the yearly "Le Salon Vu Par Les Pieds!") were favorable reports of Méliès illusions like "La Stroubaïka Persane," "Le Valet de Trèfle Vivant," and "Hypnotisme, Catalepsie, Magnétisme."[4] Shoes made specially to be worn onstage were a Méliès specialty, and a stage-worn pair of Méliès shoes from the Théâtre Robert-Houdin survive in the collections of the Académie de la Magie in Paris.[5]

Méliès' beginnings in magic theater coincided with the heyday of "modern magic," the most renowned exponent of which was Jean Eugène Robert-Houdin, the namesake of Méliès' magic theater. After Robert-Houdin retired from the stage in 1854, the theater had been relocated to 8, Boulevard des Italiens, where for more than thirty years, a series of his successors, including Robert-Houdin's son-in-law Hamilton, his son Émile Robert-Houdin, and a number of others, performed modern magic in the genteel style with which Robert-Houdin was identified.[6] In performances of modern magic, a magician in formal attire generally presented conjuring tricks as rational demonstrations of sleight-of-hand and manual dexterity along with illusions involving electricity, mechanics, pneumatics, optics, acoustics, and chemistry. The exact methods were concealed, but the demonstrations were nevertheless meant to be edifying as well as entertaining.

After assuming direction of the Théâtre Robert-Houdin during the summer of 1888, Méliès directed the material and technical resources of modern magic to creating what French literary and cultural historians describe as "modern laughter" (*rire moderne*).[7] Modern laughter, according to Daniel Grojnowski and a number of other commentators who have identified it as such, appeared in France after the end of the Second Empire (1830–1870) as a distinctively modern challenge to traditional modes of humor. It found its most well-documented expressions in the activities of various artistic circles and ephemeral publications, including numerous short-lived periodicals and small-print-run books and pamphlets. Even more ephemeral examples of modern laughter echoed performances of song and spoken word in Parisian cabarets, café-chantants, and variety shows during the 1880s. Modern laughter was closely tied to the spirit of *fumisterie* and the *blague* and was defined by parody, satire, derision, absurdity, and some degree of mystification.[8] Modern laughter, I argue here, is a defining element of what Méliès himself described as the "genre Méliès," a singular genre that includes, but is not limited to, many of the trick films for which he is best known.[9] Méliès used this phrase as early as 1906 in advertisements in which he credited himself as the "creator of the genre Méliès."[10]

Comedy had long been a part of many magic performances, but the modern laughter Méliès often aimed to provoke in his audiences was rather different from the comparatively gentle mirth produced by Robert-Houdin's legendary *Soirées Fantastiques*. According to magic historian Christian Fechner, Robert-Houdin's performances were "full of humor," and "tasteful good humor" at that.[11] Méliès' sense of humor was not exactly taste*less*, but he indulged the kinds of "puns and mystifications" Robert-Houdin had always been careful to avoid.[12] When Méliès purchased the Théâtre Robert-Houdin in 1888, he remodeled the modestly sized theater but retained part of Robert-Houdin's repertoire, which included a number of pieces of magical apparatus, the most notable of which were Robert-Houdin's trick automatons. In matinee performances of magic over the years of Méliès' long tenure as director, a number of different magicians performed

magic in the style of Robert-Houdin, but many of the original illusions and
magic sketches Méliès created especially for evening performances were full of
absurd humor, fantastic costumes, and frenetic action.

When Méliès presented tricks from Robert-Houdin's repertoire, he altered
their presentation. Robert-Houdin had performed "Le Dessèchement Cabalistique" (The Cabalistic Drying), for example, but whereas Robert-Houdin had
done it "as was his manner, with all the seriousness in the world," Méliès, after
"realizing the considerable comic possibilities of the trick," "profoundly altered
its presentation."[13] In this illusion, "A handkerchief borrowed from a lady, after
having been soaked in wine and stuffed into a pistol, was sent into several bound
and sealed boxes, and was discovered clean, ironed, and scented with a perfume
chosen by the audience."[14] Writing years later, Méliès emphasized that his al-
terations had primarily been verbal because it was the spoken "patter, which
provoked joy and laughter and made it a success."[15] His version of "Le Dessèchement Cabalistique" upended the high seriousness of Robert-Houdin's presentation through extensive byplay with an assistant who repeatedly responded to
the earnestness and seriousness of a magician trying hard to perform the trick
by *laughing*.[16] The radical differences between Méliès' performance style and
those of his theater's late namesake are indicated by the somewhat indignant
response the theater's longtime mechanic, Eugène Calmels, is reported to have
had to some of Méliès' illusions: "Monsieur Robert-Houdin would never have
done that!"[17] Verbal comedy was at the root of Méliès' invocations of modern
laughter, but this spoken humor left precious few traces and is known almost
entirely from his later recollections since the handful of artifacts that do survive
from Méliès' tenure at the Théâtre Robert-Houdin provide little evidence of his
outrageous comedy.

Absurdity and mystification were combined in the magic of Méliès. While Grojnowski and others have identified the locus of modern laughter in minor literary
genres, in caricatures, and in visual art, here I connect modern laughter to magic
performance. I also emphasize the structural homology between sleight-of-hand
and the joke: both belie expectations, often with a sudden unexpected reversal.
Indeed, the act of misdirection crucial for magic has affinities with the prank,
a favored Méliès antic also beloved by the Incohérents. The ensuing laughter,
moreover, was not just a bodily response Méliès expected of spectators, it was also
a physical act performed in Méliès' productions for stage and screen, including
several of his very first films—those that involved magic and those that did not.
Méliès has long been recognized as a magician-filmmaker, but the role of humor in
Méliès' magic (and in his body of work more generally) is often overlooked.

FIGURE 4.1. Émile Cohl, "Frères, il nous faut rire!" *Le Courrier français* (March 12, 1885): 24, Bibliothèque nationale de France.

Incohérent Illusions

On March 12, 1885, just a few months after Méliès returned from London to Paris, the periodical *Le Courrier français* dedicated a special issue to "Les Incohérents." The front page showed an Incohérent ball (as discussed in chapter 2), but the back page was a full-page caricature of a man's countenance that grinned at readers, exclaiming, "Brothers, we must laugh!" The caption identifies the man depicted, the ostensible speaker of these words, as "Jules Lévy, father of the Incohérents, incoherently drawn by Émile Cohl." The artist's name also appears within the frame in contrasting black-and-white mirror writing, obliging the reader to mentally invert the letters or use a mirror to read them. In Cohl's drawing, Lévy's mustachioed countenance, smile widening into laughter, is naturalistically drawn and clearly discernible, although it is set within a geometrical black-and-white pattern radiating kaleidoscopically around his head. Lévy's undersized decapitated body sits atop his detached, disproportionately large head, a topsy-turvy variation of the portrait-charge format favored by many caricaturists. Lévy paradoxically appears to be sitting atop his own oversized head, heels at his ears. As such, his clothed body—knees, toes, and one arm adorned with bells—resembles one of the hats worn by revelers at an Incohérent costume ball. In its left hand, the body holds a puppet jester. In its right hand, the body grasps a large umbrella; its handle zigzags up to the corner of the frame, tapering to form the exclamation point that punctuates the words of Lévy's exhortation. The letters that spell out the words of his imperative curve below Lévy's smiling face within the frame of the drawing (unlike the typographically printed and neatly horizontal caption below it). Cohl's caricature of Lévy is a quintessential Incohérent image. It is a mass-produced image from an ephemeral publication that was based on a drawing. It is partly caricature, and it combines text and image such that letters are both semantic as well as graphic elements. It is inherently contradictory on several levels and its representational strategies vary along a spectrum from naturalism to abstraction. It is also a two-toned mosaic that contains multiply fragmented images, each of which requires a slightly different perspective.

Laughter above all else and by any means was the fundamental precept of Incohérence. Yet, the wording of Lévy's exhortation suggests just how male-centered and fraternal were the Incohérents, who reveled in gags, pranks, parodies, inside jokes, and highly specific—but often elaborately coded—allusions that were often aimed partially—if not entirely—at other members of the group.[18] Although "modern laughter" may not have necessarily been among the "dominant forms of humor" at this time, the laughter of the Incohérents was certainly "patriarchal laughter," which, as Maggie Hennefeld points out, "tend[s] to empower the sadistic male laughing subject (while objectifying women)."[19] It was also a mode of laughter that was uncontrollable and less socially sanctioned, what she calls "convulsive laughter of the body as opposed to the thoughtful laughter of the mind."[20]

The follow-up Incohérent number of *Le Courrier français* published a year later, on April 4, 1886, aptly featured a caricature by Henri Pille of sixteenth-century satirist Rabelais on its front page. The illustration shows a crowd of celebrants in armor and other sixteenth-century garb, many holding aloft mugs, flagons, pitchers, and glasses with arms linked. Vignetted in an oval frame within the crowd is a head-and-shoulders portrait of a bearded Rabelais, identified in a legend at the bottom of the page. Above the illustration but below the masthead is a row of three-dimensional block letters, none of which are upright, between and behind which are people and several animals, spelling the word "INCOHERENT"—the theme of the issue.[21]

Pille's drawing is an illustration of Rabelaisian revelry, the "joyful and triumphant hilarity" Mikhail Bakhtin describes.[22] Bakhtin accords "an important place in the life of medieval man" to "carnival pageants," "carnival festivities," and "comic spectacles [. . .] based on laughter and consecrated by tradition [. . .] sharply distinct from the serious official, ecclesiastical, feudal, and political cult forms and ceremonials. They offered a completely different, nonofficial, extraecclesiastical and extrapolitical aspect of the world, of man, and of human relations; they built a second world and a second life outside officialdom."[23] This life "outside officialdom" was something to which the Incohérents aspired. Incohérence never had a manifesto and the Incohérents were generally averse to either categorization or to articulating theoretical justifications in support of their artistic practices.[24] Nor does their work have anything like a consistent style, no doubt because Incohérence itself generally involved an outright repudiation of aesthetic principles.[25] Indeed, Lévy's exhortation, "Brothers, we must laugh," was perhaps the closest the Incohérents ever came to anything like a manifesto.

Before taking over the direction of the Théâtre Robert-Houdin, Méliès was a relative unknown to French magicians. As an outsider to the existing community of magicians, Méliès, unlike the prior directors of the theater, was less beholden to the traditions of French magic. By contrast, Méliès' approach to illusion was shaped by his exposure to popular bohemia and the Incohérents. In his memoirs, Méliès wrote that his earliest conjuring performances took place at the Musée Grévin's Cabinet Fantastique and the Théâtre de la Galerie Vivienne.[26] The latter opened in 1886 and occupied the former site of the 1883 and 1884 Incohérent exhibitions, a fact that was frequently noted at the time.[27] The Théâtre de la Galerie Vivienne catered to a family audience with afternoon and evening programs that included magic, music, songs, pantomime, juggling, acrobatics, ventriloquism, and marionettes.[28]

Méliès credited Félix Galipaux and Coquelin *cadet,* both of whom moved in Incohérent circles, for inspiring him to add comedy to his performances during the 1880s.[29] Galipaux and Coquelin *cadet* were known for humorous monologues, which were something of an Incohérent genre at the time.[30] Madeleine Malthête-Méliès writes that during the 1880s, Méliès combined magic with humorous monologues, which she notes were "fashionable at the time."[31] After spending 1884 in London, Méliès later recalled, "It was during this period of three years as a monologuist and an illusionist" from 1885 to 1888, that marked the "origins of his artistic career" and the formation of what he called "my genre."[32]

This same three-year period also saw Méliès break with shoe manufacturing by selling his share of the Société Méliès to his two older brothers in 1886. But he did not make a clean break with the world of French footwear. At the February 12, 1887, banquet of the Chambre Syndicale de la Chaussure en Gros de Paris, the three Méliès brothers and their mother Catherine Méliès were present, even though their father Jean-Louis Méliès, who was honorary vice president of the organization, was not.[33] Arthur Taire, publisher of *Le Franc Parleur Parisien,* "gave a lecture on the history of shoes since the beginnings of compagnonnage," and Catherine Méliès sang a series of operatic selections as part of the festivities, but the highlight of the banquet was a magic show later in the evening reported in at least two different trade press organs of the French footwear industry:

> Messieurs Méliès *fils* prepared a surprise that was deemed a great success; while attendees were having coffee in lounges adjacent to the banquet hall, they set up an impromptu theater at which the youngest, Monsieur Georges Méliès, an amateur conjurer who could no doubt give pointers to Robert-Houdin were he still alive, had the crowning success of the evening thanks to the help of two ladies. [. . .] For more than an hour, Monsieur Georges Méliès took us from one surprise to another, having such a success that everyone forgot the time, and it was past two in the morning when the banquet finally broke up; everyone left promising to meet again next year.[34]

But only two of the three Méliès brothers appear to have returned the following year for the 1888 banquet of the Chambre Syndicale de la Chaussure en Gros de Paris: Méliès was not in attendance and thus there was no magic show.[35] Six months later, Méliès was directing the Théâtre Robert-Houdin.

Robert-Houdin's successors at the Théâtre Robert-Houdin each managed the theater and performed on its stage. But, after Méliès assumed its direction, he delegated the performance of magic to other magicians while relegating performances of modern magic mainly to matinee conjuring shows, which were patronized partly by an audience of children and the adults who accompanied them, along with visitors to Paris who found the Théâtre Robert-Houdin listed in guidebooks.[36] The first of Méliès' original magic theater productions coincided with his work as a professional caricaturist for *La Griffe*, and these magic shows shared the satirical quality, the comic sensibility, and the distorted character of his published caricatures.[37]

Further evidence of the importance of comedy for the magic of Méliès is suggested by a sixty-six-page book entitled *Farces et facéties de la prestidigitation* that was pseudonymously authored by "Gilles et de Phlanel." Fechner identifies this ostensibly plural nom de plume, homonymous with *gilet de flanelle* (flannel vest), a fashion reference, with Méliès. It is one of the only books published by Émile Voisin. *Farces et facéties de la prestidigitation* is less a conjuring manual than a text that makes fun of conjuring books without really revealing magical secrets. It is seemingly unique among magic books, focusing on integrating wordplay and pranks into the performance of conjuring. This is established in the book's foreword, which consists of an anecdote that puns on two meanings of *tour*: "tower" and "trick," then segues to descriptions of a series of conjuring tricks, many involving the use of simple devices in conjunction with verbal ruses. These could ostensibly be inserted at various points in a performance in order to add comedy to a routine. The second part of the book is made up of pranks that conjurers can use to mock audience members.[38]

"Gilles et de Phlanel" is also credited with writing two three-act juvenile theatricals published in Watilliaux's "Théâtre des Enfants" series during the late 1870s: a fairy tale titled *Florine, ou la Clef d'Or: Féerie en Trois Actes* and a farce titled *Les Méfaits de l'Ami Grognard: Comédie en Trois Actes*.[39] *Florine, ou la Clef d'Or*, in which Satan lures Florine, a poor young girl, into a mysterious cave with the promise of great riches, looks forward to characters, settings, and props in such Méliès films as *Les Trésors de Satan*, *Le Chaudron infernal*, *La Fée Carabosse ou le Poignard fatal*, and *Barbe-Bleue*. In *Les Méfaits de l'Ami Grognard*, which resonates with elements of the genre Méliès, the good-for-nothing "friend Grognard" plays a prank on Monsieur Coquembois after the latter refuses to loan him five hundred francs, convincing him to take on a pair of ignorant provincials as temporary replacements for his regular servant and cook. The two replacements wreak havoc on the placid bourgeois home of Monsieur and Madame Coquembois, who have a spoiled only child named Paul. *Les Méfaits de l'Ami Grognard* is animated by silly mix-ups, physical gags, and childish wordplay. One running joke is about rubber and elasticity, a recurring Méliès motif discussed in chapter 3.[40]

Laughing while Decapitated

When Méliès took over the direction of the Théâtre Robert-Houdin, it was ex-
periencing a downturn, but he made it a success with a series of new illusions
and magic sketches. Fechner divides Méliès' magic into three distinct categories: so-called *entresorts*, which were stationary optical illusions like those
seen in fairground shows; large stage illusions, generally requiring specialized
purpose-built apparatus and more than one performer; and magic sketches of
fifteen to thirty-five minutes in which tricks and illusions were joined together
by a loose narrative. Comedy was especially prominent in the magic sketches
Méliès staged between 1888 and 1897 involving "sets and costumes, with always
humorous—if not frankly comical—dialogues, and that brought the entire staff
of the theater onstage for a mysterious, exotic, poetic, or even diabolical intrigue
that became the pretext for a sequence of tricks and illusions."[41] While a number
of commentators have emphasized a link between the magic sketches Méliès
may have seen Maskelyne and Cooke perform at London's Egyptian Hall in
1884 and the magic sketches he later staged at the Théâtre Robert-Houdin, I
believe his magical aesthetic owes more to Incohérence and modern laughter.[42]
It was the combination of illusions and Incohérent comedy that was the basis of
the genre Méliès. Onstage, the genre Méliès involved dialogue, but onscreen the
genre Méliès did not since the films were silent (although wordplay sometimes
appears in the text Méliès embedded in his painted backgrounds).

Just as Méliès scholarship has long aspired to compile *the* complete Méliès
filmography (as discussed in the introduction), a similar urge has motivated efforts to compile a complete Méliès "trickography": a list of all of the illusions
Méliès staged during his long tenure as director of the Théâtre Robert-Houdin.[43]
But the surviving material record of Méliès' magic theater is even more sparse
than the corresponding traces of his work as a filmmaker. A few stage-worn
costumes, props, and illusions have survived, but most of the primary-source
documentation of Méliès' theatrical magic consists of posters, photographs, and
other publicity materials. Short notices of the Théâtre Robert-Houdin from
this period can also be found in a number of newspapers, along with specialized periodicals like *Le Moniteur de la Cordonnerie*, *Le Franc Parleur Parisien*,
and *La Griffe*, which point to Méliès' simultaneous engagement with fashion,
magic, and caricature. It is telling that the first version of Jacques Deslandes's
trucographie (whose neologism Paul Hammond later anglicized as "trickography") appeared in a periodical dedicated to "old paper" published by collectors
of ephemera.[44] Some of the paper documents from which these annotated lists

of tricks and illusions have been derived were nearly as ephemeral as the performances themselves. Yet, the primary sources that were contemporaneous with the heyday of Méliès' magic theater indicate comparatively little about the mise-en-scène of Méliès' illusions, and even less about the critical role of laughter onstage and in the theater.

During the late 1920s and early 1930s, Méliès corresponded with a number of French magicians who kept his letters for posterity because they were magic collectors who have long had a tradition of collecting unpublished documents and rare ephemera related to the history of magic. It was during this time that Auguste Drioux, the publisher and editor of the Lyon magic journal *Passez Muscade*, commissioned Méliès to write a series of articles, which eventually numbered more than two dozen published between 1927 and 1934. (Méliès wrote Drioux he had material enough to fill several volumes, but no such book was ever published.[45]) Readers of *Passez Muscade* were likely more interested in Méliès' magic than in his films, but it is nevertheless surprising to find a filmography (not called that) comprising just nine film titles appended to the biographical sketch published in *Passez Muscade*; it is followed by a comparatively long list of thirty illusions and magic sketches.[46] In his articles for *Passez Muscade*, Méliès provided histories of the Théâtre Robert-Houdin and the Chambre Syndicale de la Prestidigitation, explanations of several of his magic sketches, accounts of a number of the performers who had performed there, and exposés of a number of tricks. Although written several decades after Méliès' heyday as a magic theater director, these accounts in *Passez Muscade* are perhaps the best guides we have to the magic of Méliès. In his account of the Théâtre Robert-Houdin, Méliès highlighted the humor of Raynaly (who sometimes composed humorous verses) and the jovial performances of Harmington, but most of all the "memorable hilarity" of Folletto.[47]

Méliès' published explanation of "Le Décapité Récalcitrant" (The Recalcitrant Decapitated Man) is perhaps the most detailed account of one of his magic sketches that survives, including more than a dozen diagrams and several pages of dialogue Méliès reconstructed from memory. It also provides indications of the importance of humor in his performances: a photograph of the stage production is captioned "fantastical buffoonery," an apt condensation of the way the genre Méliès combined buffoonery with the fantastic.[48] First staged in 1891, Méliès recalled the "mad hilarity that shook spectators during this extra-burlesque scene," remembering physical reactions to this "scene of irresistible buffoonery" that was "Le Décapité Récalcitrant": adults laughing so hard that tears came to their eyes and children stomping their feet enthusiastically. While other illusionists—most notably Bénévol—performed beheading illusions provoking horror, Méliès insisted that although "Le Décapité Récalcitrant" involved an apparent decapitation, it had been absolutely hilarious.[49] What made this magic sketch even funnier was the way it appeared to involve a member of the audience, the prolix Professor Clodion Barbenfouillis (often played by Méliès himself), who interrupted a spiritualistic scene onstage and confronted the performers, who chased him around—the magic sketch ended with Barbenfouillis's beheaded body dangling from the rafters yet continuing to speak.[50]

Living heads severed from living human bodies constituted a recurring Incohérent motif.[51] When *La Revue Illustrée* published its own Incohérent special issue on March 15, 1887, the drawing on the cover by Incohérent Jan van Beers was of a minstrel in an all-white Pierrot clown costume holding his own decapitated head in one hand and a six fingered glove in the other.[52] The minstrel is depicted with familiar "white gloves, wide eyes, voracious mouth, and tricksterish resistance," as Nicholas Sammond describes the stock figure of the minstrel, but it is Incohérently (and inexplicably) beheaded, although the smiling face belies the cleanly detached head.[53] (Méliès incorporated the racialized attraction of blackface minstrelsy into *Le Cake-Walk infernal* and *L'Omnibus des toqués ou Blancs et Noirs*.[54]) Severed human heads formed a recurring motif in several of the illusions Méliès showcased at the Théâtre Robert-Houdin, including the *entresort* "La Fée aux Fleurs," in which a woman's head appeared in a bouquet of flowers, and *Auriol et Debureau*, one of Robert-Houdin's trick automatons sometimes demonstrated at the Théâtre Robert-Houdin during Méliès' tenure.[55] Decapitated heads appear in a number of Méliès' films including *Un homme de têtes*, *Le Mélomane*, and *L'homme à la tête en caoutchouc*.

The decapitation motif implied that bodily functions and capacities specific to the head—thinking, speaking, listening, smelling, eating, expressing oneself facially, laughing—could carry on quite independently of the rest of the body (and vice versa). Incohérent versions of this motif emphasized the undeniable corporeality of the organ capable of abstract thought. Perception and thought may well be immaterial, but human mental and neurological processes are mediated by living tissue that can be blown to smithereens. The fragility of this living tissue was made tragically palpable by the rue François-Miron catastrophe: the blast left one victim with a fractured skull, eyeballs hanging from their sockets, and another badly injured by shards of glass and rubble to the head. Méliès made fatal head trauma into something comical in *L'homme à la tête en caoutchouc*, and even more so in his later ex post facto drawing in which shards of brain and skull are seen exploding from his own oversized head.

Cinematic Pranks

Laughter and its connection to material culture was embedded in the very first film Méliès produced, *Une partie de cartes*, which was shot on the Méliès family property in Montreuil with the first camera Méliès and Reulos constructed. Méliès' *Une partie de cartes* is a remake of the Lumière film *Partie d'écarté*, but the differences Méliès added to the relatively simple situation shown in the film are revealing. Both films show three men seated at a table waited on by a fourth person who brings a bottle to the table; in both versions, the man seated opposite the camera pours glasses for himself and the two others. The Méliès version adds a fifth person, Méliès' eight-year-old daughter Georgette Méliès, and multiplies people's entrances and exits to the frame, making the mise-en-scène considerably more complex than the Lumière version while activating offscreen space.[56]

In the Méliès version, Méliès himself faces the camera, smoking a cigarette while looking at a newspaper and pouring drinks while the two other men seated at the table play cards (as in the Lumière version). But, in the Lumière version, after being summoned by the person facing the camera and being sent for drinks, the waiter (Antoine Féraud) returns with a bottle and three glasses on a tray, which he places on the table. As the drinks are poured, he begins pointing and laughing, seemingly appreciating the play of the cards, and the game is won by the player on the left (Antoine Lumière), who pockets his winnings and smiles as the other card player (Félicien Trewey) raises his hands and shrugs his shoulders.[57] The three men at the table raise their glasses in a toast, the waiter points and laughs again, gesticulating at each player in turn as if replaying the game and enjoying the result another time, but he is the only one laughing in the film, and he remains an observer, a kind of spectator within the film, a role that recurs in many early films, including a number of Méliès films in which a performer *in* the film on the margins of the frame cues the response of spectators *of* the film itself.

In his remake, however, Méliès used a newspaper as a prop to expand and extend the most dynamic and unpredictable action of the Lumières' *Partie d'écarté*: laughter. The waiter's laughter in the Lumière version appears to be a reaction to the game and he is the only one who is laughing. But in the Méliès version, it is something in the newspaper that starts the laughter: Méliès points to something on the page—a caricature, perhaps, whether actually printed in the newspaper or just imagined for the purposes of this little fiction—and shows it to the other two seated people, leaning across the table to show it to each in turn. Both card players tilt their chairs backward, guffawing together, and the laughter proves contagious: even the woman waiting on the table and standing beside it is smiling as the film ends.

Something in the newspaper ostensibly causes the shared laughter in Méliès' *Une partie de cartes*, but in other Méliès films from this period, it is a pratfall. Some of these pratfalls occur as direct results of magical occurrences—conjunctions of magic and comedy that point to their homology. In *Le Château hanté*, a chair suddenly disappears and reappears on the other side of the room, causing the costumed character (played by Méliès) to collapse on the floor of a castle as he tries to sit down. The same gag is reprised in *L'Auberge ensorcelée*, where a bed disappears unexpectedly just as another costumed character (played by Méliès) is about to lay down after his clothing is mysteriously spirited away, leaving him collapsed in a heap on the floor before fleeing the haunted hotel room. Here, Méliès uses the substitution splice to make furniture disappear unexpectedly, effectively pranking himself onscreen.

The prank is a prototypical scenario for modern laughter. For Henri Bergson, the "practical joke," like other humorous situations, results from "mechanical inelasticity" produced by design rather than accidentally, "the result being that [. . .] when he fancies he is sitting down on a solid chair he finds himself sprawling on the floor."[58] This comical inelasticity was the converse of the physical elasticity that Méliès pushed to its absolute breaking point in several films. Bergson continues,

> The victim, then, of a practical joke is in a position similar to that of a runner who falls,—he is comic for the same reason. The laughable element in both cases consists of a certain *mechanical inelasticity*, just where one would expect to find the wide-awake adaptability and the living pliableness of a human being. The only difference in the two cases is that the former happened of itself, whilst the latter was obtained artificially. In the first instance, the passer-by does nothing but look on, but in the second the mischievous wag intervenes.[59]

As Méliès discovered very early, an unexpected cut could play the technological role of "the mischievous wag."

Méliès found other ways to create onscreen pranks, and prank films form a recognizable subset of the genre Méliès. These prank films include *Douche du colonel*, *Un malheur n'arrive jamais seul*, *Un feu d'artifice improvisé*, *L'Hôtel des voyageurs de commerce ou les Suites d'une bonne cuite*, *Robert Macaire et Bertrand*, *les rois des cambrioleurs*, and *La colle universelle*. In each, pranks of varying levels of cruelty are perpetrated on unsuspecting individuals (often played by Méliès himself). In *Un feu d'artifice improvisé*, a drunkard (played by Méliès) who loses his way in the city at sundown "falls before a pyrotechnist," as Méliès' American catalogue description makes clear, but this danger is exacerbated by the location since he "goes to sleep under a gas-jet"—the same energy source that had caused so much damage on the rue François-Miron in 1882.[60] In a scenario that was reportedly suggested by Méliès' son André Méliès, who was four years old at the time, a band of miscreants then strap fireworks to the man and set them off, much to his painful chagrin and their great amusement.[61] The inciting incidents of Méliès films like these are acts of mischief or pranks that sometimes result in casually inflicted violence, which was a frequent occurrence in Méliès' magic theater and in numerous Méliès films. Méliès relished the asymmetry of knowledge between prankster and unknowing victim, aligning himself, and viewers of the film, with the prankster. In these prank films, Méliès puts viewers in the know by letting them in on the prank before it happens.[62]

Fabricated Deceptions

As in *Une partie de cartes*, a newspaper and a chair are also key props in a film Méliès made later in 1896, *Escamotage d'une dame chez Robert-Houdin*, which Méliès described in his memoirs as the first of his "extraordinary views."[63] In it, Méliès appears as a modern magician, dressed in black tie and tailcoat, places a newspaper on the floor, and rotates a chair on top of it, performing a variation of "The Vanishing Lady" illusion Buatier de Kolta had introduced ten years earlier. By the time Méliès made *Escamotage d'une dame chez Robert-Houdin*, "The Vanishing Lady" was something of a cliché. According to magician Charles Bertram, whom de Kolta had licensed to perform the illusion in London, writing in 1896, "Of course, hundreds of imitators sprung up. No place of entertainment was complete without its vanishing lady."[64] Along with countless theatrical imitations, two American film producers made cinematic variations of "The Vanishing Lady" before the turn of the century: one by Biograph in 1897 and another by Edison in 1898, the latter featuring magician-filmmaker and quick-sketch artist Albert E. Smith.[65] Méliès' version combined "The Vanishing Lady" with two other illusions, the appearance of a skeleton in the empty chair, and the transformation of the skeleton into the person who had just vanished.[66] The second of these three illusions is a surprise that occurs unexpectedly, and seemingly contrary to the magician's wishes, a prank-like disruption to the disappearance and appearance of the woman.[67] Skeletons were often featured in magic acts, and some appeared to move of their own accord, like the skeleton in Méliès' magic sketch "Le Décapité Récalcitrant" and the skeleton in the Lumière film *Le Squelette joyeux*, but this skeleton simply intrudes on the reappearance of the woman in the chair remaining momentarily motionless.

The woman who vanishes in the film is Jehanne d'Alcy, who had performed at the Théâtre Robert-Houdin as a magician's assistant even before Méliès became the director, and who later became Méliès' second wife. Typically, the vanished woman reappeared from the wings of the stage or in the theater, as she does in the 1934 British film *Sing As We Go!* in which the trick was accomplished onscreen using de Kolta's theatrical method (and the very chair he used to perform the illusion onstage).[68] But, in Méliès' film version, she reappears in the chair from which she vanished, only after a skeleton has momentarily taken her place.

The film's title suggests that the titular act of *escamotage* will be performed in the manner of Robert-Houdin, but its presentation suggests instead that it is presented as it might have been at the Théâtre Robert-Houdin during Méliès' tenure. Indeed, Méliès performs the illusion comically by having the magician conjure up a skeleton instead of the woman by mistake. The unexpected appearance of the skeleton seems to catch the magician off guard and he recoils in performed surprise and waves it emphatically away, pausing for the laughter of an implied audience before making the vanished woman reappear. Only when he drapes the fabric over the skeleton in the chair does the woman reappear beneath the cloth with a well-placed substitution splice. While the fabric covers the disappearance and the reappearance of the woman, the appearance of the skeleton occurs in full view. This is yet another departure from the typical way of presenting "The Vanishing Lady," and one that emphasizes the unexpected appearance of the skeleton as a humorous interruption to an illusion performed in the nominal style of Robert-Houdin.

In many versions of "The Vanishing Lady" performed onstage, the covering placed over the woman disappeared the moment it was removed: The person and the cloth *appeared* to vanish at the same moment, leaving only the chair and the newspaper beneath it.[69] Bertram insisted, "the trick was never complete without the veil being made to vanish [. . .] simultaneously with the lady's disappearance, [. . .] which caused an especial interest to the audience, and made our performance stand out in contrast to all imitations."[70] In Méliès' version, the fabric does not disappear: he casts it aside and then picks it up again to cover the skeleton as it is transformed into d'Alcy, then casts it aside again as d'Alcy

rises from the chair. Managing the fabric was reportedly one of the most difficult parts of performing the illusion. Like Méliès, many magicians omitted the
cloth vanish since it was more difficult to perform than vanishing the woman,
and thus more likely to fail. Whereas many of the props in a magic show and in
countless trick films are brought onstage, used in a trick, and then removed (or
else made to disappear), the fabric remains and is central for the mise-en-scène
of two distinct nonconsecutive illusions.

Professor Hoffmann's 1890 book *More Magic*, the sequel to his 1876 book
Modern Magic, concludes with a detailed explanation of "The Vanishing Lady"
illusion that parses the advantages and disadvantages of vanishing the veil, "an
additional effect [. . .] performed by Buatier and the more ambitious of his imitators": "If all goes well, the effect is extremely magical, the visible disappearance
of the veil enhancing the marvel of the invisible disappearance of the lady. [. . .]
In my own opinion, the additional effect of success is not sufficient to coun-
terbalance the risk of failure, and this element of the feat is best omitted."[71] As
Bertram, who performed the illusion with the vanishing of the veil, pointed out
in 1899, "Many performers tried the trick afterwards: and most of them could
'vanish' the lady, but they could not cause the disappearance of the large silk covering."[72] The sheer size of the fabric, unlike the much smaller handkerchiefs and
silks typically used in conjuring, made it difficult to manipulate and especially
challenging to vanish.

If the explanation found in *More Magic* is accurate, the fabric had to be "very
thin soft silk, so as to be capable of being folded or crumpled into very small
dimensions" and then rapidly pulled up the sleeve by means of an elastic cord.[73]
The draping of the silk was also a crucial part of "The Vanishing Lady" stage
illusion inasmuch as it was used to suggest that she was still in the chair while
she was in fact in the process of exiting the stage—to then reappear in the wings
or in the theater audience. A framework of metal wire held the silk in the shape
of the woman's seated silhouette as she descended through a trap door in the
stage; it dropped out of sight when the silk was removed. A newspaper placed
beneath the chair ostensibly prevented the use of a trap door, but the newspaper
was either specially cut and lined up with the opening of the trap door or made
of rubber with a concealed slit large enough for a person to slip through.[74]

In Méliès' *Escamotage d'une dame chez Robert-Houdin*, the fabric appears to
be rather thicker than silk and it appears to have been somewhat difficult to
manage at several points in the film. As Méliès raises the fabric up after draping
it over d'Alcy as she is seated in the chair, he leaves part of her uncovered, and she
disappears in an instant. Similarly, as he drapes the fabric over the skeleton, he

leaves a corner of the chair uncovered, and in an instant the fabric shifts to block
our view of the chair entirely—at that very instant, d'Alcy is back in the chair.
These seemingly inadvertent mishandlings of the fabric betray the fact that the
film is not a spatial illusion, but instead is a trick that relies on manipulating tem-
porality. Like onstage, the woman's disappearance occurs before the magician's
gestures signal it has occurred. Likewise, she takes the place of the skeleton just
as the magician starts to drape the fabric over the bones and she remains seated
beneath the cloth while he makes magic passes over her head and pulls off the
cloth with a flourish.

The fabric of the costumes worn by women who performed "The Vanishing
Lady" onstage and screen is also relevant. Bertram, who began performing the
illusion at the Egyptian Hall in London in August 1886, shortly after de Kolta
first performed it in Paris, specifies that his assistant, Mademoiselle Patrice, wore
a "long white silk Grecian costume, trimmed with gold lace, and with a long
yellow silk cloak hanging from her shoulders."[75] This costume presumably made
it easier for Mademoiselle Patrice to slip through the trap door quickly after a
"large red silk shawl, seven feet square [. . .] was lightly placed over her head and
tied at the back [. . .] so as to completely envelope her."[76] By contrast, the dress
worn by d'Alcy in *Escamotage d'une dame chez Robert-Houdin* is rather full,
with puff sleeves and a darker bodice ornamented at the bosom. The dress may
well have belonged to d'Alcy rather than being a theatrical costume. Many early
film performers wore their own clothing, and Méliès did not obtain a stock of
costumes until after his first Montreuil filmmaking studio was operational.[77]
Filmed in direct sunlight, the white fabric and dotted print of the dress makes
d'Alcy's lower body stand out eye-catchingly from the gray background. This
costume choice compels us to follow d'Alcy's entrances and exits from the scene
with our eyes and makes for a noticeable void when she disappears. An empty
chair and then a seated skeleton occupy the center of the frame subsequently,
but neither really fills the visual void left by d'Alcy and her gown. D'Alcy's dress
should serve as a *material* reminder of all that is tangible and tactile in a medium as insubstantial and ephemeral as the cinema, even at the very instant of
a disappearance.

Conjuring with Celluloid

Méliès' film magic relied on celluloid, an industrially produced nitrocellulose
compound (formed under high pressure in high heat) that provided the base for
photographic emulsion on both motion-picture negative film and positive film

prints.[78] Celluloid was thin and durable enough to move smoothly and quickly through motion picture cameras and projectors in strips.[79] Made possible by modern organic chemistry, the production of celluloid increased exponentially in France during the Second Industrial Revolution as part of what Michael Stephen Smith calls the "industrialization of chemicals."[80] Evidence suggests that Méliès initially obtained his celluloid from a producer of nitrocellulose with a factory in Lagny, although he is also reported to have purchased raw film stock produced by George Eastman in London, which he perforated himself.[81] Later, multinational corporations employing "many thousands of workers" together "create[d] the material conditions for the existence of cinema," as Paolo Cherchi Usai explains. "The sheer complexity of the process involved in manufacturing motion picture film on a large scale required a vast amount of space, energy, materials, and qualified personnel."[82]

Méliès also depended on other products of modern organic chemistry. These included the chemical baths used to develop film negatives in his several laboratories and the chemicals for formulating the film cement that Méliès used to join together individual lengths of film negative. The multicolored aniline dyes that hundreds of hand-colorists applied to positive prints of Méliès' films with innumerable brushstrokes with tiny camel's hair brushes were also products of modern organic chemistry.[83] Many of Méliès' films were punctuated by chemically produced pyrotechnic effects—smoke, fire, and explosions—he created himself.[84] Artificial clouds of smoke in front of the camera were often used to punctuate the cinematic appearances and disappearances Méliès would later create by splicing the negatives on which these scenes had been shot. Joined by a carefully placed substitution splice, objects and people in identically framed shots appear and disappear in thick clouds of smoke when the finished film was projected onscreen. Both the smoke and the film cement were products of modern organic chemistry.

Chemical pyrotechnics also made possible the effect of things quickly and spectacularly bursting into flames. Examples range from the reconstructed actuality *Éruption volcanique à la Martinique*, in which an ersatz Mount Pelée spews smoke before incinerating a miniature version of the city of St. Pierre in a fiery conflagration, to the sensational crime melodrama *Les Incendiaires*, in which bandits rob a farmhouse and murder several of its inhabitants before setting the structure ablaze and fleeing. Some of these cinematic pyrotechnics were made even more spectacular onscreen by the addition of hand-coloring to these parts of the film prints. In a hand-colored print of *Le Chaudron infernal*, for example, flames, smoke, and fireballs blaze in brilliant orange as a pair of green-skinned demons (one played by Méliès) force a series of women clad in pink dresses into the fiery cauldron of the film's title. The use of pyrotechnics during filming was not without its hazards. Stéphanie Méliès recalled, "One day they set the garden on fire with some explosive powder."[85]

The profilmic use of explosives was matched by the explosive properties of nitrate films, which were a major fire hazard, as Méliès learned in 1896 when a tent show he was involved with went up in smoke after a box of films caught fire.[86] The danger of fire, of which the public became more cognizant after an 1897 inferno engulfed a cinematograph show at the Bazar de la Charité in Paris, obligated Méliès to add a projection booth to the Théâtre Robert-Houdin, according to Stéphanie Méliès, who recalled, "he was forced to build a special projection booth. It was the law. So he got the booth, right after the fire at the Bazar de la Charité."[87] The space improvised as a projection booth was more like a narrow corridor across which a plank was fixed: the space was so confining that the person operating the projector had to duck under the plank on which the projector rested to pass from one side to the other, with the projected film collected in a basket for rewinding later.[88] Eugène Calmels, the theater's mechanic, acted as projectionist.[89]

Analog film projection involves a continual alternation between a projected still image and a fraction of a second of darkness on the screen when the shutter covers the lens. In *Escamotage d'une dame chez Robert-Houdin*, however, this alternation is thematized between life and death: d'Alcy is replaced by a skeleton, but then replaces the skeleton a moment later; the transformations are covered by a veil that makes d'Alcy and the skeleton, respectively, momentarily invisible—not unlike the shutter that flickered behind the lens of the projector showing the film. (The mechanism must have been familiar to Méliès since he deconstructed one of Robert W. Paul's projectors in order to transform it into a camera.[90])

The substitution splice was a physical and a chemical process with which Méliès joined together two strips of film to create an onscreen effect. We see an illustration of this process in the drawing André Méliès later made of his father hunched over a table—back turned to the "no smoking" sign signed by G. Méliès on the wall behind him—lit cigarette dangling from his lips and magnifying glass in hand, peering at a strip of (highly flammable nitrate) film illuminated by a bare light bulb, trying to find just the right spot to place the cut; scissors and a small bottle of chemicals bearing the letters "ACE" are on the table within Méliès' reach, along with an ashtray filled with cigarette butts. We can surmise that these letters refer to the chemicals specified in the 1911 *Handbook*

FIGURE 4.2. André Méliès' drawing of Méliès cutting
films, private collection, rights reserved.

of Kinematography, "A reliable formula for film cement consists of commercial
Acetone and Amyl Acetate in equal parts."[91]

More direct evidence of the physical editing process can also be seen in surviving positive prints of Méliès' trademark "Star" Films. The visible splices in
these prints reveal how Méliès' most important trick was done, even though its
method was far from secret. (Numerous commentators have nevertheless mis-
takenly called it the "stop-motion" trick, which misleadingly ascribes the illusion
more or less entirely to the stoppage of the camera and the rearrangement of the
mise-en-scène, unlike the phrase "substitution splice.") *The Handbook of Kinematography* is one of the many places where it can be found under the heading
"joining films." To make a splice, one first had to cut the strip of film slightly

past the last desired frame and scrape the emulsion off. After the frame lines and sprocket holes were properly aligned and film cement was applied, another strip of film could be laid over and affixed.[92] This overlap resulted in a thick join that left a mark visible in subsequent generations of positive prints.[93]

The transformation from living person to skeleton in *Escamotage d'une dame chez Robert-Houdin* allegorizes the tension between life and death that was part of the chemical composition of the celluloid film on which *Escamotage d'une dame chez Robert-Houdin* was originally recorded, printed, and duplicated. As a 1913 book about the nitrocellulose industry explained: "Broadly speaking, the framework of the individual cell—the predominating constituent of plant tissues—the structural basis of all vegetable organisms—is cellulose. It is the plant itself minus its protoplasmic contents."[94] Celluloid was the stuff of life itself. It may not have been alive, but it had not vanished. Instead, it had been transmuted into film, coated with photographic emulsion, and given new onscreen life by camera and projector.

CHAPTER 5

The New Profession of the Cinéaste

I N AN AUTOBIOGRAPHICAL ACCOUNT that was published in 1938 shortly after his death, Méliès wrote that, beginning in 1896, he had added "the new profession of the cinéaste" to his several other occupations.[1] André Gaudreault insists that "the word *cinéaste* did not exist at the time"—at least not in 1896, when Méliès added it to his other occupations. But, it did when Méliès wrote his memoirs "in the 1930s," at which point "the term *cinéaste*" had become "common."[2] Méliès' choice of the term *cinéaste*, applied retrospectively, has meaningful implications because, during the 1930s, the word encompassed not only the aesthetic but also the technical and the economic aspects of filmmaking, unlike the phrase *metteur en scène*, for example, which he used elsewhere.[3] Yet, with a few notable exceptions, technological, economic, and material factors have been given comparatively short shrift in existing studies of Méliès. This chapter offers a closer look at the work of the new profession of the cinéaste as Méliès conceived it both in his prime and with the benefit of several decades of hindsight.

Méliès sometimes used the word *auteur* to define his role in the filmmaking process. Indeed, one of the earliest uses of the term in a cinematic context was from Méliès' 1907 essay "Les Vues Cinématographiques," which was published as a "discussion" (*causerie*) in the *Annuaire général et international de la Photographie* near the peak of his productivity as a film producer.[4] For Méliès, the new profession of the cinéaste encompassed a variety of skills: "The stage, drawing, painting, sculpture, architecture, mechanical skills, manual labor of all kinds—all are employed in equal measure in this extraordinary profession."[5] This discussion is the fullest account Méliès provided of the new profession of the cinéaste, and his emphasis on "manual labor" here and elsewhere is noteworthy.

Decades later, in correspondence from the 1920s and 1930s, Méliès also occasionally used the term "auteur," but his use of the word should not be confused with the later critical concept and practice of *auteurism*.[6] The term "auteur" tends to imply working within—or independent from—a system of film production that did not exist at the time Méliès was making films. Nothing comparable to the French "tradition of quality" or the Hollywood studios—the poles between which the *"auteur* policy" was defined during the 1950s—was in existence between 1896 and 1913 when Méliès was making films. As Jane M. Gaines writes, "we search for signs of the auteur-director in vain in this early period when there was no such concept."[7]

For the period of early cinema, both "auteur" and film "director" are anachronisms, as Gaudreault emphasizes. These distinctions are especially relevant to considerations of Méliès because, for Gaudreault, "the essential problem of coordinating the various agents involved in the manufacture of animated views is posed to a greater extent in his films than in any others. His films were generally more complex than those of his competitors, and they generally required a greater number of people in their manufacture."[8] Gaudreault argues, "Méliès establishes the existence and precedence of a figure [. . .] who is in some sense fundamentally responsible for all the operations that go into the work" of filmmaking, but this figure is not identifiable with the role of the director or even the metteur en scène. Instead, it might better be captured by archaic terms like "cinematographist," although I have used the term "filmmaker" in this book to avoid further overburdening the text with obsolete and unfamiliar terms. Here, I follow Méliès in his retrospective use of the term "cinéaste," although I could also have chosen the phrase "film manufacturer."[9]

Rather than further parsing possible terminology with which to capture Méliès' role in the filmmaking process as it was organized at his Montreuil studios (a special challenge for English-language historical writing), I identify his film authorship, like he and the law did at the time, more simply and directly with his trademark. "The trademark star," Richard Abel points out, "was an extension of his signature," both of which are materially present in and on most of Méliès' films.[10] Indeed, the signs of Méliès' authorship are not recurring patterns derived from an "analysis of the whole *corpus*" produced by a filmmaker, but instead the quite literal signatures and trademarks materially present in and on the films themselves.[11]

Méliès was a veritable "one-man band," as his extraordinary film *L'Homme-orchestre* (which combines multiple exposures of Méliès in a carefully coordinated long shot that makes it appear he is filling all seven seats in a musical ensemble himself) metaphorically suggests.[12] As a filmmaker, Méliès was responsible for a great many parts of the production process, including acting and direction. But he also expected many of his closest collaborators to be "jacks of all trades." Working apart from a clearly specified division of labor, Méliès was also a one-man *brand*. He identified not with any specific aspect of film production or single role within the process but instead with the finished product as a whole. Thus, the material signs of Méliès' authorship are manifest in the trademark he embedded within film backdrops and imprinted on the leader, along with his signature, on many of the film commodities that emerged from his laboratories. Like the name stamped on the soles of Méliès brand shoes and boots, the "Star" Films trademark differentiated the products Méliès and his collaborators manufactured from unauthorized knockoffs.

Méliès was particularly proud of the fact that he had financed his filmmaking operations entirely with his own funds. Unlike Lumière, Gaumont, and Pathé, Méliès did not seek external capitalization to expand his business, infamously declining funds from Claude Grivolas, a wealthy industrialist who was an amateur magician and a fellow member of the Chambre Syndicale de la Prestidigitation.[13] "Star" Films was not really a company but instead existed principally as a registered trademark, as Jacques Malthête has pointed out.[14] Other than a brief partnership with Lucien Reulos in 1897, Méliès had no other filmmaking partners.[15] Brother Gaston Méliès, Méliès insisted, was not his partner but rather his employee, listed as the "general manager" of the New York branch office in Méliès' American catalogues.[16] In a 1930 letter to Merritt Crawford, Méliès emphasized that Gaston Méliès "worked [. . .] with me for 10 years, as my representative (nothing else) [. . .] he was not my <u>partner</u>, having not brought a penny in the business, but only a 'manager' paid, and having a part on [*sic*] the profits."[17]

Méliès claimed the term "cinéaste" for himself retrospectively while contrasting his work as an "author" of films during the early period with what he described as the "modern cinéaste" working within a fairly strict division of labor to produce a relatively standardized product.[18] In 1930, Méliès wrote he was "very well posted regarding matters in the motion picture field."[19] Although neither newspapers nor magazines were sold in either of the two kiosks he worked in at the Gare Montparnasse, Méliès appears to have taken an interest in the film industry through what he read in various periodicals. Alberto Cavalcanti, who spoke with Méliès "three or four times" during this period, recalled, "Méliès knew through the newspapers everything that was happening in the cinemas of Paris."[20] Méliès also contributed to film industry trade journals and film magazines like *Ciné-Journal* and *Cinéa et ciné pour tous réunis* during the late 1920s and early 1930s.[21]

Méliès criticized films of the 1930s that were produced in modern studios as "the result of a collaboration of a crowd of specialists" rather than "being conceived and executed by a single author."[22] Méliès thus defined his authorship

diachronically. Rather than contrasting his mode of production with the emerging methods of his immediate contemporaries in France like Lumière, Pathé,
and Gaumont (as many film historians would later do), Méliès differentiated
how he made films from the standardization and overspecialization that he ascribed to sound filmmaking in the French and American studio systems. In
other words, the "new profession of the cinéaste" as it had taken shape in Méliès'
hands was a far cry from the "modern cinéaste."[23]

Nowhere was this more clearly articulated than in Méliès' correspondence
with American film journalist Merritt Crawford, who tantalized Méliès with
the prospect of making sound films in the United States.[24] Méliès' epistolary
exchanges with Crawford and Eugène Lauste, a film pioneer who similarly supported Méliès' planned comeback while seeking his own retrospective recognition as an innovator of sound film technology, make clear how Méliès understood his own authorship diachronically and, to a lesser extent, transnationally
also. Méliès had come to some conclusions about how his conception of the profession of the cinéaste (no longer new) might be made to work in Hollywood
after reading Maurice Dekobra's series of dispatches from Hollywood published
in the Paris daily newspaper *Le Journal*.[25] Despite being sixty-nine years of age
in 1931, Méliès believed he was "strong enough for undertaking the trip and producing again some good work" were a "contract with Hollywood" offered, provided the contract was "sufficiently profitable for allowing my wife and myself
to live, when returned to France."[26] Méliès, however, was concerned by what he
described (in English) as "the 'standardization' studios in Hollywood," which,
he claimed, made sure "American films are all the same. This is exactly what
worries me and what I would have to look out for if they want me to make Star
films again. That is to say, to make films which are particularly characteristic as
to conception and execution."[27]

Part of what had made Méliès' "Star" Films "particularly characteristic" was
Méliès' specific personal contributions to multiple aspects of the filmmaking
process. Pointing out that Maurice Chevalier, an émigré from France, had
achieved success in Hollywood despite being, according to Méliès, "only a music
hall singer, and not a motion picture man," Méliès promised to deliver much
more as a filmmaker.[28] As he explained to Crawford:

> And let me tell you that I am always perfectly able, not only to give "sug-
> gestions" for cinematographic films, but to compose the scenarios, estab-
> lish and imagine the sceneries, paint the sketches, draw the costumes,
> draw, on paper, all the mechanic stage works, survey their construction,

and also take the direction of the actors in the studio; even, if required for certain difficult tricks, to perform myself. I can also, if necessary, paint some fancy sceneries. I have not lost at all my faculties for hand works; and I work quickly.[29]

Aside from such "hand works," which Méliès still apparently felt quite capable of doing despite his age, another part of what had made Méliès' "Star" Films "particularly characteristic" was his approach to collaboration. Thus, Méliès was extremely keen to find out if his preferred mode of "collaboration could suit a motion picture co[mpany]" in the United States.[30] Evidently not. Like Auguste Drioux's suggestion that the Théâtre Robert-Houdin be reopened in 1934 in a new location, nothing came of the idea of Méliès making a film in the United States.[31]

New Second Industrial Revolution Métiers

Abel describes Lumière, Méliès, Pathé, and Gaumont as "The Big Four" of early French cinema.[32] But, it seems telling that in his correspondence of the 1930s, Méliès only named the last three of the four as "creators of this industry" while excluding Lumière. Méliès' rationale for this exclusion was, "I know Lumière, and he is unable to work the simplest tool," adding that the Cinématographe had been "invented by Moi[s]son, and constructed by Charpentier, a French engineer."[33] For Méliès, the new profession of the cinéaste was a hands-on métier that combined the use of the cinematograph, a Second Industrial Revolution technology, with skilled manual labor by himself and a coterie of collaborators working with Second Industrial Revolution materials in contexts supported by Second Industrial Revolution infrastructure. It was, in short, one of the "new métiers" specific to the Second Industrial Revolution in France.[34]

Méliès acknowledged that Lumière should be given credit for the invention of the cinematic apparatus but claimed for himself the distinction of "the creator of cinematographic spectacle," a phrase he identified with the new profession of the cinéaste.[35] For Laurent Creton, one of the few scholars to consider Méliès from an economic standpoint, Méliès represents the "artistic" while Lumière represents the "technical" and Pathé represents the "industrial" in early French cinema, but this convenient historiographic heuristic is far too schematic because Méliès' operations involved both industrial and technological components.[36] When challenged in 1909 by one of his competitors that he was "just an artist" and failed to understand business, Méliès reportedly

retorted that if not for artists like himself, businessmen would have nothing
to sell and their stores would go out of business.[37] This remark is sometimes
used to oppose art and commerce while aligning Méliès with the former, but
Méliès' response articulates a symbiosis of making and selling. Méliès was an
artist *and* a businessman himself, and before he went out of business, he operated not one, but two commercial storefronts: a storefront in the Passage de
l'Opéra (located first at number 13, then at number 14, and finally at number
16) in Paris and a storefront at 204 East 38th Street in New York, where "Star"
Films were sold.[38] As his collaborator Francois Lallement put it, "he produced
and he sold."[39]

Creton dismisses Méliès' "brief stint in the family business" as inconsequen-
tial, instead characterizing Méliès' métier as "theatrical."[40] While I have argued
the contrary about Méliès' years in the family footwear manufacturing business
throughout this book, the second part of Creton's claim partly accords with
Méliès' description of the new profession of the cinéaste in "Les Vues Cinématographiques," where he credits cinema's international "popularity" to what he describes as "artificially arranged scenes [. . .] in which the action is prepared as
it is in the theater and performed by actors in front of the camera."[41] Maurice
Noverre (who carried on a fairly extensive correspondence with Méliès) perhaps
put it better by crediting Méliès with having founded "the first industrial theatrical cinema business," a phrase that differentiated Méliès' mode of filmmaking
from actuality-based uses of the medium like the Lumières, while still acknowledging that Méliès' film practice was in fact industrial.[42]

The first of Méliès' two studios, which is better documented than the second,
about which less is known, conforms to François Caron's definition of the factory as "a place for mobilizing and gathering together different professions."[43]
Under Méliès' supervision, the new profession of the cinéaste generated a number of new métiers that were exercised inside of, and adjacent to, the spaces of
the studios. In Méliès' mode of production, these new métiers often overlapped.
Indeed, many of Méliès' most important contributors took multiple roles in the
film production process and were also responsible for tasks related to not only
the production of films but also their distribution and exhibition as well. These
tasks, many of which emerged as distinct new métiers of their own, extended
beyond Méliès' studios to storefronts in the Passage de l'Opéra where laboratory work was done and positive prints were made and sold, and to the Théâtre
Robert-Houdin where films were screened. Lucien P. Tainguy, for example, did
secretarial work managing Méliès' business correspondence but also worked

FIGURE 5.1. Méliès' costume shop, *Annuaire général et
international de la Photographie* (1907), 378.

selling film prints and operated the camera.[44] Personnel from the theater and
the laboratory were also sometimes enlisted to perform in the studios by taking
roles in Méliès' larger film productions.[45]

No one's role in the production process was more fluid than that of Méliès. He
was not only "the person who directs the operators, assistants, stagehands, actors, and extras" but he also (as he later recalled) "work[ed] as a joiner or carpen-
ter [. . .] for years, when I made everything myself."[46] Additionally, he appeared
in front of the camera in numerous roles. Despite the crazy roles he sometimes
played onscreen, André Méliès recalled his father as "extremely organized," with
a rather rigid approach to scheduling who wanted days to run like clockwork,
down to the minute, and expected his family and his employees to conform to
this exactitude.[47] Significantly, André Méliès described Méliès as "gifted" both
from an "industrial point of view" as well as from an "artistic point of view."[48] An
important part of Méliès' organizational and time management skills involved

collaborating with others, whom he treated as fellow "compagnons" rather than friends or employees, cultivating a remarkable atmosphere of teamwork, which André Méliès recalled.[49] Méliès prided himself on mastery of many parts of the film production process but necessarily delegated tasks to others.

Like the Société Méliès, which had involved multiple members of the extended Méliès family, the Manufacture de Films pour Cinématographes G. Méliès was likewise a family business. It involved Méliès' brother Gaston Méliès, Gaston Méliès' son Paul Méliès, and both of Méliès' children. Daughter Georgette Méliès began as a child actor in several of Méliès' first films, *Une partie de cartes*, *Un petit diable* [lost], *Bébé et fillettes* [lost], and *Entre Calais et Douvres*.[50] According to Méliès, she was "the first woman projectionist and the first 'camera woman'; also one of the first motion picture actresses."[51] Méliès' son André Méliès acted in a number of Méliès' publicity films and played child roles in *La Légende de Rip Van Vinckle* [incomplete], *Conte de la grand-mère et Rêve de l'enfant*, *Le Locataire diabolique*, and *À la conquête du Pôle*.[52] He was also a frequent observer of filmmaking in the Montreuil studios. Others who were not directly related to the Méliès family sometimes came into the business through family connections. For example, Maurice Astaix, one of Méliès' employees, explained, "My parents were already acquainted with Méliès. My mother was the nurse of the children of Mr. and Mrs. Méliès."[53]

Much like shoe manufacturing at the factory of the Société Méliès, the work of the new profession of the cinéaste in Méliès' studios required the labor of multiple people and involved fairly complex machinery. But, there was fluidity in how the work was divided and allocated. As Astaix explained,

> Yeah, in 1900 I was assistant. I was dealing with such things as lab printing [...] Lallemand [*sic*] and I stayed at the laboratory, at Passage de l'Opéra, behind the Théâtre Robert-Houdin. At the same time, we were screening films for Méliès' clients, the itinerant exhibitors. Every time a client came, we went with him at [*sic*] the Théâtre Robert-Houdin, and screened films for him. [...] We were also helping with the editing, the set decoration, the machineries.[54]

Méliès abhorred overspecialization. Looking back on his work as a filmmaker from the vantage of the 1920s and 1930s, when studio systems defined commercial film production, Méliès was sharply critical of their extreme division of labor. Modern cinema, Méliès complained "is the product of a collaboration of very numerous technicians (too numerous in fact)," resulting in standardized commercial products.[55]

These criticisms provided a belated echo of commentators on French shoe manufacturing during the 1880s who had warned that overly specialized workers were prone to being replaced by the mechanization of their specific tasks. An 1887 editorial in the trade journal *Le Franc Parleur Parisien* argued that a true professional needed to learn and maintain a range of skills encompassing "the whole profession," not just one isolated technique, or risk being unemployed during economic downturns or material shortages. The French footwear industry, it was asserted, could use more workers with the kind of holistic training that compagnons had received during apprenticeships on the Tour de France. This is exactly what Jean-Louis Méliès had espoused in a professional gathering of cordonniers some two decades earlier.[56] But, in 1887, craftspeople who possessed the necessary competencies to construct a pair of shoes or boots by themselves also had to be well-acquainted with modern methods, machines, and materials.[57] Méliès brought a similar approach to filmmaking, adapting the ethos of the master craftsperson in footwear manufacturing to Second Industrial Revolution materials and machinery like his father Jean-Louis Méliès to create the new profession of the cinéaste.

"Les Vues Cinématographiques," Illustrated

In 1897, a studio, which Méliès described as "a combination, made of iron and glass, of a photographic studio (on a gigantic scale) and a theatrical stage" was constructed on Méliès' portion of his family's land in Montreuil.[58] Over the next decade, the studio was progressively expanded to include a balcony, lateral spaces directly adjacent to the main playing area, as well as a scene shop, a costume shop, and dressing rooms.[59] Around 1906, Méliès acquired the other two-thirds of the property and the buildings on it from his two older brothers and knocked down the walls that had formerly separated their respective subplots.[60] In 1907, much of the house that had been on the land since the seventeenth century was demolished to make way for a second, larger studio.[61] As part of this renovation, a wing of the building was retained and converted into dressing rooms, office space, and a film developing laboratory.[62] Much of the work associated with the new profession of the cinéaste took place in and around the studio. The studio was the centerpiece of Méliès' account of filmmaking in "Les Vues Cinématographiques," which provides a behind-the-scenes account of "the thousand and one difficulties professionals must surmount" in producing "cinematographic views."[63]

"Les Vues Cinématographiques" is a classic of the primary-source literature of early cinema that has been republished more than a dozen times, including in

English, German, and Italian translations.[64] However, Roland Cosandey points out, "None of these editions reproduces the [. . .] illustrations of the original version, which constitute nevertheless an invaluable primary iconographic source."[65] Some of the forty-one original illustrations are reproductions of "original production stills (13.2 × 16.6 cm) from Méliès' films, taken under the direction of Méliès himself before and during the shooting in the Montreuil studio from 1897 to 1908."[66] In addition to these production stills, a number of the other illustrations originally published in 1907 with "Les Vues Cinématographiques" are photographs depicting the material processes and the new métiers that were involved in the manufacture of cinematographic views. These illustrations provide a series of snapshots of the new profession of the cinéaste at work. Working on various tasks inside of and around Méliès' Montreuil studio, Méliès' multiple collaborators (most of whom have not yet been definitively identified) show that film production was a collaborative enterprise that required "the metteur en scène, the stagehands, the actors, and the operator taking the view," along with numerous others.[67] Méliès emphasized his own role as "the metteur en scène" who "directs the operators, assistants, stagehands, actors, and extras," adding that the scale of some of his largest and most ambitious productions could require "20 to 30 actors, 150 to 200 extras, a couple of dozen stagehands, dancers, wardrobe people and hairdressers, costumers, and the rest."[68]

Illustrations published with "Les Vues Cinématographiques" show actors rehearsing scenes, individuals constructing props, operating cameras, cranking stage machinery, sewing costumes, and drying motion picture film. Seeing the article in context illustrates just how much Méliès' mode of film production depended on multiple individuals and an array of technological and material resources. Several photographs depict the work of fabricating props, scenery, and backdrops, including a photograph of Méliès stooped over at work in a straw hat alongside five collaborators fabricating wooden properties. André Méliès identified Claudel, Parvillier, and Lecuit-Monroy as primary collaborators who assisted Méliès in working on décors, recalling an idiosyncrasy of each, but little more is known about them, including whether or not they are any of the individuals in these photographs. The stage machinery inside of the studio was operated by Salmon, Garroust, and Gallois although it is likewise difficult to determine who is depicted in the corresponding photographs.[69]

"Méliès was sometimes behind the camera in the early days of his career."[70] But, given his many other responsibilities (including many onscreen roles) in an increasingly complex mode of production that involved more people, he was replaced by others whom he presumably trained himself, and the Kinétographe was replaced by a Gaumont-Demenÿ camera.[71] Méliès' camera operators

FIGURE 5.2. Manual labor outside of Méliès' studio, *Annuaire
général et international de la Photographie* (1907), 377.

included François Lallement, Théophile Michault, Lucien P. Tainguy, Lucien
Bardou, Georgette Méliès, an actor whom posterity knows only as Manuel, and
perhaps others, although neither the details of their work nor their biographies
are especially well documented.[72] After Méliès began making films in the studio,
the camera rarely moved from its position firmly anchored in the booth at the
back of the studio, which had been added during one of its several renovations
over the years.[73] Notable exceptions are the series of films Méliès shot using what
would later be called a "bird's-eye shot" as a trick effect to seemingly defy the
laws of gravity onscreen in *L'Homme-Mouche*, *La Femme volante*, and *L'Équili-
bre impossible*, although Méliès does not appear to have used the effect again.[74]
Méliès and his collaborators seldom ventured beyond the studio for filming, one
of the most notable post-1897 exceptions being the exterior shots made for *Les
Incendiaires*, for which Méliès sought official permission from the municipality
of Montreuil.[75]

Méliès described the new profession of the cinéaste as continually "struggling
against material problems of all sorts," and this began with the skilled manual
labor of the camera operator.[76] Realizing the benefits of having two negatives of
each individual film title he produced (rather than filming the subject over again

or making duplicate negatives of inferior visual quality) in 1902, Méliès began shooting with two different cameras, each requiring a different camera operator, but later rigged a special apparatus that allowed a single camera operator to film two negatives in parallax by conjoining two Lumière Cinématographes.[77] This was an "enormous apparatus" that required four people to move, and it was nicknamed *le moulin* (the grinder) or the *Moulin de café* (coffee grinder), monikers that alluded to the heft of the apparatus, which was about as large as a commercial coffee grinder. Operating le moulin must have required some amount of physical vigor to turn since its single crank advanced the mechanisms of two side-by-side motion-picture cameras, moving two strips of negative film through the twinned machines.[78] One negative was developed and used to strike domestic prints. The other negative was shipped to the branch office in New York, incurring duties on a single canister of film in transit. Paolo Cherchi Usai notes, "Méliès' method was quickly imitated by others, and became standard practice for many production companies of the silent era."[79]

One of the principal challenges of the camera operator was turning the crank with the cadence needed to properly expose the negative relative to lighting conditions and the speed of the action in front of the camera. This varied, as Méliès specified, "Generally, the images are taken at a speed of 12, 16, or 18 per second [. . .] according to the speed at which the camera is being cranked."[80] Stéphanie Méliès recalled that Leclerc "helped make the films; he was taking measurements, counting during the shooting."[81] A metronome was sometimes used to orchestrate the timing of trick shots involving multiple exposures, which Méliès idiosyncratically referred to as "superpositions."[82]

In "Les Vues Cinématographiques," Méliès described the constituent elements of the studio as follows:

> The camera booth and operator are located at one end, while at the other end is a floor, constructed exactly like a theater stage and fitted with trapdoors, scenery slots, and uprights. Of course, on each side of the stage there are wings with storerooms for sets, and behind it there are dressing rooms for the actors and extras. Under the stage are the workings for the trapdoors and buffers necessary for the appearances and disappearances of the diabolical gods in fairy plays and slips in which flats can be collapsed during scene changes. Overhead, there is a grate with the pulleys and winches needed for maneuvers requiring power (flying characters or vehicles, the oblique flights of angels, fairies, and swimmers, etc.). Special rollers help to move the canvas panoramas while electric lamps are used to cast the image of apparitions.[83]

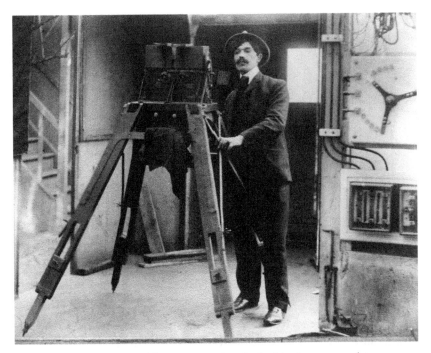

FIGURE 5.3. Lucien Tainguy operating the double-cinematograph in Méliès' studio, David Pfluger Collection (Basel, Switzerland).

Méliès contended that preparing to film a scene was almost "exactly like preparing a play for the theater," although acting for the camera involved a different set of skills than the theater actor because film "actors [. . .] have to make themselves understood [. . .] while remaining completely silent."[84] According to Méliès, "kinematographic miming requires extensive training and special qualities. There is no longer an audience for the actor to address, either verbally or with gestures. The camera is the only viewer, and nothing is worse than looking at it and performing to it," even though Méliès would frequently violate this very axiom himself in trick films like *Les Cartes vivantes*, among many others.[85] Méliès referred to the film actors and actresses who performed in his studio as *poseurs* and *poseuses*, underscoring the importance of expressive bodily performances.[86] The performance style in which Méliès schooled his actors centered on the expressive use of pose and gesture: "Their performances must not be showy and yet be very expressive. Few gestures are used, but they must be very distinct and clear. They must create perfect physiognomies and strike just the right pose."[87] According to André Méliès, Méliès hated to waste

FIGURE 5.4. Méliès' film laboratory, David Pfluger Collection (Basel, Switzerland).

film, so rehearsed scenes repeatedly, rarely shooting retakes if he could help it, making sure all was orchestrated exactly as he wanted before the crank was turned.[88] Méliès had the patience for many rehearsals but became exasperated, sometimes to the point of rage, he himself recalled, with "bad takes, due either to poor acting or to the stupidity of inexperienced extras, who have remembered nothing of the instructions lavished on them before shooting, even after countless rehearsals."[89]

Méliès' film developing laboratories were an essential adjunct to the studios but have been comparatively less well documented, although published photographs of two of Méliès' three laboratories offer glimpses of how equipment and labor were organized in these spaces.[90] The first of Méliès' film laboratories was located in the Passage de l'Opéra, the second was in the New York branch office storefront on 38th Street in Manhattan, and the third was adjacent to Méliès' second, larger studio in Montreuil.[91] Laboratory work to develop negatives and strike positive prints in Paris was done by Lallement, Astaix, Michault, and someone called Père Bach.[92] The New York laboratory appears to have been staffed by Gaston Méliès and his son Paul Méliès, who also worked the adjoining retail space. They were assisted by Augusta Faës and Claire Faës, sisters of Méliès' future second wife who came from Paris to New York for employment.[93] Little is known about the Montreuil laboratory or the workers in that location.

An Incohérent International Screen Identity

Méliès' cinematic activities rested on a historical foundation that was technological, material, and chemical as well as infrastructural. Indeed, the new profession of the cinéaste was enabled in fundamental ways by Second Industrial Revolution investments in infrastructure and energy at municipal, regional, national, and international levels. The Théâtre Robert-Houdin was wired for electricity provided by a 110-volt current through circuits accessible backstage.[94] Electrical service to the Passage de l'Opera allowed Méliès to film the singer Paulus (who was associated with the Incohérents) there using artificial light. Although adequate exposures were apparently achieved on several films, this early attempt at indoor filming, however, overloaded the available circuits, melting the transformer.[95] Short circuits in the early electrical system installed in the Théâtre Robert-Houdin also caused several small fires, although none resulted in much damage. But, on January 30, 1901, the theater was badly damaged by a fire that began in the photographic studio above the theater—damages that were caused as much by the water used to put out the fire as by the fire itself. It took nine months to reconstruct the theater to Méliès' specifications.[96]

Méliès' Montreuil studios were constructed of glass (another material that became more widely available and more economical during the Second Industrial Revolution) in order to take full advantage of available sunlight for natural lighting; the facility was later wired for electricity to allow for electric lighting.[97] A photograph of the interior of the studio taken in 1907 shows an electrical panel visible behind the double-cinematograph and its operator.[98] Detailed maps drawn by André Méliès indicate that the Montreuil property was served by an electrical transformer on the rue François Debergue.[99]

Méliès also depended on the transportation, postal, and electrical communication networks that took shape during the Second Industrial Revolution.[100] Since there were no direct transportation routes between Paris and Montreuil, commuting from the Théâtre Robert-Houdin and his adjacent offices in the Passage de l'Opéra to his Montreuil studios involved transferring from the Métro to a trolley, or else taking a horse-drawn carriage or a taxi.[101] Although the specifics are difficult, if not impossible, to document with certainty, Méliès must have relied on many of the same French and international postal systems that the Société Méliès had used for footwear to ship his films domestically and internationally.

Méliès' offices in Paris and New York both took orders by telegraph, and by 1905, the New York branch office also took orders by telephone. Purchasers could order films by telegraph through the "Starfilm-Paris" address or the "Starfilm-New York" address; American catalogues noted, "A Z French and A B C 18th Edit. Codes Used," respectively. Purchasers were advised to avoid erroneous orders (and limit their cable charges) by ordering specific titles by referring to catalogue numbers rather than titles. Customers could also telephone the New York branch office located at 204 East 38th Street in Manhattan by connecting to number 1955 in the 38th street exchange.[102] Filling the orders represented on surviving "Star" Films receipts and invoices must have involved numerous postal transactions and the shipping of equally numerous packages that have left few other specific traces indicating exactly how Méliès' film prints got from Paris and New York to various other locations in France, the United States, and beyond.

Méliès' films were intended for an international audience, and he did much to try to reach that audience through a set of strategies that I have explored elsewhere.[103] Perhaps the most important of these was the small network of sales agents Méliès created by dispatching his brother and his nephew to New York to set up a branch office, and by partnering with several international film entrepreneurs as authorized sales agents. Beginning in 1903, customers could purchase authorized prints of Méliès' films from Charles Urban in London, from Baltasar Abadal in Barcelona, and O. Richeux in Berlin.[104] Through these and other distribution channels, Méliès' films were seen in many places around the world, including in Russia.[105]

A material history of the transnational distribution of Méliès' films is unfortunately beyond the scope of this book and would involve researching exactly how Méliès and his employees received payment for orders that were placed by telegraph or telephone and how they packaged and shipped film prints. Some details can be gleaned from Méliès' sales catalogues. Prints dispatched from the New York office were sent on the following payment and shipping terms: "Net cash with orders; or C. O. D. when a deposit of one-half of the amount is placed with the order. All orders filled in order received."[106] Itemizing the full scope of how Méliès' films were distributed would also need to account for the unauthorized copies of Méliès' films, which were numerous, originating with Edison, Lubin, and others around the turn of the century (and with countless others after that in every conceivable format right up to the present time). Such a history would be keen to track the circulation of Méliès' films along the itineraries of traveling exhibitors, and how specific Méliès films were distributed after 1908 and 1911, respectively, by Gaumont and Pathé, the latter as part of preconstituted programs rented to exhibitors.[107] It would also consider how film prints transited through rental, subrental, and resale transactions as physical commodities, while also being subject to theft, abandonment, and disposal.

Lacking the material and evidentiary resources for such a history, abstraction is needed, and an anecdote must suffice. Taking care to set the scene, Méliès writes of an encounter that purportedly took place after the turn of the century, when the genre Méliès was known throughout the world:

> At the time when I performed these crazy and amazing scenes, full of tricks and improbable comedy, I received the visit of an American showman, a customer unknown to me who purchased my films indirectly. Passing through Paris, he had wanted to set eyes on the bald guy with bushy moustache and pointed beard whose head was known in all of the cinemas at the time. That guy was me. The American was astounded to have before him a man like any other, perfectly calm. Doubtless he had thought to himself that offstage I was out of my mind, a lunatic, a crazy fool, the devil or the sorcerer whom he had seen on the screen. He was very disappointed and it was obvious that I had lost his regard.[108]

James Lastra, one of few film scholars to treat the anecdote as a form of historical evidence demanding interrogation, writes: "these stories do not tell us much about whether audiences believed the images they saw on screen to be real, but they do tell us other things, indirectly. In their variety and repetition, these stories attempt to grasp the peculiar and novel relationship the film image established between its audience and its represented worlds."[109] For Lastra, whether or not an anecdote is apocryphal is of less consequence than the ways anecdotes reveal specific cultural anxieties and concerns.

Unlike some of Méliès' other anecdotes, in which lines of dialogue are provided for conversational exchanges that ostensibly took place decades earlier, the events of an episode that ostensibly had taken place in the Passage de l'Opéra, the epicenter of Méliès' film distribution operations, are narrated in entirely visual terms. Instead of witty rejoinders or bon mots like other Méliès anecdotes, this one turns on faces and visual recognition, and its succinct narration has something like a cinematic quality. This anecdote is a throwaway fragment that might otherwise be ignored, overlooked, or discarded—a marginal paragraph in a marginal history. The anecdote with which I conclude suggests how cinematic mediation might actually upstage palpable lived reality, rendering a transnational encounter with the "real thing" an utter disappointment in comparison with memories of cinematic marvels. It also indicates the ways in which

Méliès' "one-man brand" was widely recognizable, but its existence was in the
end highly virtual, existing more in the imaginations of innumerable viewers
than in specific material objects or physical bodies—even the body of Méliès
himself, whose countenance and whose onscreen performances had become
perhaps even more widely known than the "Star" Films trademark painted on
backdrops and stamped on film prints.

CONCLUSION

Toy Stories

ACCORDING TO MADELEINE MALTHÊTE-MÉLIÈS, "the first spectacle conceived and executed by Méliès dates from 1877": at age fifteen,
Méliès constructed a marionette theater from scratch and used it to
put on a show for his extended family in which an ogre was cured of stomach-
aches by becoming a vegetarian.[1] Méliès used this marionette theater to perform
original productions but later kept it padlocked inside a large wooden box in a
corner of the attic of the Montreuil house where he stored some of his filmmaking props. Méliès' son André Méliès was not permitted to play with it until he
turned ten. Many years later, he could still recall his amazement when his father
finally opened the box to reveal an elaborate miniature theater, complete with
working theatrical machinery, sets, and scenic backdrops—a "little marvel" that
anticipated Méliès' later "*féeries* for the screen."[2] Although it does not appear
to have survived, André Méliès recalled several of the settings his father had
created, "One represented an alchemist's laboratory in a medieval chamber. [...]
Another represented an ominous prison with trap doors out of which devils
emerged."[3] These recollected settings anticipate such Méliès films as *L'Antre des
esprits* (in which a crocodile hangs from the ceiling of a sorcerer's chamber) and
Faust aux enfers (in which Mephistopheles, played by Méliès, descends through
a trap door into the depths of hell clutching Faust).[4]

Although the place of toys in Méliès' childhood and the childhoods of his two
children is otherwise undocumented, this biographical episode points to a more
expansive lineage for film and for the cinema of Méliès in particular that follows
the lead of work in media archaeology.[5] How was tactility embedded within the
material experience of pre-cinematic and para-cinematic media? How were interactivity and different kinds of play mobilized in relationship to the material
practices that constellated around these archaic and largely obsolete media objects? Making films was most certainly not child's play, as Méliès insisted. But,
watching Méliès' films, one often gets the sense of their maker toying with the
new medium, trying out different possibilities in ways that come across as playful

(like the two versions of *L'Illusionniste fin de siècle* mentioned in the introduction or the trilogy filmed with an overhead camera discussed briefly in chapter 5). Méliès' mode of filmmaking referenced play even more directly through the use of puppets, marionettes, and vehicles and its emphasis on costume, dressing up, and pantomime, all of which are also potentially interactive forms of play.

This sense of play is closely connected to an unmistakably tactile quality that Antonia Lant has usefully described as "haptical cinema."[6] One gets the sense that all of the objects we see onscreen, including the painted backdrops and props—and indeed the films themselves—were purposefully crafted from palpable materials by skilled hands. Yet, these objects lie just beyond our grasp, like the miniature theater Méliès kept locked in a box until his son was "old enough" to play with it, or like a pair of leather boots or bottines, the details of which we can see, but never touch, much less try on. (The inherently tactile and intrinsically embodied quality of fit is an important part of a wearer's experience of footwear and in fact Méliès brand footwear was known not only for fashionableness, but also for "true comfort."[7]) Despite their tactile interface, the hand-cranked projector behind the back wall of the auditorium and many of the props onstage at the Théâtre Robert-Houdin that were expressly constructed for use only by the magicians and their assistants lest a closer examination betray their illusions were likewise out of reach of historical spectators. What then were the historical possibilities for tactile engagement and interactive play, which are such an integral part of our own contemporary media culture, for Méliès' later customers? The work of Meredith A. Bak provides a framework for thinking about these possibilities, which I explore through a material culture approach that considers a number of turn-of-the-twentieth-century objects that I position as adjacent to early cinema, and adjacent to the cinema of Méliès in particular.

Film historians have typically privileged the importance of optical toys as technological and/or perceptual precursors of projected cinematic moving images, but Bak insists on a broader field of "playthings [. . .] like puzzles, paper dolls, and spinning tops, forming constellations that 'make . . . new sense' of these objects."[8] Bak's juxtapositions are suggestive and this conclusion offers its own constellation of historical objects selected from turn-of-the-century Paris material culture that relate to the life and work of Méliès. This specific constellation offers an expanded history of cinema that focuses less on what Charles Musser has described as "screen practices" than on handheld amusements involving interactivity and play.[9] Traces of some of these specific practices can be glimpsed in Méliès films like *L'Anarchie chez Guignol* [incomplete] and *La Lanterne magique*, discussed below.

Manually Manipulated

The continuities between puppetry and early cinema that oral histories of the Méliès family suggest were more fully historicized and theorized in *Notes for a General History of Cinema* by Sergei M. Eisenstein, which was unpublished during his lifetime. Eisenstein had direct experience with Méliès, remembering seeing the film *Les Quat' Cents Farces du diable* at the Théâtre Robert-Houdin around 1906, at the age of eight. Years later, he could still recall "the intricate evolutions of the half-skeleton horses pulling the carriage."[10] These evolutions were effected by the operations of what was, in effect, an oversized marionette animated by several stagehands pulling ropes from which a carriage and large skeleton horse-puppet were suspended from the roof beams of Méliès' studio.[11] In *Notes for a General History of Cinema*, Eisenstein contended that puppets were connected to cinema inasmuch as puppetry represented an example of the "mechanization of motion" in which the "moving mechanism [was] outside."[12]

Puppet shows were a part of Méliès' adulthood just as they had been part of his childhood. Puppets and marionettes were staples of the Théâtre de la Galerie Vivienne where Méliès is reported to have first performed magic professionally. They were also featured at the Théâtre Robert-Houdin prior to and during Méliès' tenure as director since the theater's small scale was especially well suited to puppets and marionettes.[13] Additionally, trick automatons exhibited at the Théâtre Robert-Houdin functioned like puppets and marionettes manipulated by an assistant concealed offstage, even though they were presented as self-working autonomous devices. Méliès described them more accurately as "mechanical pieces" since "true automatons" only required manual assistance to wind and set in motion.[14] By contrast, the trick automatons at the Théâtre Robert-Houdin were operated by "Eugene Calmels, who had been an apprentice clockmaker to Robert-Houdin, [and who] served as chief mechanic of the theatre and operated all of the automata."[15] Méliès' history of the Théâtre Robert-Houdin makes mention of a number of the "mechanical pieces" exhibited during his time as director, many of which had been part of Robert-Houdin's repertoire.[16] Two of the most celebrated were *Antonio Diavolo* and *Le Pâtissier du Palais-Royal*, small mechanical figures that appeared to heed the magician's commands, respectively, by performing acrobatic feats on a trapeze before dismounting and retrieving requested treats from inside of a tabletop mechanical model of a pastry shop.[17]

Wealthy consumers could purchase doll-sized or smaller self-working automatons for display in their homes. These automatons took various forms, including simulacra of animals and people animated by clockwork mechanisms to repeat movement in three dimensions. Many automatons were powered by coiled springs that also drove music boxes housed in the base. Acrobats and magicians were common automaton figures. Many of the late nineteenth-century makers of French automatons were family-owned firms (Théroude, Vichy, Roullet et Decamps, Phalibois, Lambert, and Renou) located not far from the Théâtre Robert-Houdin in the Marais district, clustered along adjacent streets in the second arrondissement.[18] Méliès made several films that nominally featured automatons, automated figures, or moving dolls, including *Gugusse et l'automate* [lost], *Coppélia ou la Poupée animée* [lost], and *La Poupée vivante* [lost].[19]

Films like these likely showed people interacting with objects that took on lives of their own. How this might have been depicted onscreen is suggested by Méliès' film *L'Anarchie chez guignol* [incomplete], which showed puppets coming violently to life. Although the film survives as a fragment, the missing part of the film is evoked by the published catalogue description:

> The performance begins, and the marionettes delight the children with their antics. They start to beat one another with sticks, and in their excitement, they leap out of the box on to the floor in front, meanwhile becoming living midgets, without letting up on their scrapping. The manager of the show comes out from behind the curtains and strives passionately to beat back his marionettes into their places where they ought to have remained. But they push the impresario aside and suddenly become the size of natural men. Then they rush at him with redoubled blows, and finally hurry away. Afterwards the children pummel the unfortunate director and bury him in confetti.[20]

Menacing puppets appear in *Faust aux enfers* and *À la conquête du Pôle*, comprising a recurring thematic in Méliès' cinema.

For users, puppets and marionettes could be manipulated to enact imaginative fictions with dialogue, and/or sound effects created entirely by the puppeteer(s). Sets, scenery, and props could be purchased, fabricated from scratch, or improvised with available items. More finished fictions could be performed using published scripts and/or puppet theaters. Toy theater sheets, often printed in color or hand-colored, were illustrations of backdrops, scenery, people, animals, furniture, and other objects to be cut out and mounted on cardboard, which Méliès remembered constructing as a child.[21] Méliès' cinematic mise-en-scène has a distinctively two-dimensional quality that often juxtaposes flat painted backdrops with flat painted scenic elements and flat painted props. Moreover, the iconography of a number of Méliès' films has an affinity with lithographed toy theater images printed in Épinal by the Pellerin firm, making

Figure C.1. "Décors de Théâtre: Salons et Coulisses," private collection, rights reserved.

certain Méliès film tableaus look like toy theater productions enlarged to the scale of real people.[22]

Conjuring has historically relied on handheld objects and implements. Although Méliès reportedly attended the Théâtre Robert-Houdin as a child as early as 1871, whether or not he ever owned a magic set during his youth is

unrecorded.[23] Beginning in the mid-nineteenth century, boxed magic sets manufactured in France and Germany that varied in size, quality, and cost were com-
mercially available. Boxed magic sets that contained small apparatus with which
to perform simple conjuring tricks were sold by toy stores, department stores,
and specialized retailers.[24] For many years during Méliès' heyday as director of
the Théâtre Robert-Houdin, at 8, Boulevard des Italiens, spectators exiting mat-
inée performances of magic had only to pay a visit next door to the Magasin
des Enfants at 10, Boulevard des Italiens, to purchase a boxed magic set.[25] For
individuals with sufficient interest and means, purchase and use of conjuring
apparatus allowed them to transfer some element of what they saw at the Théâtre
Robert-Houdin to their own personal and private domestic spaces—one example of how, as Bak points out, "many of the entertainments that captivated public
audiences were adapted for the home."[26]

Méliès had connections to Paris magic dealers Émile Voisin, who briefly directed the Théâtre Robert-Houdin shortly before Méliès became its director and
who owned a magic shop on the rue Vieille-du-Temple founded by his grandfather André Voisin, and Charles De Vere, who ran a magic shop near the Folies
Bergères.[27] Méliès sometimes contributed to the magic journal L'Illusionniste,
which featured him on the cover of one issue.[28] The publisher of L'Illusionniste
was Jean Caroly, proprietor of the eponymous Maison Caroly, which sold conjuring supplies and large stage illusions, including versions of several trick automatons seen onstage at the Théâtre Robert-Houdin.[29] A number of magicians
(including fairground exhibitors like Bénévol and Gallici-Rancy) screened films
as part of their performances and thus Caroly also advertised a "large selection"
of "cinematographic views" for sale at his magic shop.[30]

Handheld Moving Images

As objects, many moving image devices were made and marketed as toys and
handheld amusements. Émile Reynaud patented the Praxinoscope in 1877, a device made of a drum that rotated around a spindle within a polygon of angled
mirrors. When a strip of sequential images (printed in color with chromolithog-
raphy), a dozen of which came with the device, was placed within the drum
and the drum was spun, a repeating illusion of motion was visible reflected in
the mirrors. Reynaud commercialized the device in partnership with Laurent
Péan, a Paris toymaker who specialized in optical toys (and who produced his
own Animateur, patented in 1874 as an improvement on the Phénakistoscope

and the Zootrope). Thus, Péan's initials were printed at the center of the circular label affixed to the Praxinoscopes he made.[31] Reynaud also produced a considerably larger, more elaborate, and more expensive Praxinoscope-théâtre, which combined a projecting Praxinoscope with a miniature proscenium resembling a toy theater in which the moving images were projected. Reynaud used a much larger version of the projecting Praxinoscope for his large-screen "Pantomimes Lumineuses," which had an eight-year run during the 1890s at the Musée Grévin's Cabinet Fantastique (where Méliès had reportedly given some of his earliest performances of magic during the 1880s).[32] Predating the Lumière Cinématographe and other motion-picture machines by several years, Reynaud's apparatus projected long chains of motion-sequenced images painted on individual pieces of glass onto a large screen and thus represent the beginnings of animated cinema if not cinema itself, albeit in the form of a completely artisanal installation that could never be mechanically reproducible.[33]

Imitations of the Praxinoscope were manufactured by Gebrüder Bing, who, with Ernst Planck and Georges Carette, was one of several German toymakers producing "toy projectors [. . .] alongside their large and varied output of ordinary magic lanterns."[34] While some toy magic lanterns projected still images, other models projected moving images printed on short translucent strips of drawn images. One such strip, made to be projected on one of "these toy cinematographs," according to magic lantern historian and Méliès scholar David Robinson, "shows a bearded magician performing a conjuring trick. It is unmistakeably Méliès, both in looks and movement."[35]

An oversized toy magic lantern that projects moving images is the central prop in Méliès' film *La Lanterne magique*, which is set in "the interior of a toyshop."[36] *La Lanterne magique* is a vivid illustration of the childhood fantasy of toys coming to life that involves living, moving versions of the pantomime characters Polichinelle, Pierrot, Harlequin, and Colombine, who were each commonly modeled as toys, puppets, marionettes, dolls, and automatons that could be animated in three dimensions.[37] In *La Lanterne magique*, Polichinelle and Pierrot come onscreen dancing, the actors' limbs moving as if they were marionettes. Polichinelle and Pierrot then pull out a pedestal on which they construct a magic lantern that is made out of four flat panels (like a toy requiring some assembly). A lens protrudes from one of the panels and the top of the lantern descends, its conical corrugated shape similar to those that topped ornate box-shaped magic lanterns made in France by Carré and Riche. Polichinelle and Pierrot tilt the front of the lantern up, then open the back panel and insert a lamp, which they light with an oversized match (which really burns). Polichinelle removes the lens cap, "thereby throwing upon the wall a large white disc, within which pictures in varying subjects begin to appear," including moving "pictures of Pierrot and Punchinello [known as Polichinelle in France] highly magnified."[38]

The oversized toy magic lantern projects moving pictures onto a wall, but even more marvelous are the series of individuals that subsequently emerge from the body of the lantern. Its panels fold down and a sextet of dancers come forth "do[ing] a four-step," followed by a high-kicking dancer who somersaults and turns multiple cartwheels after the lantern is moved aside. After the high-kicking dancer, the magic lantern is brought back, and Harlequin and Colombine emerge from the back panel in their traditional motley, and dance off together. The panels of the lantern fold down to produce "an entire corps de ballet" of ten ballerinas pirouetting, followed by the high-kicking dancer, who is interrupted by Harlequin and Colombine tussling, sending the dancers scampering offscreen. Four toy soldiers march onscreen and stop the fight. Harlequin and Colombine then climb into the lantern and are transformed into a jack-in-the-box that is extending wildly, feet firmly planted but body extending elastically as if it contained a spring. The toy soldiers brandish their sabres as the jack-in-the-box threatens to head-butt them. They flee and the dancers return, dancing a circle around the jack-in-the box as it continues to extend itself wildly.[39]

"In one playful film, Méliès brings together characters from the ancient pantomime, nineteenth century ballet, and the music hall," John Frazer writes, "The inserted matte shot on a white ground, more than a technical stunt, is a movie within a movie."[40] The film is also an imaginative catalogue of turn-of-the century French toys, beginning with the magic lantern, which comprised a distinctive specialty in the toy industry.[41] Everything that emerges from the eponymous magic lantern in *La Lanterne magique* is a life-sized anthropomorphized version of an object that was sold in quantity in turn-of-the-century French toy stores: Pierrot and Polichinelle marionettes, pirouetting and acrobatic automatons, Harlequin and Colombine dolls, toy soldiers, and a jack-in-the-box, the latter known in France as a *diable en boîte* or a *boîte à diable*.[42] Among the toys depicted on the background of *La Lanterne magique*, there is even a mechanism, presumably part of a mechanical toy.

Méliès complained that French jurisprudence categorized moving pictures as *bimbeloterie*, which included certain kinds of toys.[43] Yet, some of the images he made were made into *bimbelots*. Indeed, Méliès appears to have filmed a number of the chronophotographic sequences that were published by Léon Beaulieu around the turn of the century as flip books, appearing in several. More than a dozen of the flip books published by Beaulieu show very brief scenes, each consisting of 121 grainy reproductions of photographs that may have been derived from films made by Méliès and/or his collaborators.[44] These flip books are examples of handheld, inherently tactile, interfaces for moving pictures that flourished during Méliès' heyday. Flip books could easily be placed in one's pocket, and indeed one of these flip books was found in Méliès' coat pocket after his death.[45]

Connections to other kinds of tactile and interactive amusements are suggested by the variety of publications printed by Watilliaux, the publisher of two juvenile theatricals authored by "Gilles et de Phlanel"—the pseudonym identified with Méliès—discussed in chapter 4. The Maison Watilliaux was a specialty producer of card games, board games, three-dimensional puzzles, toys, and other kinds of two-dimensional and three-dimensional ephemera.[46] The range of Watilliaux's games included specialized card games of various sorts, including transportation, military, and word games each requiring specially printed packs of cards.[47] Watilliaux also produced three-dimensional dexterity puzzles, flip books (called "folioscopes"), as well as toy animals, toy figures, and toy theaters.[48] In 1897, Watilliaux and Claparède patented the Cinébaroscope, "a device which gives the illusion of movement through a succession of photographs or drawings."[49] In 1902, Watilliaux was listed as a "publisher of folioscopes or small pocket cinematographs for riffling with the thumb."[50]

Watilliaux produced a number of different travel games that involved multiple players moving tokens or playing cards that simulated the itineraries of trips to exotic locations. These included the railroad game *Jeu des Chemins de fer*, played along continental railroad lines, and the steamship game *Jeu des Paquebots*, played along oceanic shipping lanes. Global exploration was the theme of other Watilliaux games including *Jeu des Explorateurs, En Afrique: Nouveau Jeu de Voyages*, and *Le Voyage à Pekin par air, par fer, par terre et par mer*, which offered interactive multiplayer gaming experiences. In the latter, "Players [...] travel by air, sea, horse, or train, depending on the roll of a teetotum. [...] An unlucky roll could lead to the traveler's death in a storm, off a precipice, in an explosion, or in a shipwreck."[51] Such chance trajectories across turn-of-the-century game boards are comparable to the episodic itineraries of Méliès films like *Le Raid Paris—Monte-Carlo en automobile, Voyage à travers l'impossible, Le Raid New York-Paris en automobile* [lost] and others that take viewers to the far reaches of planet Earth: *Les Aventures de Robinson Crusoé, Le Rastaquouère Rodriguez y Papaguanas* [lost], and *À la conquête du Pôle*. Unlike the Lumière operators who traveled to multiple continents during the 1890s, filming "foreign lands we have probably never seen [...] for the pleasure of people who do not like to stir" (as Méliès put it) and unlike the fiction and nonfiction films Gaston Méliès shot on location in Southeast Asia, Australia, and New Zealand during the 1910s, Méliès' films offered strictly imaginary journeys to faraway places like contemporaneous travel games.[52]

Toy Merchant of La Gare Montparnasse

Toys were big business in France, and Paris was the international capital of the toy industry. In his 1887 *Histoire des jouets et des jeux enfants*, Edouard Fournier estimated that between four hundred and five hundred toy makers employing some three thousand workers could be found in Paris.[53] Henry d'Allemagne's 1902 *Histoire des jouets* noted, "manufacture of toys was, undoubtedly, one of the most important branches of French industry."[54] According to Léo Claretie, toys "create a little world" that have "a relationship to reality" while comprising a "history of our time written by and for children."[55] But, Claretie reminded readers that behind the glossy sheen of the toy shop and its treasures were artisans and workers, some of whom labored in dangerous and deplorable conditions. Like the ready-to-wear clothing and footwear industries, the toy industry exploited outwork through the so-called sweating system whereby parts of the toymaking process were outsourced to home laborers working long hours on a piecework basis rather than daily factory shifts.[56] French toy manufacturing employed many children as well as imprisoned convicts.[57] Whatever joy these toys were able to bring to children, Claretie stressed that the toy industry concealed a great deal of misery.

Although Méliès' working conditions were not as dire or as exploitive as these, the seven years he sold candy and toys in the Gare Montparnasse during the late 1920s and early 1930s were far from joyful despite his being surrounded by playthings. Some of the most poignant images of Méliès, reenacted cinematically by Georges Franju for *Le Grand Méliès* as well as by Martin Scorsese for *Hugo*—the latter based on Brian Selznick's drawings in *The Invention of Hugo Cabret*—were derived from photographs of the early 1930s.[58] These scenes show Méliès as an older man, as Colin Williamson evocatively puts it, "surrounded by an almost unwieldy collection of toys [...] a part of the assemblage of wondrous odds and ends collected and put on display for the delight of curious children [...] [in] a toy booth in the Gare Montparnasse in Paris."[59] Williamson ruminates that Méliès' placement "within an assemblage of trifling toys" conjures a "reflection of the collection of once wondrous devices, spectacles, and techniques that became ordinary and sometimes fell into obscurity as technological innovations changed the landscape of the cinema."[60] Like Williamson, I am very interested in these images, but I read them not only as media archaeology metaphors but also (more literally) as further evidence of the ways that Méliès was proximate to toys of various kinds throughout his career. Méliès' film production and exhibition enterprises were geographically proximate to toy manufacturing and sales. Montreuil was home to several doll factories, including Jumeau, a leading international de luxe producer, and Paris-Bébé.[61] There were also toy stores located around the corner from the Théâtre Robert-Houdin in the Passage de l'Opéra.[62]

During the mid-1920s, some years after becoming a widower, Méliès reunited with Stéphanie Manieux (née Charlotte Faës), who had performed at the Théâtre Robert-Houdin using the stage name Jehanne d'Alcy, and had appeared in *Escamotage d'une dame chez Robert-Houdin*, discussed in chapter 4, among several Méliès films.[63] Méliès and Manieux married in 1925, and both worked the concession she had previously been granted at the Gare Montparnasse by the French national railway.[64] The terms of her 1922 lease granted Manieux the exclusive right to sell candy in the train station; while it expressly forbade her from selling pastries or tobacco, it did permit her to sell so-called articles de Paris, which included souvenirs, trinkets, and bimbeloterie. The only known photograph of the first kiosk, which survives as an unidentified newspaper clipping bearing a handwritten 1928 date, shows Méliès standing in front of a semipermanent wooden structure jam-packed with toys. It was a "minuscule boutique"—so small it was officially called a "kiosk" (*kiosque*).[65] The kiosk is topped by a sign that reads "Tout est Bon Confiserie."[66] Although this kiosk looks too small to accommodate a seat, it was situated in a high traffic area near the ticket counter within the Gare Montparnasse, a better location for attracting customers than where the concession was relocated in 1930 while the train station was being renovated.[67]

A number of different photographs of the second kiosk, which bears the sign "Confiserie et Jouets," survive and were the basis of corresponding scenes in the films *Le Grand Méliès* and *Hugo*. The words on the sign notwithstanding, toys are more visible than candy in these photographs. Balls and toys hang overhead in mesh sacks; toy musical instruments hang below; dolls and pull toys can also be seen. In some photographs, outdoor playthings like wheelbarrows, shovels, and toy sailboats were ostensibly on display in warm-weather months to appeal to children departing the Gare Montparnasse on trains for the seaside. Malthête-Méliès also recalled puppets and yo-yos being sold.[68]

Figure C.2. Newspaper clipping showing a reproduction of a photograph
of the first of Stéphanie Méliès' two kiosks at the Gare Montparnasse,
the "Tout est Bon Confiserie," private collection, rights reserved.

Known photographs of the Mélièses' kiosks were taken with black-and-white
film, rather than, for example, the autochrome natural color photography process perfected by Lumière.[69] Many of the toys were likely to have been brightly
colored, even though toy manufacturers and consumers had long been aware

that some of the chemical colorants used for that purpose were poisonous if ingested.[70] Thus, the array of commodities passersby saw within the two kiosks that Méliès and Stéphanie Méliès operated in the Gare Montparnasse would probably have been even more eye-catching than what can be seen in black-and-white photographs.

In surviving correspondence, Méliès often complained about how uncomfortable working in the kiosks were. He called the first and smaller of the two kiosks a "wooden cage (commonly: a cubicle)."[71] Although Marie Loudou, Stéphanie Méliès' cook, relieved Stéphanie Méliès and Méliès by tending the kiosk part time, she was let go when it was relocated.[72] The second of the two kiosks was "open in front, very cold and windy, without fire, and, principally, very dark in winter," Méliès wrote.[73] A drawing Méliès made around this time is a self-portrait that shows him hunched over a counter, seated on a stool, chained by a collar to the stone wall of a prison cell; above him is the sign, "Gare Montparnasse."[74] Adopting a classic caricatural trope, Méliès represented the inside of the kiosk as a space of confinement and monotony. While working in the kiosk, which was "open to the outside air," Méliès was subject to uncomfortable variations in temperature that made it "glacial in winter, torrid in summer."[75] (Méliès had been subject to similar temperature extremes while filming in his Montreuil studio, which was equipped with a large stove for heating and did have some provisions for ventilation, but was an "uncomfortable place" subject to "polar cold" temperatures in winter and "scorching heat"—temperatures greater than 110 degrees—in summer.[76])

However claustrophobic, monotonous, and uncomfortable it might have been to work in, photographs of the second kiosk make it look like a place of playful possibilities, visibly overflowing with toys promising different kinds of physical and imaginative play. In one of the least posed of these photographs, Méliès is standing in front of the second kiosk showing a toy limousine, which appears to be a German-made Lehmann model wind-up toy, a fairly de luxe imported transportation toy, to another man. Unlike other photographs showing the second kiosk, Méliès is smiling. He never owned a car but was instead reliant on public transportation or rides in other people's vehicles. We are left to our imaginations in thinking about what preceded or followed the taking of this photograph, but the gleam in Méliès' eye suggests it might have involved humor, laughter, or fun, if not actual play.

It is unclear whether or not this type of toy was ever sold in the kiosk, but we do know that more toys were housed nearby in two small rooms directly adjacent to Stéphanie Méliès' apartment on the second floor of 18, rue Jolivet

Figure C.3. Photograph of Méliès at the Gare Montparnasse, Cinémathèque Française.

where she and Méliès resided during a fairly impoverished period of both of their lives. Méliès' granddaughter Madeleine Fontaine lived there too after her mother Georgette Méliès was hospitalized, later dying. Young Madeleine Fontaine slept in the corner of a storage room filled with backstock, surrounded by "puppets, toy drums, and toy trumpets."[77] One wonders what dreams or nightmares—a recurring motif of Méliès' cinema—might have come to a young girl sleeping night after night amid a jumble of toys in such life circumstances.

Business in the kiosk worsened as the Great Depression deepened, and in 1932, Stéphanie Méliès' lease was terminated for nonpayment, at which point the contents of the kiosk and all of the remaining backstock were presumably sold.[78] Most of these toys were likely eventually broken or disposed of, although it is possible that some of the toys sold by Méliès (or at least toys like them) were not destroyed, like a number of the drawings Méliès made while working in these kiosks, which survive at the Cinémathèque Française and in private collections. Perhaps one of the "puppets, toy drums, and toy trumpets" like those that Madeleine Malthête-Méliès (née Madeleine Fontaine) could still remember more than sixty years later can still be found, tucked away in the corner of an attic or storage space somewhere, like Méliès' homemade marionette theater, or the "Star" Films that have turned up in flea markets, or the seventeen examples of original Incohérent art that were found in 2020.[79]

Maybe the toy limousine Méliès cradled in his hands or the riding boots that appear to walk up a wall in *L'Auberge du bon repos* were suitably de luxe and/or personally meaningful enough to someone to have survived. We can approximate holding these things in our hands or wearing them on our feet by looking at photographs and watching films, but toys and boots involve a tactile and material engagement, a bit like holding this book in your hand or digitally turning its electronic "pages" with a keystroke, the touch of a button, or the swipe of a screen. Perhaps some element of the experience of watching hand-colored films projected with hand-cranked projectors onto fabric screens, which left spectators marveling at the wonderful work of Méliès, comes through in the end.

NOTES

Introduction

1. All translations from French throughout the book are mine unless otherwise noted. Paolo Cherchi Usai, "The Institute of Incoherent Cinematography: An Introduction," in Paolo Cherchi Usai, ed., *A Trip to the Movies: Georges Méliès, Filmmaker and Magician (1861–1938)* (Rochester, N.Y.: George Eastman House, 1991), 23.

2. François Caron, *Les deux révolutions industrielles du XXe siècle* (Paris: Albin Michel, 1997); Michael Stephen Smith, *The Emergence of Modern Business Enterprise in France, 1800–1930* (Cambridge, Mass.: Harvard University Press, 2006).

3. Ulrich Lehmann, *Tigersprung: Fashion in Modernity* (Cambridge, Mass.: MIT Press, 2000), xii.

4. Lehmann, *Tigersprung*, xiv. See also Peter Wollen, "The Concept of Fashion in *The Arcades Project*," *boundary 2* 30, no. 1 (2003): 131–142.

5. Walter Benjamin, *The Arcades Project*, trans. Howard Eiland and Kevin McLaughlin (Cambridge, Mass.: Belknap Press, 1999); Susan Buck-Morss, *The Dialectics of Seeing: Walter Benjamin and the Arcades Project* (Cambridge, Mass.: MIT Press, 1989); David Harvey, *Paris, Capital of Modernity* (New York: Routledge, 2003).

6. Letter from Georges Méliès to Paul Gilson, August 16, 1929, reprinted in Jacques Malthête, ed., "Correspondance de Georges Méliès (1904–1937)," in André Gaudreault and Laurent Le Forestier, with Stéphane Tralongo, eds., *Méliès, carrefour des attractions, suivi de correspondance de Georges Méliès (1904–1937)* (Rennes: Presses Universitaires de Rennes, 2014), 370. Georges Sadoul noted this legacy in other terms in *Georges Méliès* (Paris: Éditions Seghers, 1961), 10.

7. Madeleine Malthête-Méliès, *Georges Méliès, L'Enchanteur* (Grandvilliers, France: La Tour Verte, 2011), 31.

8. *Archives commerciales de la France* (August 25, 1886): 1063; "Tribunaux de Commerce," *Franc Parleur Parisien*, no. 103 (September 5, 1886): 8; Jacques Deslandes, *Le boulevard du cinéma à l'époque de Georges Méliès* (Paris: Éditions du Cerf, 1963), 20. According to Paul Méliès, the son of Gaston Méliès, this buyout was the idea of Jean-Louis Méliès. "Recherches Historiques du samedi 22 juillet 1944: Paul Méliès," 21–22, Fonds Commission de Recherche Historique, Cinémathèque française.

9. Madeleine Malthête-Méliès, *Magnificent Méliès: The Authorized Biography*, ed. Matthew Solomon, trans. Kel Pero (Ann Arbor: University of Michigan Press, 2022).

10. In his memoirs, Méliès recalled that after his father refused to support his study of the fine arts, he had reluctantly gone to work at the Société Méliès factory, but he elaborated on his experiences there only to say he developed mechanical skills that later proved useful. Georges Méliès, *La vie et l'œuvre d'un pionnier du cinéma*, ed. Jean-Pierre Sirois-Trahan (Paris: Éditions du Sonneur, 2012), 30–31. Maurice Noverre likewise emphasized the mechanical aptitude Méliès developed between 1882 and 1886 in "L'œuvre de Georges Méliès: Etude retrospective sur le premier « Studio cinématographique » machiné pour la prise de vues théâtrales," *Nouvel Art Cinématographique*, 2d ser., no. 3 (July 1929): 85. See also Pierre Arias, "Méliès mécanicien," in Madeleine Malthête-Méliès, ed., *Méliès et la naissance du spectacle cinématographique* (Paris: Editions Klincksieck, 1985), 37–80.

11. Émile Goudeau, *Dix ans de bohème* (1888; Paris: Champ Vallon, 2000).

12. Advertisement, *Leeds Times* (December 27, 1884). Advertisements in the *Kilburn Times* (October 29, 1886) and *The Queen* (January 28, 1888) touted "Hand-Sewn French Boots" for men, women, and children. Thank you to David Pfluger for these references.

13. Daniel Grojnowski and Denys Riout, *Les arts incohérents et le rire dans les arts plastiques* (Paris: Éditions Corti, 2015), 101; Catherine Charpin, *Les Arts Incohérents (1882–1893)* (Paris: Éditions Syros Alternatives, 1990), 60–61, 77, 98; Luce Abélès and Catherine Charpin, eds., *Arts incohérents: Académie du dérisoire* (Paris: Editions de la Réunion des musées nationaux; Spadem, Adagp, 1992), 75; Sophie Herszkowicz, *Les Arts incohérents, suivi de Compléments* (Arles: Éditions de la Nuit, 2010), 15–16.

14. Given the international reputation of Méliès riding boots, some may possibly survive in private and/or public collections of equestriana. The de luxe boots manufactured by Méliès likely bore but scant resemblance to the pair of secondhand work boots Vincent van Gogh painted in 1886, which have generated considerable aesthetic, philosophical, and art historical discussion. See Cliff Edwards, *The Shoes of Van Gogh: A Spiritual and Artistic Journey to the Ordinary* (New York: Crossroad Publishing, 2004), and Donald Preziosi, ed., *The Art of Art History: A Critical Anthology*, rev. ed. (Oxford: Oxford University Press, 2009), 284–300. On shoes *in* film, see Elizabeth Ezra and Catherine Wheatley, eds., *Shoe Reels: The History and Philosophy of Footwear in Film* (Edinburgh: Edinburgh University Press, 2020).

15. Charpin, *Les Arts Incohérents*, 83–93; Abélès and Charpin, *Arts incohérents*; Herszkowicz, *Les Arts incohérents*. See also Phillip Dennis Cate and Mary Shaw, eds., *The Spirit of Montmartre: Cabarets, Humor, and the Avant-Garde, 1875–1905* (New Brunswick, N.J.: Zimmerli Art Museum, 1996); Jorgelina Orfila, "*Blague*, Nationalism, and Incohérence," in June Hargrove and Neil McWilliam, eds., *Nationalism and French Visual Culture, 1870–1914* (Washington, D.C.: National Gallery of Art, 2005), 172–193; and Marc Partouche, *La lignée oubliée: Bohèmes, avant-gardes et art contemporain de 1830 à nos jours* (Paris: Hermann Éditeurs, 2016).

16. Matthew Solomon, "Georges Méliès: Anti-Boulangist Caricature and the Incohérent Movement," *Framework* 53, no. 2 (2012): 305–327; French translation published

as "Méliès, l'Incohérent," trans. Stéphane Tralongo, in Gaudreault and Le Forestier, with Tralongo, eds., *Méliès, carrefour des attractions*, 203–216.

17. Grojnowski and Riout, *Les arts incohérents*, 118. See also Noël Richard, *À l'aube du symbolisme* (Paris: Nizet, 1961).

18. Peter Wollen, "The Two Avant-Gardes," *Readings and Writings: Semiotic Counter-Strategies* (London: Verso, 1982), 94–95, 102.

19. Wollen, "The Two Avant-Gardes," 93–94.

20. Wollen, "The Two Avant-Gardes," 94.

21. Quoted in Oksana Bulgokawa, *Sergei Eisenstein: A Biography*, trans. Anne Dwyer (Berlin: Potemkin Press, 2001), 39, emphasis in original. See also Sergei M. Eisenstein, "The Montage of Attractions" and "The Montage of Film Attractions," trans. Richard Taylor and William Powell, *The Eisenstein Reader*, ed. Richard Taylor (London: British Film Institute, 1998), 29–52, and Matthew Solomon, "Sergei Eisenstein: Attractions/Montage/Animation," in R. Barton Palmer and Murray Pomerance, eds., *Thinking in the Dark: Cinema, Theory, Practice* (New Brunswick, N.J.: Rutgers University Press, 2015), 78–80.

22. Wanda Strauven, ed., *The Cinema of Attractions Reloaded* (Amsterdam: Amsterdam University Press, 2006); Gaudreault and Le Forestier, with Tralongo, eds., *Méliès, carrefour des attractions*.

23. André Gaudreault, *Film and Attraction: From Kinematography to Cinema*, trans. Timothy Barnard (Urbana: University of Illinois Press, 2011), 7.

24. Gaudreault, *Film and Attraction*, 3, 8.

25. Lee Grieveson, *Policing Cinema: Movies and Censorship in Early-Twentieth-Century America* (Berkeley: University of California Press, 2004), 149.

26. Paul C. Spehr, "Unaltered to Date: Developing 35mm Film," in John Fullerton and Astrid Söderbergh-Widding, eds., *Moving Images: From Edison to the Webcam* (Eastleigh: John Libbey, 2001), 3–28.

27. Paolo Cherchi Usai, *Silent Cinema: A Guide to Study, Research and Curatorship* (London: British Film Institute, 2019), 22.

28. Robert Friedel, *Pioneer Plastic: The Making and Selling of Celluloid* (Madison: University of Wisconsin Press, 1983), 95.

29. Lee Grieveson, *Cinema and the Wealth of Nations: Media, Capital, and the Liberal World System* (Berkeley: University of California Press, 2017), 20.

30. Anna Malinowska and Karolina Lebek, "Introduction: The Popular Life of Things," in Anna Malinowska and Karolina Lebek, eds., *Materiality and Popular Culture: The Popular Life of Things* (New York: Routledge, 2017), 2.

31. Malinowska and Lebek, "Introduction," 1.

32. Brian R. Jacobson, "Introduction: Studio Perspectives," in Brian R. Jacobson, ed., *In the Studio: Visual Creation and Its Material Environments* (Berkeley: University of California Press, 2020), 7.

33. Caetlin Benson-Allott, *The Stuff of Spectatorship: Material Cultures of Film and Television* (Berkeley: University of California Press, 2021), 6.

34. Brian R. Jacobson, *Studios Before the System: Architecture, Technology, and the Emergence of Cinematic Space* (New York: Columbia University Press, 2015), 55–86, 225–233.

35. Jacobson, "Introduction: Studio Perspectives," 4–5.

36. Maurice Bessy and [Giusuppe Maria] Lo Duca, *Méliès, mage* (Paris: Prisma, 1945); *Méliès, un homme d'illusions* (Paris: Centre Nationale de la Photographie, 1986); Paolo Cherchi Usai, ed., *A Trip to the Movies*; Jacques Malthête, *Méliès, images et illusions* (Paris: Exporégie, 1996); Laurent Mannoni and Jacques Malthête, eds., *Méliès, magie et cinéma* (Paris: Paris-Musées, 2002); Laurent Mannoni, *Georges Méliès: La Magia del Cine* (Barcelona: Obra Social "la Caixa," 2013); Laurent Mannoni, *Georges Méliès, la magie du cinéma* (Paris: Cinémathèque Française, 2020). See also my discussion of Méliès in *Disappearing Tricks: Silent Film, Houdini, and the New Magic of the Twentieth Century* (Urbana: University of Illinois Press, 2010), 40–59, 140–146; my "Fairground Illusions and the Magic of Méliès," in Martin Loiperdinger, ed., *Travelling Cinema in Europe, KINtop Schriften* 10 (2008): 34–45; and my "Méliès und die Materialität Moderner Zauberei," trans. Katharina Rein, *Zeitschrift für Medien und Kulturforschung* 7, no. 1 (2016): 169–184.

37. *Complete Catalogue of Genuine and Original "Star Films" (Moving Pictures)* (New York: Geo. Méliès, 1903), 5; *Complete Catalogue of Genuine and Original "Star Films" (Moving Pictures)* (New York: Geo. Méliès, 1905), 2. John Frazer used this phrase as the title for his book, *Artificially Arranged Scenes: The Films of Georges Méliès* (Boston: G. K. Hall, 1979).

38. Jacques Malthête, "La vie et l'œuvre de Georges Méliès: Petit précis spatiotemporal," in Mannoni and Malthête, eds., *Méliès, magie et cinéma*, 22–23; "A Vendre," *L'Industriel Forain*, no. 365 (August 2–8, 1896); no. 366 (August 9–16, 1896); no. 368 (August 25–29, 1896); no. 369 (August 30–September 5, 1896); no. 370 (September 6–12, 1896); no. 371 (September 13–19, 1896); no. 372 (September 20–26, 1896); no. 373 (September 27–October 3, 1896); no. 374 (October 4–10, 1896).

39. James A. Schmiechen, *Sweated Industries and Sweated Labor: The London Clothing Trades, 1860–1914* (Urbana: University of Illinois Press, 1984), 27.

40. "Machines À Coudre," *L'Innovateur* 7, no. 11 (March 15, 1857): 85.

41. Louis Lumière even claimed that dreaming about a sewing machine had inspired an important mechanism incorporated into the Cinématographe. Quoted in Vincent Pinel, *Louis Lumière, inventeur et cinéaste* (Paris: Nathan Université, 1994), 19–20.

42. Georges Brunel, *La Photographie et la projection du mouvement: Historique—Dispositifs, Appareils, Cinématographiques* (Paris: Charles Mendel Éditeur, 1897), 94–95. When functioning as a camera rather than a projector, the exposed film fell into a cloth sack after passing through the Kinétographe.

43. Jacques Malthête and Laurent Mannoni, *L'Œuvre de Georges Méliès* (Paris: Éditions de la Martinière, Cinémathèque Française, 2008), 89.

44. Madeleine Malthête-Méliès, Anne-Marie Quévrain, and Jacques Malthête, *Essai de Reconstitution du Catalogue Français de la Star-Film, Suivi d'une Analyse*

Catalographique des Films de Georges Méliès Recensés en France (Bois d'Arcy, France: Services des Archives du Film du Centre National de la Cinématographie, 1981), 7; Frazer, *Artificially Arranged Scenes*, 83.

45. *Complete Catalogue of Genuine and Original "Star" Films* (1903), 8.

46. Titles are based on Jacques Malthête, "Filmographie Complète de Georges Méliès," in Mannoni, *Georges Méliès, la magie du cinéma*, 306–313. See also Malthête-Méliès, Quévrain, and Malthête, *Essai de Reconstitution du Catalogue Français de la Star-Film*, and Madeleine Malthête-Méliès, *Analyse Descriptive des Films de Georges Méliès Rassemblés entre 1981 et 1996 par la Cinémathèque Méliès* (Paris: Les Amis de Georges Méliès, 1996).

47. See, for example, Kristin Thompson, *Exporting Entertainment: America in the World Film Market, 1907–1934* (London: British Film Institute, 1986); Ivo Blom, *Jean Desmet and the Early Dutch Film Trade* (Amsterdam: Amsterdam University Press, 2003); and Frank Kessler and Nanna Verhoeff, eds., *Networks of Entertainment: Early Film Distribution, 1895–1915* (Eastleigh: John Libbey, 2007).

48. *L'Orchestre* (May 1, 1902).

49. Solomon, "Fairground Illusions and the Magic of Méliès," 34–45; Jean-Jacques Meusy, *Paris-palaces, ou les temps des cinémas (1894–1918)* (Paris: CNRS Éditions, 1995), 98–103.

50. Paul S. Moore, "'Bought, Sold, Exchanged and Rented': The Early Film Exchange and the Market in Secondhand Films in *New York Clipper* Classified Ads," *Film History* 31, no. 2 (2019): 1–31.

51. Malthête-Méliès, Quévrain, and Malthête, *Essai de Reconstitution du Catalogue Français de la Star-Film*, 66–67; Malthête-Méliès, *Analyse Descriptive des Films de Georges Méliès*, 16–17; Marie-Hélène Lehérissey-Méliès, with Anne-Marie Quévrain, "Deux Films Retrouves au Marche aux Puces: Le mystère s'intensifie...," *Cinémathèque Méliès*, no. 15 (1989): 21–26; Matthew Solomon, review of *Georges Méliès: First Wizard of Cinema (1896–1913)* and *Georges Méliès: Encore (1896–1911)*, *Moving Image* 12, no. 2 (2012): 190.

52. Richard Abel, *The Red Rooster Scare: Making Cinema American, 1900–1910* (Berkeley: University of California Press, 1999), 40–46; Bregtje Lameris, "Pathécolor: 'Perfect in Their Rendition of the Colours of Nature,'" *Living Pictures* 2, no. 2 (2003): 47–48; Joshua Yumibe, *Moving Color: Early Film, Mass Culture, Modernism* (New Brunswick, N.J.: Rutgers University Press, 2012), 45–48; Joshua Yumibe, "French Film Colorists," in Jane Gaines, Radha Vatsal, and Monica Dall'Asta, eds., *Women Film Pioneers Project* (New York: Columbia University Libraries, 2013), https://wfpp.columbia.edu/essay/french-film-colorists/; Tom Gunning, Giovanna Fossati, Joshua Yumibe, and Jonathon Rosen, *Fantasia of Color in Early Cinema* (Amsterdam: Amsterdam University Press, 2015).

53. Frank Kessler, "The *Féerie* between Stage and Screen," in André Gaudreault, Nicolas Dulac, and Santiago Hidalgo, eds., *A Companion to Early Cinema* (Oxford: Wiley-Blackwell, 2012), 64–79; Frank Kessler, "*A Trip to the Moon* as *Féerie*," in Matthew

Solomon, ed., *Fantastic Voyages of the Cinematic Imagination: Georges Méliès's Trip to the Moon* (Albany, N.Y.: SUNY Press, 2011), 115–128; Paul Ginisty, *La Féerie* (Paris: Michaud, 1910).

54. *Complete Catalogue of Genuine and Original "Star Films"* (1905), 37–38. These two films were titled *Faust and Marguerite* and *The Damnation of Faust*, respectively, in Méliès' American catalogues.

55. Thomas Elsaesser, "L'Appel des sons: *Weihnachtsglocken* de Franz Hofer et les transformations des genres musicaux dans le cinéma allemand des premiers temps," *1895*, no. 50 (2007): 94–122. See also Richard Abel and Rick Altman, eds., *The Sounds of Early Cinema* (Bloomington: Indiana University Press, 2001); Rick Altman, *Silent Film Sound* (New York: Columbia University Press, 2004); and Martin Barnier, *Bruits, cris, musique de films: Les projections avant 1914* (Rennes: Presses Universitaires de Rennes, 2010).

56. *Complete Catalogue of Genuine and Original "Star Films"* (1905), 43.

57. *Résumé à lire au public pendant la projection: La légende de Rip Van Vinckle, grande pièce fantastique en 3 parties et 17 tableaux* (Paris: Imprimerie Thivet, 1905).

58. *Complete Catalogue of Genuine and Original "Star Films" (Moving Pictures)* (New York: Geo. Méliès, 1908), 87–92; *La Légende de Rip Van Vinckle: Grande pièce fantastique en 17 tableaux* (Paris: Manufacture de Films pour Cinématographes G. Méliès, 1905).

59. See my "Negotiating the Bounds of Transnational Cinema with Georges Méliès, 1896–1908," *Early Popular Visual Culture* 14, no. 2 (2016): 162–166, and my review of *Georges Méliès*, 191.

60. My understanding of the tremendous variation of silent film projection speeds benefited from Paolo Cherchi Usai, email communication to the author, October 17, 2016. Silent film speed continues to be a vexed issue about which there are many competing opinions. Kevin Brownlow wrote one of the only studies of this issue, "Silent Films—What was the Right Speed?" in Thomas Elsaesser, with Adam Barker, eds., *Early Cinema: Space/Frame/Narrative* (London: British Film Institute, 1990), 282–290. Elsewhere Brownlow is reported as saying, "The only rule is to transfer it at the speed at which it looks right, not at the speed [it] is supposed to be shot at." Quoted in Gilbert Bianchi, "Méliès—Initiés et Profanes," *Cinémathèque Méliès*, no. 19 (1991): 37.

61. Cherchi Usai, *Silent Cinema: A Guide*, 182.

62. Georges Méliès, "Kinematographic Views," in Gaudreault, *Film and Attraction*, 137.

63. *L'Orchestre* (September 28, 1902). This published program also gives the length of the film as three hundred meters—in contrast to the 260-meter length specified in Méliès' published film lists. Because no longer versions of *Voyage dans la Lune* have been reported, I suspect this version, which was screened at the Théâtre Robert-Houdin shortly after the film was completed, was actually 260 meters in length, which corresponds to the 845-foot length that is indicated in Méliès' American catalogues, which specify "Duration of exhibit sixteen minutes." *Complete Catalogue of Genuine and Original "Star Films"* (1903), 25; *Complete Catalogue of Genuine and Original "Star Films"* (1905), 18. See also my Introduction to Solomon, ed., *Fantastic Voyages*, 7–8.

64. *Complete Catalogue of Genuine and Original "Star Films"* (1908), 87.

65. Cherchi Usai, *Silent Cinema: A Guide*, 180. This is considerably slower than the speeds at which silent films are screened or have generally been transferred, which can vary greatly. Most projectors powered by electricity cannot be set to a speed of less than sixteen frames per second.

66. Cherchi Usai, *Silent Cinema: A Guide*, 247.

67. Georges Méliès, "Reply to Questionary" (1930), in Solomon, ed., *Fantastic Voyages*, 233.

68. Cherchi Usai, *Silent Cinema: A Guide*, 245. See also Joanne Bernardi, Paolo Cherchi Usai, Tami Williams, and Joshua Yumibe, eds., *Provenance and Early Cinema* (Bloomington: Indiana University Press, 2021).

69. See my Introduction to Solomon, ed., *Fantastic Voyages*, 8–11.

70. *Eine phantastische Reise nach dem Monde* appears on the DVD published with Solomon, ed., *Fantastic Voyages*. This is the "tinted positive of undetermined generation," which Cherchi Usai mentions in *Silent Cinema: A Guide*, 245.

71. Mannoni, *Georges Méliès, la magie du cinéma*, 184; *Complete Catalogue of Genuine and Original "Star Films"* (1903), 25; Mannoni, *Georges Méliès: La Magia del Cine*, 186.

72. Cherchi Usai, *Silent Cinema: A Guide*, 246.

73. Cherchi Usai, *Silent Cinema: A Guide*, 213.

74. Stéphanie Salmon, *Pathé: À la conquête du cinéma, 1896–1929* (Paris: Éditions Tallandier, 2014), 217–218.

75. Georges Sadoul, *Les pionniers du cinéma, 1897–1909*, rev. ed., ed. Bernard Eisenschitz (1948; Paris: Editions Denoël, 1978), 486, quoting G. Maréchal in *L'Industriel Forain* (March 4, 1909).

76. Malthête, *Méliès, images et illusions*, 11.

77. Charles Pathé, *Écrits Autobiographiques: Souvenirs et conseils d'un parvenu; De Pathé frères à Pathé-Cinéma*, ed. Pierre Lherminier (Paris: L'Harmattan, 2006), 158–160, 166; Laurent Creton, "Figures de l'entrepreneur, filières d'innovation et genèse de l'industrie cinématographique: Lumière, Pathé et Méliès," in Jacques Malthête and Michel Marie, eds., *Georges Méliès, l'illusionniste fin de siècle?* (Paris: Presses de la Sorbonne Nouvelle, 1997), 154n47, 162–164; Jean-Pierre Sirois-Trahan, "Les relations entre Pathé et Méliès: Aux sources du cinéma industriel et du cinéma indépendant (1908–1913)," *Cinema & Cie*, no. 21 (2013): 95–107; Salmon, *Pathé*, 572n45.

78. Malthête-Méliès, *Georges Méliès*, 399–425; André Méliès, "Mémoires et Notes d'André Méliès," ed. Marie-Hélène Lehérissey-Méliès, *Cinémathèque Méliès*, no. 20 (1992): 17–25; Malthête, *Méliès, images et illusions*, 173–201; Marie-Antoinette Dameron, "Souvenirs d'une jeune choriste du théâtre des Variétés Artistiques de Montreuil dirigé par Mademoiselle Georgette Méliès," *Cinémathèque Méliès*, no. 16 (1990): 19–21; Henri Jeanson, [untitled transcription of 1945 radio broadcast], *Cinémathèque Méliès*, no. 16 (1990): 28–29; La Rédaction, "Georges Méliès," *Passez Muscade* 12, no. 40 (1927): 486; Blée, "Le Théâtre des Variétés," in *Exposition commemorative du centenaire de Georges Méliès* (Paris: Musée des Arts Décoratifs, 1961), 44.

79. Uncredited typescript translation of letter from G. Méliès to [Eugène] Lauste, January 23, 1930, reproduced in Eileen Bowser, ed., *The Merritt Crawford Papers* (Lanham, Md.: University Publications of America, 1986), microfilm, reel 3. See also letter from G. Méliès to Robelly [pseud., Robert Rouet], April 30, 1937, reprinted in Malthête, ed., "Correspondance de Georges Méliès," 480.

80. Manuscript letter from [Méliès] to [Merritt] Crawford, April 8, 1931, reproduced in Bowser, ed., *Merritt Crawford Papers*, reel 3.

81. Malthête-Méliès, *Georges Méliès*, 427; Méliès, *La vie et l'œuvre d'un pionnier du cinéma*, 33. The demolition of this area had been planned since 1857—it was part of Baron Haussmann's original plan to widen Paris thoroughfares. The extension of the Boulevard Haussmann between the rue Taitbout and the rue Drouot was approved in 1910. "Les Grands Travaux de Paris," *L'Illustration*, no. 3499 (March 19, 1910): 273–274. See also Jacques Hillairet, *Dictionnaire Historique des Rues de Paris*, vol. 1 (Paris: Editions de Minuit, 1963), 623.

82. Georges Pillement, "Le nouveau Boulevard Haussmann," *Almanach de la Femme et l'Enfant* (1927): 69.

83. Geo. Méliès, "Documents pour Compléter l'Histoire du Théâtre Robert-Houdin," *Passez Muscade*, no. 9 (August 1934): 126–127. It was reported that a gambling enterprise took up temporary residence on the former site of the Théâtre Robert-Houdin after it was vacated while work on the extension of the Boulevard Haussmann was ongoing. *Candide*, no. 47 (February 5, 1925).

84. Creton, "Figures de l'entrepreneur," 135, 135fn6.

85. Marie-Hélène Lehérissey, email communication to the author, December 22, 2020.

86. André Méliès, "Suite de la publication des Mémoires et notes d'André Méliès," ed. Marie-Hélène Lehérissey-Méliès, *Cinémathèque Méliès*, no. 14 (1989): 15–16; no. 20 (1992): 24; Jacques Malthête, "Les deux studios de Georges Méliès," in Mannoni and Malthête, eds., *Méliès, magie et cinéma*, 135–159; André Méliès, "Mémoires et notes d'André Méliès," ed. Marie-Hélène Lehérissey-Méliès, *Cinémathèque Méliès*, no. 20 (1992): 16.

87. André Méliès, "Mémoires et notes d'André Méliès," *Cinémathèque Méliès*, no. 20 (1992): 24; Noverre, "L'œuvre de Georges Méliès: Etude retrospective sur le premier « Studio cinématographique »," 83. Before vacating the property, a neighboring girls' school allowed Méliès to store some of his things, including costumes and several of Robert-Houdin's mechanical pieces.

88. André Méliès, "Suite de la publication des Mémoires et notes d'André Méliès," *Cinémathèque Méliès*, no. 14 (1989): 17. See also André Méliès, "La féerie familière," in Sadoul, *Georges Méliès*, 146.

89. Malthête-Méliès, *Georges Méliès*, 424. See also Madeleine Malthête-Méliès, "Vains essais de sauver la maison de Georges Méliès à Montreuil," *Cinémathèque Méliès*, no. 32 (1998): 28–32.

90. Malthête-Méliès, *Georges Méliès*, 427.

91. Cherchi Usai, *Silent Cinema: A Guide*, 211. See also Paolo Cherchi Usai, *Silent Cinema: An Introduction* (London: British Film Institute, 2000), 13, 44.

92. Malthête-Méliès, *Georges Méliès*, 428.

93. Solomon, "Negotiating the Bounds of Transnational Cinema," 159–162.

94. André Méliès, "Mémoires et notes d'André Méliès (suite)," ed. Marie-Hélène Lehérissey-Méliès, *Cinémathèque Méliès*, no. 18 (1991): 37.

95. André Méliès, "Mémoires et notes d'André Méliès," *Cinémathèque Méliès*, no. 20 (1992): 25.

96. Michel Juignet, *La Chaussure: Son Histoire, Ses Légendes, Son Compagnonnage et Se Cordonniers Célèbres* (Paris: Imprimerie du Compagnonnage, 1977), 210–211; "Brevets d'Invention," *Bulletin des lois de la République française*, no. 248 (1875): 295. In 1887, Henri Méliès and Gaston Méliès patented a method of nailing protective wear guards called "*bons-bouts*" to the corners of shoe heels. "Brevets d'Invention," *Franc Parleur Parisien*, no. 129 (October 5, 1887): 149.

97. Malthête-Méliès, *Georges Méliès*, 428; André Méliès, "Mémoires et notes d'André Méliès," *Cinémathèque Méliès*, no. 20 (1992): 25.

98. Manuscript letter from G. Méliès to [Merritt] Crawford, December 8, 1930, reproduced in Bowser, ed., *Merritt Crawford Papers*, reel 3.

99. Letter from Méliès to Crawford, December 8, 1930.

100. Paul S. Moore, "Ephemera as Medium: The Afterlife of Lost Films," *Moving Image* 16, no. 1 (2016): 134–138.

101. Malthête, "Filmographie Complète de Georges Méliès," 309, 313. Several dozen of Méliès' films were uncatalogued, including between fifteen and twenty advertising films produced in 1900, and the prestaging of the coronation of England's King Edward VII, which Méliès was specially commissioned by Charles Urban to make in 1902. Additionally, catalogue numbers were not assigned to a number of other Méliès films, including several dated 1908, and the films Méliès produced in 1911–1913 for distribution by Pathé.

102. Allyson Nadia Field, *Uplift Cinema: The Emergence of African American Film and the Possibility of Black Modernity* (Durham, N.C.: Duke University Press, 2015), 23.

103. Field, *Uplift Cinema*, 23.

104. Jacques Malthête, ed., *158 scénarios de films disparus de Georges Méliès* (Paris: Association "Les Amis de Georges Méliès," 1986), 46–47; Malthête, *Méliès, images et illusions*, 30; Paul Hammond, *Marvellous Méliès* (London: Gordon Fraser, 1974), 17; *Complete Catalogue of Genuine and Original "Star Films"* (1903), 24; *Complete Catalogue of Genuine and Original "Star Films"* (1905), 17.

105. Kemp R. Niver, *The First Twenty Years: A Segment of Film History*, ed. Bebe Bergsten (Los Angeles: Locare Research Group, 1968), 31–32, 38–40, 43–44, 51–53. See also Kemp R. Niver, *Early Motion Pictures: The Paper Print Collection in the Library of Congress*, ed. Bebe Bergsten (Washington, D.C.: Library of Congress, 1985). Compare Hammond, *Marvellous Méliès*, 54.

106. Cherchi Usai, *Silent Cinema: A Guide*, 230.

107. Cherchi Usai, *Silent Cinema: A Guide*, 35.

108. Lisa Gitelman, *Paper Knowledge: Toward a Media History of Documents* (Durham, N.C.: Duke University Press, 2014), 3.

109. Gitelman, *Paper Knowledge*, 24.

110. Gitelman, *Paper Knowledge*, 26, 40.

111. Michael Twyman, "The Long-Term Significance of Printed Ephemera," *RBM: A Journal of Rare Books, Manuscripts, and Cultural Heritage* 9, no. 1 (2008): 20. Twyman adds, "This was so in France in the late nineteenth century. A law on the liberty of the press of 29 July 1881 (art. 3) specifically exempted from legal deposit [. . .] ballot papers, trade or industrial circulars, and jobbing printing or ephemera."

112. Jacques Malthête, "La *Jeanne d'Arc* de Georges Méliès," *1895*, no. 36 (2002): 118fn7; Malthête, "Les *Vues spéciales de l'Exposition de 1900* tournées par Georges Méliès," *1895*, no. 36 (2002): 99fn1.

113. Mannoni, *Georges Méliès: La Magia del Cine*, 137; Mannoni and Malthête, eds., *Méliès, magie et cinéma*, 267.

114. Henry Raine, "The Importance of Ephemera," in Simon Eliot and Jonathan Rose, eds., *A Companion to the History of the Book*, 2d ed. (London: John Wiley, 2020), 642.

115. Twyman, "The Long-Term Significance of Printed Ephemera," 19. Twyman adds, "The French term for 'jobbing printing' was 'ouvrages de ville,' later 'travaux de ville.'" Most promotional materials printed to promote Méliès' films do not indicate a printer—one that does was printed by the Imprimerie Thivet at 26, Passage de l'Opéra, not far from Méliès' first film developing laboratory.

116. None lists the name of a printer, only the names of the copyright holder, "Geo. Méliès, Paris—New York," and "Gaston Méliès, General Manager" of the "New York Branch." See, for example, *Complete Catalogue of Genuine and Original "Star Films"* (1903), 6.

117. Georges Sadoul, "Georges Méliès et la première élaboration du langage cinématographique," *Revue internationale de filmologie*, no. 1 (1947): 23–30. Compare Elizabeth Ezra, *Georges Méliès: The Birth of the Auteur* (Manchester: Manchester University Press, 2000), 35.

118. Gérard Genette, *Paratexts: Thresholds of Interpretation*, trans. Jane E. Lewin (Cambridge: Cambridge University Press, 1997), 344. See also Marta Braun and Charlie Keil, "'As Pleasing as It Is Incomprehensible': Film Catalogues as Paratext," in Kessler and Verhoeff, eds., *Networks of Entertainment*, 218–222.

119. Genette, *Paratexts*, 3–4.

120. Letter from G. Méliès to Auguste Drioux, December 16, 1927, reprinted in Malthête, ed., "Correspondance de Georges Méliès," 342; "Georges Méliès et le mythe des 4000 films," *Cinémathèque Méliès Lettre d'Information*, no. 52 (January 2019): 2.

121. Malthête, *Méliès, images et illusions*, 49–50. Méliès may have been dubbed "the man of a hundred-thousand images," but the actual number of film frames he produced was more like two million. Compare Paul Gilson and Nino Frank, "L'Homme aux cent mille images," *Revue du cinéma*, no. 11 (March 1948): 3–27.

122. Georges Sadoul, "An Index to the Creative Work of Georges Méliès [1896–1912]," *Special Supplement to Sight & Sound*, no. 11 (August 1947): 3–32. A revised and expanded version, which included more discursive paragraphs about Méliès' life and career and contextual information about individual film titles and groups of titles, was published as "Bio-Filmographie," in Sadoul, *Georges Méliès*, 162–234.

123. Sadoul, "An Index to the Creative Work of Georges Méliès," 3; Sadoul, *Georges Méliès*, 52.

124. Georges Sadoul, "Lettre à Jay Leyda," *Rencontres 1: Chroniques et Entretiens*, ed. Bernard Eisenschitz (Paris: Éditions Denoël, 1984), 15.

125. Joanne Morra and Marquard Smith, introduction to Joanne Morra and Marquard Smith, eds., *Visual Culture: Critical Concepts in Media and Cultural Studies*, vol. 1 (New York: Routledge, 2006), 10. Their list is slightly longer; I eliminated all of "the objects and subjects and media and environments" that postdate Méliès' lifetime.

126. Morra and Smith, introduction to Morra and Smith, eds., *Visual Culture*, vol. 1, 9, 15.

127. Thomas Elsaesser, *Film History as Media Archaeology: Tracking Digital Cinema* (Amsterdam: Amsterdam University Press, 2016), 25.

128. Jussi Parikka, *What Is Media Archaeology?* (Cambridge: Polity Press, 2012), 15–16.

129. See, for example, Siegfried Kracauer, *Theory of Film: The Redemption of Physical Reality* (New York: Oxford University Press, 1960), 30–33.

130. For their part, a number of Lumière films involved what were often carefully staged and choreographed presentational performances.

131. See esp. Georges Sadoul, *Les pionniers du cinéma (de Méliès à Pathé)*, rev. ed., ed. Bernard Eisenschitz (1947; Paris: Éditions Denoël, 1973).

132. Mannoni and Malthête, eds., *Méliès, magie et cinéma*, 87.

133. Mannoni and Malthête, eds., *Méliès, magie et cinéma*, 55. On costume in Méliès' films more generally, see Priska Morrissey, "La garde-robe de Georges Méliès: Origines et usages des costumes des vues cinématographiques," in Gaudreault and Le Forestier, with Tralongo, eds., *Méliès, carrefour des attractions*, 177–188.

134. See also my "'Twenty-Five Heads under One Hat': Quick-Change in the 1890s," in Vivian Sobchack, ed., *Meta-Morphing: Visual Transformation and the Culture of Quick-Change* (Minneapolis: University of Minnesota Press, 2000), 1–20, esp. 19n37–20n37.

135. One wonders in what ways *High-Life Taylor* [lost] may have dealt with fashion. The film's title may allude to either the High Life Tailor, located at 112, rue Richelieu, or the Cordonnerie du High-Life, located at 30, boulevard des Italiens, the same street as the Théâtre Robert-Houdin. The storefront beneath the Théâtre Robert-Houdin was for many years the tailor shop of Lejeune. David Pfluger, email communication to the author, September 1, 2021. See the production stills of *High-Life Taylor* [lost] reproduced in Malthête, *Méliès, images et illusions*, 143, and Malthête and Mannoni, *L'Œuvre de Georges Méliès*, 238, and the map drawn by André Méliès reproduced in *Cinémathèque Méliès*, no. 17 (1990): 22–23.

136. Katherine Groo, "Let It Burn: Film Historiography in Flames," *Discourse* 41, no. 1 (2019): 19.

137. *Le Voyage à travers l'Impossible* (Paris: Imprimerie Thivet, n.d.), 1; *Complete Catalogue of Genuine and Original "Star" Films* (1905), 60. See also Malthête-Méliès, Quévrain, and Malthête, *Essai de Reconstitution du Catalogue Français de la Star-Film*, 201. In England, however, *Voyage à travers l'impossible* was released as *Whirling the Worlds* by the Charles Urban Trading Company, an authorized "Star" Films distributor,

and the opening scene was described in publicity materials as taking place at a meeting of the less fancifully named "The Geographical Society." *"Whirling the Worlds": Adventuous Voyage of The 'Exploring Club' By Train, Motor-car, Air-ship, and Sub-marine* (London: Scott, Herbert, and Co., n.d.), 1. This ephemeral publication describes the film as "Jules Verne Outdone [. . .] 'The Most Fantastic Picture Series Ever Conceived' . . . Invented and Arranged by Mr. Geo. Melies [*sic*]."

138. *Complete Catalogue of Genuine and Original "Star Films"* (1905), 60.

139. *Complete Catalogue of Genuine and Original "Star" Films* (1905), 67.

140. *Complete Catalogue of Genuine and Original "Star" Films* (1905), 67–68.

141. The description of these tableaus looks forward to the conclusion of Méliès' film *À la conquête du Pôle*, in which a group of arctic explorers are irresistibly pulled toward the North Pole, represented by an actual pole, to which they adhere like so many pieces of metal.

142. Madeleine Malthête-Méliès, "La Cinémathèque Méliès: Son histoire et ses activités," *Journal of Film Preservation*, no. 48 (1994): 39–42; Anne-Marie Quévrain, "Rapatrier l'œuvre de Georges Méliès: La collection de Madeleine Malthête-Méliès," *Journal of Film Preservation*, no. 99 (2018): 96–106.

143. Éric LeRoy, "Méliès à l'aube du domaine public," *Journal of Film Preservation*, no. 77/78 (2008): 73–76.

144. Solomon, review of *Georges Méliès*, 187–192.

Chapter 1

1. Vachon, "Revue des Chaussures Françaises," *L'Innovateur* 6, no. 3 (July 15, 1855): 19; Vachon, "Exposition Universelle: Compte-Rendu général des Chaussures françaises à l'Exposition," *L'Innovateur* 6, no. 5 (September 15, 1855): 38.

2. Félix Guénin, "Botterie Française: Le cordonnier—Le bottier," *Moniteur de la Cordonnerie* 37, no. 2 (January 16, 1886): 2–3.

3. On compagnonnage, see Cynthia M. Truant, *The Rites of Labor: Brotherhoods of Compagnonnage in Old and New Regime France* (Ithaca, N.Y.: Cornell University Press, 1994); Jean-Pierre Bayard, *Le Compagnonnage en France* (Paris: Payot, 1977); and Raoul Dautry, ed., *Compagnonnage par les compagnons du Tour de France* (Paris: Plon, 1951). My understanding of compagnonnage benefited from Michel Juignet, telephone conversation with the author, August 25, 2020.

4. Madeleine Malthête-Méliès, *Georges Jean-Louis Méliès, L'Enchanteur* (Grandvilliers, France: La Tour Verte, 2011), 22–25. Méliès adopted the compagnon name "Carcassonne-l'Ami-du-Courage." Michel Juignet, *La Chaussure: Son Histoire, Ses Légendes, Son Compagnonnage et Se Cordonniers Célèbres* (Paris: Imprimerie du Compagnonnage, 1977), 210.

5. Jacques Malthête, "La vie et l'œuvre de Georges Méliès, petit précis spatiotemporel," in Laurent Mannoni and Jacques Malthête, eds., *Méliès, magie et cinéma* (Paris: Paris-Musées, 2002), 14–15. The category of "cordonnier en chambre" is defined in *Journal du*

Palais: Répertoire Général Contenant la Jurisprudence de 1791 à 1857, l'Histoire du Droit, la Législation et la Doctrine des Auteurs (Paris: Bureaux de l'Administration, 1857), 584.

6. Quoted in Malthête, "La vie et l'œuvre de Georges Méliès," 15. The earliest commercial addresses for "Méliès, bottier" are 32, rue Montmartre, and 7, rue Feydeau in the second arrondissement. *Annuaire Général du Commerce, de l'Industrie, de la Magistrature et de l'Administration, ou Almanach des 500,000 Adresses de Paris, des Départements et des Pays Etrangers* (Paris: Firmin Didot Frères, 1853), 343, 518, 1074, 1144; *Annuaire Général du Commerce, de l'Industrie, de la Magistrature et de l'Administration, ou Almanach des 500,000 Adresses de Paris, des Départements et des Pays Etrangers* (Paris: Firmin Didot Frères, 1854), 356, 533, 1003, 1200; *Almanach-Bottin du Commerce de Paris, des Départements de la France et des Principales Villes du Monde* (Paris: Bureau de l'Almanach du Commerce, 1854), 347, 458, 493, 713; *Almanach-Bottin du Commerce de Paris, des Départements de la France et des Principales Villes du Monde* (Paris: Bureau de l'Almanach du Commerce, 1855), 325, 493, 532, 755; *Annuaire Général du Commerce, de l'Industrie, de la Magistrature et de l'Administration, ou Almanach des 500,000 Adresses de Paris, des Départements et des Pays Etrangers* (Paris: Firmin Didot Frères, 1855), 331, 488, 1055.

7. "Exposition Universelle," *L'Innovateur* 5, no. 12 (April 15, 1855): 96; "Exposition Universelle—Empire Français," *L'Innovateur* 6, no. 2 (June 15, 1855): 12; Vachon, "Revue des Chaussures Françaises," *L'Innovateur* 6, no. 3 (July 15, 1855): 18; Vachon, "Exposition Universelle: Compte-Rendu général des Chaussures françaises à l'Exposition," *L'Innovateur* 6, no. 5 (September 15, 1855): 38; Vachon, "Exposition Universelle: Compte-Rendu général des Chaussures françaises à l'Exposition (Suite et Fin)," *L'Innovateur* 6, no. 6 (October 15, 1855): 46; "France," *L'Innovateur* 6, no. 7 (November 15, 1855): 64; *Exposition des Produits de l'Industrie de Toutes les Nations: Catalogue Officiel*, 2d ed. (Paris: E. Panis, Éditeur, 1855), 178.

8. An 1878 account indicates that the Maison Méliès started making women's footwear some ten years earlier. Félix Guénin, "Exposition Universelle 1878," *Moniteur de la Cordonnerie* 29, no. 19 (October 1, 1878): 4.

9. *Complete Catalogue of Genuine and Original "Star Films" (Moving Pictures)* (New York: Geo. Méliès, 1905), 23.

10. Tom Gunning, "The Ghost in the Machine: Animated Pictures at the Haunted Hotel of Early Cinema," *Living Pictures* 1, no. 1 (2001): 10.

11. Gunning, "Ghost in the Machine," 11, quoting Karl Marx, *Capital: A Critique of Political Economy*, ed. Frederick [*sic*] Engels, trans. Samuel Moore and Edward Aveling, vol. 1 (New York: International Publishers, 1967), 71.

12. Gunning, "Ghost in the Machine," 11.

13. Georges Moynet, *La Machinerie théâtrale: Trucs et décors, explication raisonnée de tous les moyens employés pour produire les illusions théâtrales* (Paris: Librairie Illustrée, 1893), 104–106. See also Joseph Sokalaski, "From Screen to Stage: A Case Study of the Paper Print Collection," *Nineteenth Century Theatre* 25, no. 2 (1997): 128–130.

14. Marx, *Capital*, 1:354.

15. Marx, *Capital*, 1:165.

16. Marx, *Capital*, 1:315.

17. Marx, *Capital*, 1:354.

18. J.-P. Damourette, *Matériel des Industries du Cuir: Tannerie, Corroierie, Mégisserie, Maroquinerie, Fabriques de Courroies et de Chaussures* (Paris: Hennuyer et fils, 1869).

19. Peter McNeil and Giorgio Riello, "Walking the Streets of London and Paris in the Enlightenment," in Peter McNeil and Giorgio Riello, eds., *Shoes: A History from Sandals to Sneakers* (Oxford: Berg, 2006), 101.

20. Animals provided raw material for Méliès footwear and were butchered to produce the so-called sweetbreads (*ris de veau*), which cousin Adolphe Méliès imported from England to France. Malthête-Méliès, *Georges Méliès*, 90–91. Adolphe Méliès' "sweetbread" profits helped finance *La Griffe*, but Adolphe Méliès et Cie was officially liquidated on April 2, 1897. *Archives Commerciales de la France* 24, no. 105 (December 31, 1897): 114.

21. Anne-Marie Malthête-Quévrain, email communication to the author, April 16, 2021, citing research by Avraham Jean-François Malthête.

22. Philippe Ponsot, *Tanneries et Tanneurs du Cinglais, 1746–1962* (Cully, France: OREP Editions, 2005), 10–25.

23. *Grande Exposition de Cuirs et Peaux des Fabricants Français & Étrangers (Tannerie, Corroierie, Mégisserie, Hongroierie, Maroquinerie): Notice et Compte-Rendu de l'Exposition* (Paris: Imprimerie Ch. Schiller, 1867), 26. Croiser is listed as "Madame veuve Croisier aîné."

24. Thorstein Veblen, *The Theory of the Leisure Class* (1899; New York: Augustus M. Kelley, 1975), 83, 167.

25. Veblen, *Theory of the Leisure Class*, 173.

26. A. Privé, "Petite Cause, Grands Effets," *Franc Parleur Parisien*, no. 41 (February 5, 1884): 1.

27. Diana de Marly, *Worth: Father of Haute Couture*, 2d ed. (1980; New York: Holmes & Meier, 1990), 119.

28. De Marly, *Worth*, 119.

29. De Marly, *Worth*, 126, 128.

30. Marie-Josèphe Bossan, *The Art of the Shoe* (New York: Parkstone Press, 2004), 67. See also O. Eychenne, "Les Inventions," *Franc Parleur Parisien*, no. 69 (April 5, 1885): 4–5.

31. Napoléon Gaillard, *Memoire Descriptif de la Chaussure Française en Gutta-Percha* (Neuilly: Imprimerie de A. Poilleux, 1858); E. Lihard, "Caoutchouc," *Moniteur de la Cordonnerie* 6, no. 10 (February 15, 1856): 85–86; 6, no. 11 (March 15, 1856): 93; Adolphe Gairaud, "De le Gutta Percha et Son Application à la Chaussure," *Moniteur de la Cordonnerie* 6, no. 8 (December 15, 1855): 70; 6, no. 9 (January 15, 1856): 77–78.

32. Elizabeth Semmelhack, *Heights of Fashion: A History of the Elevated Shoe* (Toronto: Bata Shoe Museum, 2008), 30.

33. Pinet is the subject of an excellent monograph by Xavier Gille, *François Pinet: Bottier des élégantes, 1817–1897* (Chemillé-sur-Indrois, France: Éditions Hugues de Chivré, 2011). See also Valerie Steele and Colleen Hill, *Shoe Obsession* (New York: Fashion Institute of Technology, 2012), 30. Pinet received the Legion of Honor, an honor that eluded Jean-Louis Méliès. Unlike Jean-Louis Méliès, whose company was defunct by the time he died in 1898, Pinet's brand outlived his 1897 death and the subsequent sale of the company by his sons Albert Pinet and Maurice Pinet: it still exists.

34. Léon Joly, "Le Compagnonnage," *Franc Parleur Parisien*, no. 49 (June 5, 1884): 4–5; no. 50 (June 20, 1884): 5–6; no. 51 (July 5, 1884): 2–3; no. 54 (August 20, 1884): 7; no. 55 (September 5, 1884): 4–5; no. 56 (September 20, 1884): 6–7; no. 59 (November 5, 1884): 4. See also letter from G. Toussant, April 17, 1860, *Moniteur de la Cordonnerie* 10, no. 12 (April 20, 1860): 6.

35. Mollet-Perrotat, "Correspondance Au sujet des ateliers en cordonnerie du compagnonnage, sur le tour de France," *Moniteur de la Cordonnerie* 37, no. 6 (March 16, 1886): 3–4.

36. Alain Plessis, "Au temps du Second Empire, de l'entreprise de luxe au sommet des affaires," in Jacques Marseille, ed., *Le Luxe en France du siècle des « Lumières » à nos jours* (Paris: Association pour le développement de l'histoire économique, 1999), 51.

37. Jean Castarède, *Histoire du luxe en France: Des origines à nos jours* (Paris: Groupe Eyrolles, 2007), 223–236.

38. Bossan, *Art of the Shoe*, 76.

39. Mannoni and Malthête, eds., *Méliès, magie et cinéma*, 14.

40. Madeleine Malthête-Méliès, Anne-Marie Quévrain, and Avraham Jean-François Malthête, conversation with the author, December 2, 2015. See also A[rthur] T[aire], "Nécrologie," *Moniteur de la Cordonnerie* 49, no. 4 (February 13, 1898): 140; "Nécrologie," *Franc Parleur Parisien*, no. 403 (February 20, 1898): 102.

41. *Rapports des Délégués des Ouvriers Parisiens à l'Exposition de Londres en 1862* (Paris: Imp. Poupart-Devyl et Comp., 1862–1864), 41; *Rapport de l'Administration de la Commission Impériale sur la Section Française de l'Exposition Universelle de 1862* (Paris: Imprimerie de J. Claye, 1864), 249.

42. Charles Vincent, "Quatrième Group," *Moniteur de la Cordonnerie* 29, no. 19 (October 1, 1878): 4.

43. *Artisans de l'élégance* (Paris: Réunion des Musées Nationaux, 1993), 146.

44. "Le Progrès! Toujours le Progrès!" *Petit Journal* (December 4, 1883): 3; "Musique de Style," *La Mode de Style* 16, no. 45 (November 4, 1891): 360; E. de L., "Auguste Frétin," *Auto-Vélo*, no. 22 (October 10, 1897): 3; "La Grande Manufacture de chaussures: Cousues à la main et visées Auguste Frétin," *La Justice* (October 10, 1897).

45. *Franc Parleur Parisien*, no. 42 (February 20, 1884): 12; *Franc Parleur Parisien*, no. 49 (May 20, 1884): 12; "Un Exemple À Suivre," *Franc Parleur Parisien*, no. 56 (September 20, 1884): 2–3; "Progrès Industriel: La Fabrication des Chaussures Françaises," *Moniteur de la Cordonnerie* 38, no. 22 (November 16, 1887): 4; "Vue générale des Magasins et

Ateliers de M. Frétin," *Franc Parleur Parisien*, no. 155 (November 5, 1889): 165. Frétin's employees wore green aprons, which were associated with his brand and later with shoe sales more generally.

46. Un Vieux Brave, "Les Conseils d'Un Vieux Brave," *Franc Parleur Parisien*, no. 119 (May 5, 1887): 68–69.

47. Business conditions and recent developments in the international footwear industry were summarized in a lengthy multinational "Revue Étrangère" published in issues of *Le Franc Parleur Parisien*. Much of this information was gathered from other trade publications, the sheer number of which indicates the global reach of the industry and the importance of specialized periodicals in linking different national contexts. These specialized but highly ephemeral publications served as essential conduits of information helping to bind the international footwear industry together.

48. A. Privé, "Commerce & Bazar," *Franc Parleur Parisien*, no. 39–40 (January 5–20, 1884): 2; Arthur Taire, "La Guerre Aux Bazars," *Franc Parleur Parisien*, no. 91 (March 5, 1886): 2; Arthur Taire, "Impots et Contribuables," *Franc Parleur Parisien*, no. 96 (May 20, 1886): 2; Bénard, "Toujours Les Grands Magasins," *Franc Parleur Parisien*, no. 210 (July 1, 1890): 145. These stores included the Louvre, Bon Marché, Belle Jardinière, Printemps, Ville de Saint-Denis, Pygmalion, and Place Clichy. For a study of one Paris department store, see Michael B. Miller, *The Bon Marché: Bourgeois Culture and the Department Store, 1869–1920* (Princeton, N.J.: Princeton University Press, 1981). On the response from shopkeepers, see Philip G. Nord, *Paris Shopkeepers and the Politics of Resentment: Protest in Nineteenth-Century Paris* (Princeton, N.J.: Princeton University Press, 1986).

49. Malthête-Méliès, *Georges Méliès*, 26–31. Although the identities of most of these workers are unknown, reports from the 1860s furnish us with the names of several whose craftsmanship was outstanding enough to merit being singled out for individual praise: Grasse, Maubèche, and Sablayrolles. In 1867, Sablayrolles was awarded a bronze medal in which it was noted that he had spent fifteen years working for Méliès. *Rapports des Délégués des Ouvriers Parisiens à l'Exposition de Londres en 1862*, 41; "Liste des Récompenses," *Moniteur de la Cordonnerie* 18, no. 14 (July 25, 1867): 1.

50. *Archives Commerciales de la France* 5, no. 5 (January 17, 1878): 66.

51. Félix Guénin, "Exposition Universelle 1878," *Moniteur de la Cordonnerie* 29, no. 19 (October 1, 1878): 4.

52. Philip Scranton, *Endless Novelty: Specialty Production and American Industrialization, 1865–1925* (Princeton, N.J.: Princeton University Press, 1997), 61. Scranton's focus is the American context but French business history was characterized by comparable developments.

53. Scranton, *Endless Novelty*, 3, 8.

54. Scranton, *Endless Novelty*, 3.

55. H. Touzet, "Rapport," *Franc Parleur Parisien*, no. 51 (July 5, 1884): 4–6; E. Robichon, "Les Cordonniers," *Franc Parleur Parisien*, no. 70 (April 20, 1885): 3; Julien

Turgan, "Manufacture de Chaussures F. Pinet À Paris," *Les grandes usines de France: Études industrielles en France et à l'étranger*, vol. 13 (Paris: Calmann-Lévy, 1881), 1.

56. Malthête, "La vie et l'œuvre de Georges Méliès," 14–15, 22–23; Jacques Malthête, "Méliès: des nèfles?" *Cinémathèque Méliès*, no. 23 (1993): 43–44. *Guide-Annuaire Illustré du Cuir et de la Chaussure* (Paris: Imprimerie Veuve Édouard Vert, Charles Vincent & Murat, 1883–1884), 82; *Guide-Annuaire Illustré du Cuir, de la Chaussure, de la Sellerie et de la Bourrellerie* (Paris: Charles Vincent & Murat, 1885), 83; *Guide-Annuaire Illustré du Cuir, de la Chaussure, de la Sellerie et de la Bourrellerie* (Paris: Charles Vincent & Murat, 1887), 61. People who worked for the Société Méliès in different capacities whose names have survived for posterity are Mme. Bajavon, J. Faucheron, Octave Bigot, Jean Méliès, Pierre Cussacq, Jean-Prosper Hénault, Eugène-Louis Beuniche, Joseph-Ferdinand Jourdain, Joseph Bordier, Bernard Lannegrand, Auguste-Joseph Pescheteau, and Amand Maurice. *Exposition Universelle Internationale de 1878, À Paris, Catalogue Officiel: Liste des Récompenses* (Paris: Imprimerie Nationale, 1878), 222; *Journal Officiel de la République Française* (October 2, 1889): 4884; (July 14, 1890): 3648; (January 1, 1891): 13; (September 21, 1892): 4661–4662; (July 25, 1893): 3853, 3856–3857; (July 22, 1897): 4165.

57. Laurent Mannoni, *Georges Méliès, la magie du cinéma* (Paris: Cinémathèque Française, 2020), 87; Jacques Malthête and Laurent Mannoni, *L'Œuvre de Georges Méliès* (Paris: Éditions de la Martinière, Cinémathèque Française, 2008), 315; Mannoni and Malthête, eds., *Méliès, magie et cinéma*, 15.

58. Brian R. Jacobson, *Studios Before the System: Architecture, Technology, and the Emergence of Cinematic Space* (New York: Columbia University Press, 2015), 12. Jacobson explains that this allowed "expand[ed] stage sizes without the need for the internal support columns that might block camera angles or cast unwanted shadows."

59. Jacobson, *Studios Before the System*, 57. Jacobson does not make a distinction between the First Industrial Revolution and the Second Industrial Revolution here, but does in "Introduction: Studio Perspectives," in Brian R. Jacobson, ed., *In the Studio: Visual Creation and Its Material Environments* (Berkeley: University of California Press, 2020), 9.

60. Duchatelet, "La Halle Aux Cuirs," *Moniteur de la Cordonnerie* 1, no. 1 (May 20, 1854): 3–4; "Nouvelle Halle aux Cuirs, rue Santeuil à Paris," *Revue générale de l'architecture et des travaux publics*, vol. 25 (Paris: Ducher, 1867); M. R. Vaubourdolle and M. J. Cauvy, "La Nouvelle Gare de Paris-Montparnasse," *Revue Générale des Chemins de Fer* 14 (1965): 645–654.

61. Sean Wilentz, *Chants Democratic: New York City and the Rise of the American Working Class, 1788–1850* (New York: Oxford University Press, 1984), 126.

62. James A. Schmiechen, *Sweated Industries and Sweated Labor: The London Clothing Trades, 1860–1914* (Urbana: University of Illinois Press, 1984), 27.

63. *Guide-Annuaire Illustré du Cuir et de la Chaussure* (1883–1884), 180.

64. Arthur Taire, "Les Chaussures sans Couture," *Franc Parleur Parisien*, no. 48 (May 20, 1884): 2.

65. Mme. [Stéphanie] Méliès, quoted in "Transcripts of the Roundtable on Georges Méliès Held at the Cinémathèque Française (Paris, June 17, 1944)," in Paolo Cherchi Usai, ed., *A Trip to the Movies: Georges Méliès, Filmmaker and Magician (1861–1938)* (Rochester, N.Y.: George Eastman House, 1991), 139.

66. Many years later, another magician-filmmaker, Orson Welles, insisted to Peter Bogdanovich that this part of the filmmaking process be called "cutting," not "editing," telling him, "Never use the word editing. [. . .] The word is cutting a picture. [. . .] The word editing is pompous." Welles-Bogdanovich interview transcription, Wilson-Welles Papers, Box 2, folder 7, Special Collections Research Center, University of Michigan.

67. The French footwear industry was slow to abandon made-to-measure shoemaking and bootmaking, which supported its own organization, the Chambre Syndicale de la Cordonnerie du Détail, well into the twentieth century.

68. *Guide-Annuaire Illustré du Cuir et de la Chaussure* (1883–1884), 82; *Guide-Annuaire Illustré du Cuir, de la Chaussure, de la Sellerie et de la Bourrellerie* (1885), 83; *Guide-Annuaire Illustré du Cuir, de la Chaussure, de la Sellerie et de la Bourrellerie* (1887), 61; *Moniteur de la Cordonnerie* 39, no. 23 (December 1, 1888): 3; *Moniteur de la Cordonnerie* 39, no. 24 (December 15, 1888): 23.

69. E. Robichon, "Les Cordonniers," *Franc Parleur Parisien*, no. 70 (April 20, 1885): 3.

70. E. Robichon, "Paris Qui Travaille: Les Piqueuses des Bottines," *Franc Parleur Parisien*, no. 87 (January 5, 1886): 4.

71. Gille, *François Pinet*, 3.

72. E. Robichon, "Paris Qui Travaille: Les Piqueuses des Bottines (Suite)," *Franc Parleur Parisien*, no. 88 (January 20, 1886): 4.

73. Compare Gille, *François Pinet*, 97–99. Bottines are an especially desirable women's fashion item in Émile Zola's cycle of novels set during the Second Empire.

74. Peter McNeil and Giorgio Riello, "The Male Cinderella: Shoes, Genius and Fantasy," in McNeil and Riello, eds., *Shoes*, 397–398.

75. Marshall McLuhan, "Clothing: Our Extended Skin," *Understanding Media: The Extensions of Man* (1964; Cambridge, Mass.: MIT Press, 1994), 119–120.

76. McLuhan, "Clothing," 119.

77. In France, these straps and belts were largely the handiwork of leather tanners who were called corroiers.

78. Quoted in Raymond Borde and Etienne Chaumeton, *A Panorama of American Film Noir*, trans. Paul Hammond (1955; San Francisco: City Lights Books, 2004), 3. Sternberg's original quotation comes from *Le Figaro* (May 8, 1951): 4n5.

79. Stefania Ricci, "Made in Italy: Ferragamo and Twentieth-Century Fashion," in McNeil and Riello, eds., *Shoes*, 313.

80. [Dziga Vertov], "On the Significance of the Nonacted Cinema," *Kino-Eye: The Writings of Dziga Vertov*, ed. Annette Michelson, trans. Kevin O'Brien (Berkeley: University of California Press, 1984), 37. This text is an abridged report of a talk Vertov gave as part of a public debate on September 26, 1926, that was not published until 1966,

twelve years after Vertov's death (322). The instigating remark about "the seventeenth [episode of] *Kino-pravda*" being a "disgrace" seems to have been made in 1923 (36).

81. [Vertov], "On the Significance of the Nonacted Cinema," 36.

82. [Vertov], "On the Significance of the Nonacted Cinema," 36–37. See also Devin Fore, "Dziga Vertov, The First Shoemaker of Russian Cinema," *Configurations* 18, no. 3 (2010): 363–381.

83. J.-A. Deprat, *Manuel Complet de Cordonnerie*, 3d ed. (Paris: Moniteur de la Cordonnerie, 1905).

84. Félix Guénin, "Petites Études Professionelles Sur l'art de la coupe," *Moniteur de la Cordonnerie* 37, no. 12 (June 16, 1886): 3–4.

85. Roland Barthes, *The Fashion System*, trans. Matthew Ward and Richard Howard (1967; Berkeley: University of California Press, 1990), 3.

86. Barthes, *Fashion System*, 4.

87. Gille, *François Pinet*, 92–93. This despite the fact that *Le Franc Parleur Parisien* boasted "several thousand subscribers" in 1884. Quotation from "La Chaussure dans l'armée: Les Fournitures Militaires et les adjudications," *Franc Parleur Parisien*, no. 39–40 (January 5–20, 1884): 3. With a few exceptions, the pictures in published fashion plates are labeled by styles rather than identified with specific makers, making it difficult to find even "image clothing" of specific articles of Méliès footwear.

88. Barthes, *Fashion System*, 5.

89. Elizabeth Semmelhack, conversation with the author, June 14, 2010.

90. Paolo Cherchi Usai, "The Institute for Incoherent Cinematography: An Introduction," in Cherchi Usai, ed., *A Trip to the Movies*, 23. See also Paolo Cherchi Usai, "Un autre Méliès retrouvé: analyse de 'Le Chevalier Mystère' (1899)," *Cinémathèque Méliès* no. 15 (1989): 15–20.

91. Wendy Haslem, *From Méliès to New Media: Spectral Projections* (Chicago: Intellect, 2019), 22.

92. Haslem, *From Méliès to New Media*, 12–13, 22.

93. Gilles Duval and Séverine Wemaere, *La couleur retrouvée du* Voyage dans la Lune *de Georges Méliès* (Paris: Éditions Capricci, 2011); Roland Cosandey and Jacques Malthête, *"Le Voyage dans la Lune* (Lobster Films / Georges Méliès, 2011; "Ce que restaurer veut dire," *Journal of Film Preservation*, no. 87 (2012): 7–10; François Albera, Laurent Le Forestier, and Benoît Turquety, "De la Terre à la Lune," *1895*, no. 69 (2013): 95–135; Cosandey, "Chronique d'un débat: A propos de la remise en circulation du *Voyage dans la Lune*," *Miscellanées Méliès*, no. 1 (2015), https://www.cinematheque.ch/fileadmin/user_upload/Expo/melies/2_Chronique_debat.pdf; Martin Bonnard, "Méliès's *Voyage* Restoration: Or, the Risk of Being Stuck in the Digital Reconstruction," *Moving Image* 16, no. 1 (2016): 139–147; Haslem, *From Méliès to New Media*, 37–56; Paolo Cherchi Usai, *Silent Cinema: A Guide to Study, Research and Curatorship* (London: British Film Institute, 2019), 273–274.

94. Cherchi Usai, *Silent Cinema: A Guide*, 268.

Chapter 2

1. Bertrand Gille, *The History of Techniques*, vol. 1, trans. P. Southgate and T. Williamson (New York: Gordon and Breach Science Publishers, 1986), 589.

2. Gille, *History of Techniques*, 1:591.

3. Gille, *History of Techniques*, 1:viii, 17.

4. François Caron, *Les deux revolutions industrielles du XXe siècle* (Paris: Éditions Albin Michel, 2007), 18.

5. Caron, *Les deux révolutions industrielles*, 18.

6. Caron, *Les deux révolutions industrielles*, 22–23.

7. Roger Price, *An Economic History of Modern France, 1730–1914*, rev. ed. (1975; London: Macmillan, 1981), vii, 225.

8. Price, *An Economic History of Modern France*, 226.

9. François Caron, *An Economic History of Modern France*, trans. Barbara Bray (1979; London: Routledge, 2014), 129–130.

10. A. Privé, Le Commerce de la France, *Franc Parleur Parisien*, no. 43 (March 5, 1884): 1–2; *Le Franc Parleur*, "La Crise Industrielle," *Franc Parleur Parisien*, no. 59 (November 5, 1884): 1–2; Arthur Taire, "Le Cours de Cuirs," *Franc Parleur Parisien*, no. 119 (May 5, 1887): 65.

11. Caron, *An Economic History of Modern France*, 87.

12. E. Robichon, "Paris Qui Travaille: Les Cordonniers et la Grève de 1882," *Franc Parleur Parisien*, no. 73 (June 5, 1885): 2–3; *Les Associations Professionnelles Ouvrières*, vol. 2 (Paris: Imprimerie Nationale, 1901), 30–31.

13. Gausser, "Revuse de la Tannerie," *Franc Parleur Parisien*, no. 39–40 (January 5–20, 1884): 2–3; Un Vieux Brave, "Conseils d'Un Vieux Brave," *Franc Parleur Parisien*, no. 65 (February 5, 1885): 5–6.

14. "La Crise Industrielle," *Franc Parleur Parisien*, no. 59 (November 5, 1884): 1–2. See also Privé, "Le Commerce de la France," 1–2..

15. "La Baisse des Cuirs," *Franc Parleur Parisien*, no. 98 (June 20, 1886): 2.

16. Gausser, "Revue de la Tannerie," 2–3.

17. Gausser, "La Fraude des Cuirs," *Franc Parleur Parisien*, no. 42 (January 20, 1884): 4–5. Just as fake leather approximated the appearance of authentic properly tanned leather, some shoes made with sewing machines were misleadingly marketed as "sewn by hand." Mangeot, "De la Chaussure Cousue-Machine Vendue à la confection pour de la chaussure cousue à la main," *Moniteur de la Cordonnerie* 37, no. 14 (July 14, 1886): 3. Compare E. Robichon, "Les Cordonniers," *Franc Parleur Parisien*, no. 70 (April 20, 1885): 3–4.

18. Paul Hammond, *Marvellous Méliès* (London: Gordon Fraser, 1974), 49. Hammond specifies, "on August 12 1895, the contract was cancelled by the Ministry of War." The August 7, 1895, liquidation of Gaston Méliès et Cie was reported in *Archives Commerciales de la France* 22, no. 104 (December 28, 1895): 214. See also Laurent Mannoni, *Georges Méliès, la magie du cinéma* (Paris: Cinémathèque Française, 2020), 90–92.

19. Nadège Sougy, "De la houille au gaz: Pour une approche par l'amont des usines gazières en France au XIXe siècle," in Serge Paquier and Jean-Pierre Williot, eds., *L'industrie du gaz en Europe aux XIXe et XXe siècles: L'innovation entre marchés privés et collectivités publiques* (Brussels: Peter Lang, 2005), 85–96.

20. Henri Besnard, *L'Industrie du gaz à Paris depuis ses origines* (Paris: Éditions Domat-Montchrestien, 1942); Jean-Pierre Williot, "De la naissance des compagnies à la constitution des groupes gaziers en France (années 1820–1930)," in Paquier and Williot, eds., *L'industrie du gaz en Europe*, 147–180; "Paris Gas Company," *Journal of Gas Lighting, Water Supply, & Sanitary Improvement* (April 26, 1881): 698–701.

21. Wolfgang Schivelbusch, *Disenchanted Night: The Industrialization of Light in the Nineteenth Century*, trans. Angela Davies (Berkeley: University of California Press, 1995), 112.

22. Schivelbusch, *Disenchanted Night*, 152.

23. Caron, *Les deux revolutions industrielles*, 19.

24. Schivelbusch, *Disenchanted Night*, 51. The costliness of gaslight illumination was reportedly something that Henri Méliès commented upon when he and several other members of the Méliès family saw the Trocadero lit up at night at the 1900 Exposition Universelle in Paris. Madeleine Malthête-Méliès, *Georges Méliès, L'Enchanteur* (Grandvilliers, France: La Tour Verte, 2011), 255.

25. Schivelbusch, *Disenchanted Night*, 39–40. Estimates suggested "that in 1880 the loss by leakage considerably exceeded that in the previous year," an amount that almost entirely offset a reported 10 percent increase in gas consumption over the previous year. "Paris Gas Company," 699.

26. "Chronique judiciaire," *Le Radical* (July 23, 1882): 3; "Faits Divers," *Le Radical* (July 24, 1882): 3; "Faits Divers," *Le Radical* (July 27, 1882): 3.

27. "Serious Gas Explosion in Paris," *Journal of Gas Lighting, Water Supply, & Sanitary Improvement* (July 18, 1882): 138–139.

28. "Catastrophe de la rue François Miron," *Le Radical* (July 14, 1882): 2–3; "Faits Divers," *Le Radical* (July 19, 1882): 3; "Faits Divers," *Le Radical* (July 20, 1882): 3.

29. "Faits Divers," *Le Radical* (July 28, 1882): 3.

30. "Catastrophe de la rue François Miron," *Le Radical* (July 14, 1882): 2.

31. "Catastrophe de la rue François Miron," *Le Radical* (July 14, 1882): 2–3.

32. "France: A Gas Explosion in a Theatre," *Chicago Tribune* (March 12, 1882): 6.

33. "Catastrophe de la rue François Miron (Suite)," *Le Radical* (July 15, 1882): 3; "Faits Divers," *Le Radical* (July 18, 1882): 3; "Conseil Municipal: Séance du 19 juillet," *Le Radical* (July 21, 1882): 3; "La catastrophe de la rue François Miron," *Le Radical* (August 7, 1882): 3.

34. *Dictionnaire de la langue française* (Paris: Librairie Hachette et Cie, 1881), 582.

35. *Dictionnaire de la langue française*, 582.

36. P. Boissière, *Dictionnaire Analogique de la Langue Française: Repertoire Complet des Mots par les Idées et des Idées par les Mots*, 6th ed. (Paris: Librairie Larousse, 1890), 421.

37. "Incohérence" with a capital-I merited its own entry in the second supplement of Pierre Larousse's *Grande dictionnaire du XIXe siècle*. Catherine Charpin, *Les Arts Incohérents (1882–1893)* (Paris: Éditions Syros Alternatives, 1990), 44.

38. Paul Fresnay, "La Kermesse des Champs-Élysées," *Voltaire* (August 5, 1882).

39. Fresnay also listed "Mmes Godin, Legault, Léo, Isabelle, Elisa Lebrun, Céline Bertaud, etc." "La Kermesse des Champs-Élysées."

40. Jules Lévy, "L'Incohérence—son origine—son histoire—son avenir," *Le Courrier français* (March 12, 1885): 3.

41. *Catalogue de l'Exposition des Arts Incohérents au Profit des Grandes Sociétés d'Instructions Gratuite* (Paris: E. Bernard et Cie, 1884), 16. The brief description may allude to the rue François-Miron catastrophe, which had happened just two days before the reopening of the nearby Hôtel-de-Ville—the first public location in Paris illuminated by gas.

42. Charpin, *Les Arts Incohérents*, 34.

43. John Harvey, *Men in Black* (Chicago: University of Chicago Press, 1995), 14.

44. Charpin, *Les Arts Incohérents*, 37.

45. Mary Gluck, *Popular Bohemia: Modernism and Urban Culture in Nineteenth-Century Paris* (Cambridge, Mass.: Harvard University Press, 2005).

46. Malthête-Méliès, *Georges Méliès*, 268–269, 302, 341, 397, 443. See also Jacques Malthête and Laurent Mannoni, *L'Œuvre de Georges Méliès* (Paris: Éditions de la Martinière, Cinémathèque Française, 2008), 325.

47. Wolfgang Schivelbusch, *The Railway Journey: The Industrialization of Time and Space in the Nineteenth Century*, trans. Anselm Hollo (1977; Berkeley: University of California Press, 2014), 131.

48. G. Méliès, quoted in "Les Accidents de Chemins de Fer: L'État des Voies sur la Ligne du Nord," *Le Rappel* (September 13, 1895). Thank you to Stéphane Tralongo for sharing this item with me.

49. Georges Méliès, "Kinematographic Views" (1907), trans. Stuart Liebman and Timothy Barnard, in André Gaudreault, *Film and Attraction: From Kinematography to Cinema*, trans. Timothy Barnard (Urbana: University of Illinois Press, 2011), 147–148.

50. Jacques Malthête, May 1, 1981, letter, quoted in André Gaudreault, "Theatricality, Narrativity, and Trickality: Reevaluating the Cinema of Georges Méliès," trans. Paul Attalah, with Tom Gunning and Vivian Sobchack, in Matthew Solomon, ed., *Fantastic Voyages of the Cinematic Imagination: Georges Méliès's Trip to the Moon* (Albany, N.Y.: SUNY Press, 2011), 42.

51. "Adresses Spéciales," *L'Innovateur* 5, no. 10 (February 15, 1855): 79.

52. Charles Vincent and Lermite, *L'Enfant du Tour de France* (Paris: Imprimerie Walder, 1857); Charles Vincent, "Un Chanteur de Bohème," *Chants et Chansons de la Bohème* (Paris: Imprimerie Gardès, 1853), 66–68.

53. Jacques Chauvin, *Le Sabaron et l'Escarpin: Chaussures et métiers Poitou-Vendée, 1880–1960* (Mougon, France: Geste Éditions, 1992), 15–17.

54. Charles Vincent, "Quatrième Group," *Moniteur de la Cordonnerie* 29, no. 19 (October 1, 1878): 4; "Petites Nouvelles," *Franc Parleur Parisien*, no. 64 (January 20, 1885): 7;

Moniteur de la Cordonnerie 39, no. 23 (December 1, 1888): 3; *Moniteur de la Cordonnerie* 39, no. 24 (December 15, 1888): 23.

55. Charles Vincent, *Histoire de la Chaussure, de la Cordonnerie et des Cordonniers Célébres Depuis l'Antiquité jusqu'à nos jours* (Paris: Librairie J. Lecuir & Cie, 1880).

56. Malthête-Méliès, *Georges Méliès*, 56–57.

57. Arthur Taire, "Le Père Vivier," *Franc Parleur Parisien*, no. 68 (March 20, 1885): 6.

58. Gustave Colline, "Les Cordonniers Poètes," *Franc Parleur Parisien*, no. 59 (November 5, 1884): 5–6; no. 60 (November 20, 1884): 6. See also, for example, "Renseignements sur l'Amérique" and Juan Hierro, "Les Poémes de L'Échoppe," *Franc Parleur Parisien*, no. 41 (February 5, 1884): 6; "Un Nouveau Tissu" and Gustave Cornu, "Variété: Ma Dernière Maîtresse," *Franc Parleur Parisien*, no. 69 (April 5, 1885): 6.

59. Gluck, *Popular Bohemia*, 7.

60. Gluck, *Popular Bohemia*, 21, 23.

61. Gluck, *Popular Bohemia*, 2.

62. Gluck, *Popular Bohemia*, 1.

63. Gluck, *Popular Bohemia*, 2.

64. Gluck, *Popular Bohemia*, 10.

65. Gluck, *Popular Bohemia*, 15.

66. Gluck, *Popular Bohemia*, 16.

67. Gluck, *Popular Bohemia*, 18.

68. *La Revue Illustré*, March 15, 1887, translated in Phillip Dennis Cate, "The Spirit of Montmartre," in Phillip Dennis Cate and Mary Shaw, eds., *The Spirit of Montmartre: Cabaret, Humor, and the Avant-Garde, 1875–1905* (New Brunswick, N.J.: Jane Voorhees Zimmerli Art Museum, 1996), 40.

69. L'Administration, "À nos lecteurs," *Franc Parleur Parisien*, no. 39–40 (January 5–20, 1884): 2.

70. "La Redaction du Franc Parleur Allant Inaugurer Le Salon de la Cordonnerie À L'Exposition de 1889," *Franc Parleur Parisien*, no. 165 (April 1, 1889): 53.

71. Charpin, *Les Arts Incohérents*, 27.

72. A. Privé, "Tout À L'Incohérence," *Franc Parleur Parisien*, no. 76 (July 20, 1885): 5. The opening words of the article, "Entre Bicêtre et Charenton," appear to be an allusion to journalist and dramatist Ernest Blum's 1866 book *Entre Bicêtre et Charenton: Les aventures d'un notaire, la légende du monsieur qui avait le frisson, petites contes fantastique avec ou sans moralité* (Paris: Librairie Internationale, 1866), which was a compilation of Blum's writings for the caricature journal *Le Charivari*, of which Blum was longtime editor, and in which he had a regular column that was headed by that title, "Entre Bicêtre et Charenton." Adolphe Bitard, *Dictionnaire de Biographie Contemporaine Française et Étrangère* (Paris: A. Lévy et Cie, Éditeurs, 1887), 76–77; A. De Gubernatis, *Dictionnaire Internation des Écrivains du Jour* (Florence: Louis Nicolai, Éditeur-Imprimeur, 1891), 334. The phrase has a number of valences which start with Paris place names that begin with consecutive letters of the alphabet, although both of these place names were also closely linked to the sites of Paris's major insane asylums (the third Paris insane asylum was located in Salpêtrière, where Charcot practiced at this time). Blum was part of a loose affiliation of writers and

artists who were closely connected with the theater. The place names "Charenton-Bicetre" [*sic*] also appeared on the public conveyance depicted in *L'Omnibus des toqués ou Blancs et Noirs*. Malthête and Mannoni, *L'Œuvre de Georges Méliès*, 120.

73. J. Colline, "La Chaussure Anglais Devant La Faculté," *Franc Parleur Parisien*, no. 44 (March 20, 1884): 3–4; X. Y. Z., "Le Courrier de la Mode: Chaussures pour Hommes," *Franc Parleur Parisien*, no. 57 (October 5, 1884): 3; Georges Colline, "Dans L'Histoire: À Propos des Bouts Pointus," *Franc Parleur Parisien*, no. 64 (January 20, 1885): 2–3; Un Vieux Brave, "Les Conseils d'Un Vieux Brave," *Franc Parleur Parisien*, no. 68 (March 20, 1885): 6–7; Le Franc Parleur, "Le Bout des Chaussures," *Franc Parleur Parisien*, no. 94 (April 20, 1886): 4. French commentators were particularly critical of the English fashion for pointed toes and flat heels.

74. Quoted in "La Boite Aux Lettres," *Franc Parleur Parisien*, no. 87 (January 5, 1886): 3.

75. "La Boite Aux Lettres," 3.

76. Arth. Eriat, "Le Salon de 1884 Vu Par Les Pieds!" *Franc Parleur Parisien*, no. 48 (May 20, 1884): 5–6; no. 50 (June 20, 1884): 6–7; A. Eriat, "Le Salon de 1885 (Vu Par Les Pieds!)," *Franc Parleur Parisien*, no. 71 (May 5, 1885) 3; no. 72 (May 20, 1885): 4; no. 74 (June 20, 1885): 3; Arth. Eriat, "Le Salon Vu Par Les Pieds," *Franc Parleur Parisien*, no. 96 (May 20, 1886): 5–6; no. 97 (June 5, 1886): 5; "Le Salon de 1887 Vu Par Les Pieds," *Franc Parleur Parisien*, no. 120 (May 20, 1887): 75–76; no. 121 (June 5, 1887): 85–86.

77. A. Eriat, "Le Salon de 1885 (Vu Par Les Pieds!)," *Franc Parleur Parisien*, no. 71 (May 5, 1885) 3; A. Eriat, "Le Salon Vu Par Les Pieds," *Franc Parleur Parisien*, no. 95 (May 5, 1886): 6.

78. *Manufacture de Chaussures Pour Hommes et Pour Dames: Prix Courant des Chaussures d'Hommes* (Paris: Méliès, n.d.), unpaginated illustration.

79. Malthête-Méliès, *Georges Méliès*, 57–67.

80. David Robinson, *Georges Méliès, Father of Film Fantasy* (London: Museum of the Moving Image, 1993), 5, 56n1.

81. Georges Méliès, *La vie et l'œuvre d'un pionnier du cinéma*, ed. Jean-Pierre Sirois-Trahan (Paris: Éditions du Sonneur, 2012), 31.

82. "Les Exposition de Londres," *Moniteur de la Cordonnerie* 35, no. 14 (July 16, 1884): 3.

83. Eliacan Piquand, "Rule Brittania," *Franc Parleur Parisien*, no. 42 (February 20, 1886): 1–2.

Chapter 3

1. X. Y. Z., "Notre Planche de Mode," *Franc Parleur Parisien*, no. 44 (March 20, 1884): 8.

2. Fashion plates and patterns began appearing fairly early in the publication history of French footwear trade industry journals. See, for example, *Moniteur de la Cordonnerie* 7, no. 3 (July 15, 1856).

3. *Complete Catalogue of Genuine and Original "Star Films" (Moving Pictures)* (New York: Geo. Méliès, 1903), 5.

4. Antonia Lant, "Haptical Cinema," *October*, no. 74 (1995): 45–47.

5. Lisa Gitelman, *Paper Knowledge: Toward a Media History of Documents* (Durham, N.C.: Duke University Press, 2014), 32.

6. Gitelman, *Paper Knowledge*, 32. Surviving examples of Méliès' letterhead from the last decade of the nineteenth century and the first decade of the nineteenth century, respectively are printed with the dates "189_" and "190_." Laurent Mannoni and Jacques Malthête, eds., *Méliès, magie et cinéma* (Paris: Paris-Musées, 2002), 272.

7. Some surviving correspondence was written by Lucien Tainguy, secretary of the Théâtre Robert-Houdin, camera operator, sometime actor, and worker in the Passage de l'Opéra film developing laboratory. Mannoni and Malthête, eds., *Méliès, magie et cinéma*, 27, 31, 272.

8. Mannoni and Malthête, eds., *Méliès, magie et cinéma*, 230–231. This extended length piece of paper appears to have been a preparatory sketch for the moving backdrop used to show a motor car travel across the rugged mountains of the Alps. *Complete Catalogue of Genuine and Original "Star" Films* (New York: Geo. Méliès, 1908), 84–85.

9. Georges Méliès, "Kinematographic Views" (1907), trans. Stuart Liebman and Timothy Barnard, in André Gaudreault, *Film and Attraction: From Kinematography to Cinema*, trans. Timothy Barnard (Urbana: University of Illinois Press, 2011), 141.

10. Georges Méliès, "The Importance of the Script" (1932), trans. Paul Hammond, in Matthew Solomon, ed., *Fantastic Voyages of the Cinematic Imagination: Georges Méliès's Trip to the Moon* (Albany, N.Y.: SUNY Press, 2011), 243. See also Tom Gunning, "The Cinema of Attraction[s]: Early Film, Its Spectator and the Avant-Garde," in Wanda Strauven, ed., *The Cinema of Attractions Reloaded* (Amsterdam: Amsterdam University Press, 2006), 382; and Tom Gunning, "Lunar Illuminations," in Jeffrey Geiger and R. L. Rutsky, eds., *Film Analysis: A Norton Reader* (New York: Norton, 2006), 74–76.

11. Méliès, "The Importance of the Script," 243.

12. Two surviving sheets of paper that correspond to the films *Chez la sorcière* and *Le Rêve du paria (sujet artistique)* [lost] each contain, a drawing accompanied by a paragraph-long description, although it is unclear when in the production process these were composed. See, respectively, Jacques Malthête and Laurent Mannoni, *L'Œuvre de Georges Méliès* (Paris: Éditions de la Martinière, Cinémathèque Française, 2008), 119; and Jacques Malthête, *Méliès, images et illusions* (Paris: Exporégie, 1996), 101.

13. Jacques Malthête, ed., "Correspondance de Georges Méliès (1904–1937)," in André Gaudreault and Laurent Le Forestier, with Stéphane Tralongo, eds., *Méliès, carrefour des attractions, suivi de correspondance de Georges Méliès (1904–1937)* (Rennes: Presses Universitaires de Rennes, 2014), 446–447fn373.

14. Madeleine Malthête-Méliès, *Georges Méliès, L'Enchanteur* (Grandvilliers, France: La Tour Verte, 2011), 501. Jacques Malthête, "Les deux studios de Georges Méliès," in Mannoni and Malthête, eds., *Méliès, magie et cinéma*, 135–159, esp. 138–139, 142. Compare Mannoni and Malthête, eds., *Méliès, magie et cinéma*, 160–169.

15. Georges Sadoul, *Georges Méliès* (Paris: Éditions Seghers, 1961), 22, 32; black-and-white reproduction of "Adam et Eve" (*La Griffe*, August 29, 1889). Two other caricatures from *La Griffe*, "Trop de Pression!!!" (August 8, 1889) and "Boulangisme! Moi Je m'assieds dessus!!!" (October 3, 1889) were reproduced in black and white as unpaginated illustrations for the first edition of Madeleine Malthête-Méliès, *Méliès, L'Enchanteur* (Paris: Éditions Ramsay, 1973). The following year, Paul Hammond included a black-and-white reproduction of "Trop de Pression!!!," in *Marvellous Méliès* (London: Gordon Fraser, 1974), 27. See also Malthête-Méliès, *Georges Méliès*, 127.

16. Sadoul, *Georges Méliès*, 22. Of the eleven episodes of *Affaire Dreyfus*, copies of all but *La Dégradation* [lost] and *Dreyfus allant du lycée de Rennes à la prison* [lost] have survived. See Malthête and Mannoni, *L'Œuvre de Georges Méliès*, 22, 26, 98–100, 340.

17. See my introduction to Solomon, ed., *Fantastic Voyages of the Cinematic Imagination*, 8–12. Compare "La Raison du Plus Fort . . ." (*La Griffe*, January 23, 1890). The pollution is emphasized in a number of drawings Méliès made in connection with the film. See Malthête and Mannoni, *L'Œuvre de Georges Méliès*, 125–133, esp. 126–127; and Mannoni and Malthête, eds., *Méliès, magie et cinéma*, 193–209, esp. 197.

18. Donald Crafton, *Emile Cohl, Caricature, and Film* (Princeton, N.J.: Princeton University Press, 1990), 66. Later, Crafton briefly discusses "relevant examples of the adaptation of Cohl's social commentary (*satire de moeurs*) to the cinema" (283).

19. "The 'Cakewalk,' a new social dance that soon became the rage of white society," Phil Jamison explains, was "the first of many African American vernacular dances to be adopted by white dancers in the early twentieth century." Jamison, *Hoedowns, Reels, and Frolics* (Urbana: University of Illinois Press, 2016), 127. Indicators of the popularity of the Cakewalk in Paris in 1903 include Rodolphe Berger, "Joyeux Nègres: Cake Walk" [sheet music] (Paris: Enoch & Cie, Editeurs, 1903), and "Le Cake-Walk dans un Salon Parisian" [engraving], *L'Illustration* (January 10, 1903). On the widespread international popularity of roller skating around this time and its relationship to early film exhibition, see Jon Burrows, *The British Cinema Boom, 1909–1914: A Commercial History* (London: Palgrave, 2017), 31–39.

20. Sadoul, *Georges Méliès*, 23.

21. Hammond, *Marvellous Méliès*, 30; Paolo Cherchi Usai, "A Trip to the Movies: Georges Méliès, Filmmaker and Magician (1861–1938)," in Solomon, ed., *Fantastic Voyages of the Cinematic Imagination*, 26.

22. Georges Méliès, *La vie et l'œuvre d'un pionnier du cinéma*, ed. Jean-Pierre Sirois-Trahan (Paris: Éditions du Sonneur, 2012), 29. On Méliès' childhood love of drawing, see also Malthête-Méliès, *Georges Méliès*, 37–39.

23. Sadoul, *Georges Méliès*, 21–22.

24. During his lifetime, Méliès published a series of caricatures of fellow magicians, subgenres of magic performance, and specific illusions in *Passez Muscade* 14, no. 54 (1929): 598, 601; *Passez Muscade* 14, no. 55 (1929): 608; *Passez Muscade*, numéro spécial (1929): 8–9, 13; *Passez Muscade* 15, no. 2 (1931): 11, 13; *Passez Muscade* 15, no. 4 (1931): 32;

Passez Muscade 15, no. 5 (1931): 38. See also Malthête, *Méliès, images et illusions*, 44–45; and Malthête and Mannoni, *L'Œuvre de Georges Méliès*, 59–60. Méliès' magic caricatures were published posthumously as illustrations for Professeur Rex, *Hypnotiseurs et mystificateurs* (Geneva: Sauty, 1944).

25. Malthête and Mannoni, *L'Œuvre de Georges Méliès*, 336–337. See also *Complete Catalogue of Genuine and Original "Star" Films* (1903), 10; *Complete Catalogue of Genuine and Original "Star" Films* (New York: Geo. Méliès, 1905), 6. Among the Méliès holdings at the Cinémathèque Française are nineteen unsigned pastel drawings of political and artistic figures (Thiers, Queen Victoria, and Bismarck among them), some in the portrait-charge format, all of which are dated around 1890, but their connection with the films that include drawings of these same individuals is unclear. Malthête and Mannoni, *L'Œuvre de Georges Méliès*, 50–52; Malthête, *Méliès, images et illusions*, 27–28.

26. Donald Crafton, *Emile Cohl, Caricature, and Film* (Princeton, N.J.: Princeton University Press, 1990); Donald Crafton, *Before Mickey: The Animated Film, 1898–1928* (1982; Chicago: University of Chicago Press, 1993); Charles Musser, *The Emergence of Cinema: The American Screen to 1907* (1990; Berkeley: University of California Press, 1994).

27. See also Paolo Cherchi Usai, "Une autre Méliès retrouvé, une analyse de *Le Chevalier mystère* (1899)," *Cinémathèque Méliès*, no. 15 (1989): 15; and Matthew Solomon, "A Trip to the Fair; or, Moon-Walking in Space," in Solomon, ed., *Fantastic Voyages of the Cinematic Imagination*, 154.

28. Matthew Solomon, "Georges Méliès: Anti-Boulangist Caricature and the Incohérent Movement," *Framework* 53, no. 2 (2012): 305–327. Matthew Solomon, "Méliès, l'Incohérent," trans. Stéphane Tralongo, in Gaudreault and Le Forestier, with Tralongo, eds., *Méliès, carrefour des attractions*, 203–216.

29. Joel E. Vessels, *Drawing France: French Comics and the Republic* (Oxford: University Press of Mississippi, 2010), 31, translating François-Emile Villiers, *Journal Officiel de la République Française* (June 8, 1880): 6212–6213.

30. Erwin Panofsky, "Iconography and Iconology: An Introduction to the Study of Renaissance Art" (1939), in *Meaning in the Visual Arts* (Chicago: University of Chicago Press, 1955), 31, 35–36. Panofsky's best-known essay on film is "Style and Medium in the Motion Pictures" (1936), in Angela Dalle Vacche, ed., *The Visual Turn: Classical Film Theory and Art History* (New Brunswick, N.J.: Rutgers University Press, 2003), 69–84.

31. Reproduced in Solomon, "Georges Méliès," 319; Solomon, "Méliès, l'Incohérent," 214.

32. Reproduced in Matthew Solomon, *Disappearing Tricks: Silent Film, Houdini, and the New Magic of the Twentieth Century* (Urbana: University of Illinois Press, 2010), 41.

33. Lucy Fischer, "The Lady Vanishes: Women, Magic and the Movies," *Film Quarterly* 33, no. 1 (1979): 30–40; Karen Beckman, *Vanishing Women: Magic, Film, and Feminism* (Durham, N.C.: Duke University Press, 2003); Stephen Waldow, "Women

Objectified, Manipulated, and Exploited: The Central Attractions in Méliès's 'Cinema of Attractions,'" *Film Matters* 1, no. 3 (2010): 20–25.

34. Trewey appeared in several of the Lumières' first films, including *Partie d'écarte*, which Méliès remade as his very first film, *Une partie de cartes*, discussed in chapter 4. Trewey performed chapeaugraphy in the Lumière film *Chapeaux à transformation* and other forms of manual dexterity in the Lumière films *Assiettes tournantes, Écriture à l'envers*, and *Serpent*. See my "'Twenty-Five Heads under One Hat': Quick-Change in the 1890s," in Vivian Sobchack, ed., *Meta-Morphing: Visual Transformation and the Culture of Quick-Change* (Minneapolis: University of Minnesota Press, 2000), 9–11.

35. Michèle Hannoosh, *Baudelaire and Caricature: From the Comic to an Art of Modernity* (University Park: Pennsylvania State University Press, 1992), 6.

36. Hannoosh, *Baudelaire and Caricature*, 13.

37. Michèle Hannoosh, "Caricature," in Michael Kelly, ed., *Encyclopedia of Aesthetics*, vol. 1 (Oxford: Oxford University Press, 1998), 344.

38. Some years later, the magic dealer Maison Caroly sold a trick involving carrots that expanded to a "huge size" when pulled out of a hat. "Nouveautés de la Maison Caroly," *L'Illusionniste*, no. 12 (December 1902): 8.

39. The respective figures represent Germany, Austria-Hungary, Italy, France, and Russia, with Germany personified by Chancellor Bismarck, Austria-Hungary by Emperor Franz Joseph, and Italy by Prime Minister Crispi. This was a common way of representing the Triple Alliance. See John Grand-Carteret, *Crispi, Bismarck et La Triple-Alliance en Caricatures* (Paris: Ch. Delagrave, 1891). Compare John Grand-Carteret, *L'Actualité en Images: Les Caricatures sur L'Alliance Franco-Russe* (Paris: Ancienne Maison Quantin, n.d.).

40. Although most of these large flat props are generic representations of the respective food and drink items, the last of these items is a large magnum of champagne emblazoned with a Mercier label, which functions both as a prop and as signage advertising the signature French beverage—an example of "product placement" *avant la lettre*. Méliès used similar conspicuously branded signage in the fifteen or so advertising films he produced around 1900 for projection outside of the Théâtre Robert-Houdin. All were untitled and uncatalogued and are considered lost. Surviving photographs indicate that some of the commodities were depicted with oversized flat facsimiles of the products on which the respective brand names are clearly legible or signs. Products promoted include Bornibus mustard, Dewar's whiskey, Orbec Bock beer, Picon apertif, Veuve C. Brunot shoe polish, Robert baby bottles, Vicat insecticide, Mystère corsets, Falières phosphatine, Nestlé chocolate, Xour lotion, Moritz beer, Pilocarpine hair-growth cream, Delion hats, Menier chocolate, Poulain chocolate, and Eclipse wax. Malthête, *Méliès, images et illusions*, 129–134, 243.

41. The caption beneath the image reads, "Only the pharmacists find this amusing," and indeed the only person smiling is the figure beneath the pharmacy sign standing inside of the doorway. By placing a pharmacy in the foreground, Méliès' caricature takes satirical aim at "a host of quack therapists who suggested a range of remedies." George

Dehner, *Influenza: A Century of Science and Public Health Response* (Pittsburgh: University of Pittsburgh Press, 2012), 39–40. A sign below the pharmacy window warns sufferers not to take Béranger lozenges, seemingly a reference to products like Géraudel lozenges, which were widely advertised at the time as a cough suppressant, but ultimately proved ineffective in treating the virus. A few weeks later, Pépin [pseud., Edouard/Claude Guillaumin] similarly satirized the medical and pharmaceutical response to the pandemic in "Tout le Monde L'A ⁽ᵗᵉʳ⁾ L'Influenza! La Ronde des Médecins et des Potards," *Le Grelot* (January 12, 1890), which shows a group of people, several of whom are labeled with the name of a medicinal treatment (antipyrine, quinine, "fleurs pectorales," an herbal remedy) dancing in a circle around a doctor holding a prescription and a suffering patient in front of whom several skeletons playing musical instruments. *La Griffe* tried to raise money for victims of the pandemic and exhorted other publications to do the same. Victorine, "L'Influenza," *La Griffe* (January 16, 1890). Emile Duval composed a song, "L'Influenza," published in *La Griffe* (December 26, 1889).

42. Mannoni and Malthête, eds., *Méliès, magie et cinéma*, 234–235, 237–239; Malthête and Mannoni, *L'Œuvre de Georges Méliès*, 284–286; Jacques Malthête, "Le Géant des Neiges était-il vraiment colossal?" *Cinémathèque Méliès*, no. 28 (1996): 17–22.

43. In *Influenza*, Dehner writes, "A conservative estimate for Europe [. . .] sets the deaths at no fewer than 250,000, far higher than the number of those who died in previous nineteenth-century pandemics, including cholera outbreaks. The first pandemic wave in the fall of 1889 was followed by two more waves lasting into 1892. [. . .] This high mortality rate resulted not from any special lethality of this strain of flu [. . .] but from its high morbidity" (41). See also Mari Loreena Nicholson-Preuss, "Managing Morbidity and Mortality: Pandemic Influenza in France, 1889–1890" (M.A. thesis, Texas Tech University, 2001).

44. Dehner, *Influenza*, 39–40.

45. John Grand-Carteret, *Les Caricatures sur L'Alliance Franco-Russe* (Paris: Ancienne Maison Quantin Librairies-Imprimeries Réunis, 1893), 2.

46. Méliès' caricature "Plus le Sou!!!" (*La Griffe*, October 17, 1889) depicted a railroad employee beside the payroll window. The railroad employee is pointing the barrel of a revolver up his nose. Barbenzingue stands nearby, shrugging his shoulder and showing his empty pockets.

47. Sergei M. Eisenstein, "On Disney," trans. Alan Upchurch, *The Eisenstein Collection*, ed. Jay Leyda (London: Seagull Books, 2006), 85–175. See also my "Sergei Eisenstein: Attractions/Montage/Animation," in R. Barton Palmer and Murray Pomerance, eds., *Thinking in the Dark: Cinema, Theory, Practice* (New Brunswick, N.J.: Rutgers University Press, 2015), 82–85, and my application of this concept to some of the films made by Méliès' contemporary Segundo de Chomón in "Visible and Invisible Hands: Chomón's Claymation and Object Animations," in Réjane Vallée, Jacques Malthête, and Stéphanie Salmon, eds., *Les Mille et Un Visages de Segundo de Chomón: Truqueur, Coloriste, Cinématographiste . . . et Pionnier du Cinématographe* (Villeneuve d'Ascq, France: Presses Universitaires du Septentrion; Paris: Fondation Jérôme Seydoux-Pathé, 2019), 102–106.

48. This figure represents Alfred Naquet and conforms to the contemporaneous characterization of Naquet as being "as crafty as a hunchback." Translated in William D. Irvine, *The Boulanger Affair Reconsidered: Royalism, Boulangism, and the Origins of the Radical Right in France* (New York: Oxford University Press, 1989), 168. See also Solomon, "Georges Méliès," 312, 316–317, 320; Solomon, "Méliès, l'Incohérent," 210–211.

49. Eisenstein, "On Disney," 87–88.

50. Malthête and Mannoni, *L'Œuvre de Georges Méliès*, 292, 294.

51. For a reading of this caricature, see Solomon, "Georges Méliès," 312–313; Solomon, "Méliès, l'Incohérent," 210.

52. Paulin Desormeaux, *Nouveau Manuel Complet du Fabricant d'Objets en Caoutchouc, en Gutta-Percha et en Gomme Factice, suivi de documents étendu sur la fabrication des tissus imperméables, des toiles cirées et des cuirs vernis* (Paris: Librairie Encyclopédique de Roret, 1855), esp. 251–256.

53. "Chaussures américaines en caoutchouc," *Moniteur de la Cordonnerie* 1, no. 1 (May 20, 1854): 4.

54. Méliès was a bicyclist, as was Stéphanie Méliès. Malthête-Méliès, *Georges Méliès*, 196. See also Malthête and Mannoni, *L'Œuvre de Georges Méliès*, 325, 328.

55. Donald Crafton, *Emile Cohl, Caricature, and Film* (Princeton, N.J.: Princeton University Press, 1990), 11.

56. *Les Hommes d'aujourd'hui* advertised in *La Griffe* and Charles Pitou, a contributor to *La Griffe*, published several biographical sketches in *Les Hommes d'aujourd'hui*. Solomon, "Georges Méliès," 307.

57. Malthête and Mannoni, *L'Œuvre de Georges Méliès*, 324.

58. *Complete Catalogue of Genuine and Original "Star" Films* (1903), 23.

59. Hammond, *Marvellous Méliès*, 27; Anne-Marie Quévrain, "Rapatrier l'œuvre de Georges Méliès: La collection de Madeleine Malthête-Méliès," *Journal of Film Preservation*, no. 99 (2018): 99. This motif can also be found in the work of other caricaturists. Solomon, "Georges Méliès," 312–313; Solomon, "Méliès, l'Incohérent," 212–213.

60. Hammond, *Marvellous Méliès*, 98–100; John Frazer, *Artificially Arranged Scenes: The Films of Georges Méliès* (Boston: G. K. Hall, 1979), 91–93. On Méliès' use of the black screen, see esp. Noam M. Elcott, *Artificial Darkness: An Obscure History of Modern Art and Media* (Chicago: University of Chicago Press, 2016), 135–164.

61. *Complete Catalogue of Genuine and Original "Star" Films* (1903), 23.

62. Thierry Lecointe, with Pascal Fouché, *Des fragments de films Méliès disparus ressuscités par des flip books (1896–1901)* (New Barnet: John Libbey Publishing, 2020), 200–202.

63. Madeleine Malthête-Méliès, Anne-Marie Quévrain, and Jacques Malthête, *Essai de Reconstitution du Catalogue Français de la Star-Film, Suivi d'une Analyse Catalographique des Films de Georges Méliès Recensés en France* (Bois d'Arcy, France: Services des Archives du Film du Centre National de la Cinématographie, 1981), 102–103.

64. Stéphane Tralongo, "Faiseurs de féeries: Mise en scène, machineries et pratiques cinématographiques émerentes au tournant du XXe siècle" (Ph.D. thesis, Université de Montréal, Université Lumière Lyon 2, 2012), 227–231.

65. *Complete Catalogue of Genuine and Original "Star Films"* (1908), 83; Malthête-Méliès, Quévrain, and Malthête, *Essai de Reconstitution du Catalogue Français de la Star-Film*, 226–229. Although this character is not identified in the pamphlets used to advertise the film in France, in Méliès' American catalogues, the reckless automobilist is identified as King Leopold II of Belgium. Compare *Le Raid Paris-Monte-Carlo en Automobile* (Paris: Manufacture de Films pour Cinématographes G. Méliès, [1905]). Fernandino Gizzi, "Le Raid Paris-New York . . . en cinématographie: Traces d'adaptations 'apparemment déliberées' dans la catalogue américain de la Star Film," *1895*, no. 93 (2021): 76–80. The oppressive Belgian colonial regime of King Leopold II in the Congo was notorious for cruelly abusing native workers in the process of rubber extraction. See Adam Hochschild, *King Leopold's Ghost: A Story of Greed, Terror, and Heroism in Colonial Africa* (New York: Houghton Mifflin, 1999); and John Loadman, *Tears of the Tree: The Story of Rubber—A Modern Marvel* (Oxford: Oxford University Press, 2005).

66. Lant, "Haptical Cinema," 45–47.

67. *Complete Catalogue of Genuine and Original "Star" Films* (1905), 71

68. In the American catalogue description, this card is misidentified as the "queen of spades." *Complete Catalogue of Genuine and Original "Star" Films* (1905), 71.

69. *The Magic Collection of Jim Rawlins*, part 1 (Chicago: Potter & Potter, 2019), 31.

70. *Extrait du Catalogue Général Appareils du Prestidigitation & Trucs Pour Théâtres De Fabrication française et irréprochable mis en vente par Caroly*, no. 3 (Paris: Maison Caroly, c.1908), 16.

71. *Complete Catalogue of Genuine and Original "Star" Films* (1905), 72.

72. Malthête and Mannoni, *L'Œuvre de Georges Méliès*, 134–135.

73. Malthête-Méliès, Quévrain, and Malthête, *Essai de Reconstitution du Catalogue Français de la Star-Film*, 219.

74. Frazer describes this "miniaturization technique" effect as "accomplished with a superimposed photographic matte." Frazer, *Artificially Arranged Scenes*, 168.

75. *Complete Catalogue of Genuine and Original "Star" Films* (1905), 72.

76. *Complete Catalogue of Genuine and Original "Star" Films* (1905), 72.

77. Malthête and Mannoni, *L'Œuvre de Georges Méliès*, 176–177. See also Mannoni and Malthête, eds., *Méliès, magie et cinéma*, 257.

78. Since 1891–1892, when W. K. L. Dickson adopted 35mm film for use in Thomas Edison's laboratories, this format was remarkably stable. Paul C. Spehr, "Unaltered to Date: Developing 35mm Film," in John Fullerton and Astrid Söderbergh-Widding, eds., *Moving Images: From Edison to the Webcam* (Eastleigh: John Libbey, 2001), 3.

79. Jean Epstein, "Magnification" (1921), trans. Stuart Liebman, in Richard Abel, ed., *French Film Theory and Criticism, 1907–1939: A History/Anthology*, vol. 1 [1907–1929] (Princeton, N.J.: Princeton University Press, 1993), 235–241.

80. Christian Metz, "The Imaginary Signifier," trans. Ben Brewster, *Psychoanalysis and the Cinema: The Imaginary Signifier* (London: Macmillan Press, 1982), 44.

81. Brian R. Jacobson, *Studios Before the System: Architecture, Technology, and the Emergence of Cinematic Space* (New York: Columbia University Press, 2015), 66.

82. *Complete Catalogue of Genuine and Original "Star" Films* (1905), 2. Méliès deplored theatrical sets as wholly inadequate to the work of the filmmaker, instead likening his detailed backdrops to those used by photographers. Méliès, "Kinematographic Views," 136–137, 143–144.

83. Geo. Méliès, "Les Vues Cinématographiques," *Annuaire général et international de la Photographie*, vol. 16, ed. Roger Aubry (Paris: Plon, 1907), 376. This photograph has been reproduced in multiple places, including Richard M. Isackes and Karen L. Maness, *The Art of the Hollywood Backdrop* (New York: Regan Arts, 2016), 46–47.

84. André Méliès, "Suite de la publication des Mémoires d'André Méliès," ed. Marie-Hélène Lehérissey-Méliès, *Cinémathèque Méliès*, no. 17 (1990): 18. In the drawing André Méliès made of Méliès painting backdrops, he is wearing a long coat and a yachting cap. On the use of colors in painting scenery, see Méliès, "Kinematographic Views," 143–144.

85. Malthête, *Méliès, images et illusions*, 53; Malthête, "Les deux studios de Georges Méliès," 144.

86. Malthête, *Méliès, images et illusions*, 53–60; Henri Bousquet, "L'âge d'or," in Jacques Kermabon, ed., *Pathé, premier empire du cinéma* (Paris: Centre Georges Pompidou, 1994), 52–54, 59. See also Jean-Pierre Berthomé, "Les décorateurs du cinéma muet en France," *1895*, no. 65 (2011): 90–111.

87. The fire retardant Ignifuge was a real product formulated by the chemist A.-J. Martin. Unlike previous formulations, Ignifuge was transparent and did not discolor or harden the materials to which it was applied.

88. In it, Méliès took issue with the ostensibly overzealous measures the authorities were taking to fireproof Paris theaters in the wake of new regulations that followed several recent theater fires (including the May 25, 1887, fire that had incinerated the Opéra Comique, resulting in more than 200 fatalities). An 1887 ordinance had ordered the replacement of all gas lights in theaters with electric lights.

89. The trademark black star was briefly replaced by a black star with the letters "M" and an "R" (Méliès' and Reulos's initials) within it, which was painted into the backgrounds of films shot in 1897. After splitting with Reulos, Méliès continued to use different versions of the black five-pointed star trademark, many of which also included his name and the words "Trade Mark" and "Star." Jacques Malthête has identified seventeen different variations on the black star trademark in "Pour Une Véritable Archéologie des Premières Bandes Cinématographiques," *1895*, no. 24 (1998): 9–20, reprinted in *Cinémathèque Méliès*, no. 34 (1999): 32–36. See also Malthête and Mannoni, *L'Œuvre de Georges Méliès*, 25–29.

90. Paolo Cherchi Usai, *Silent Cinema: An Introduction* (London: British Film Institute, 2000), 187.

91. In particular, shoes manufactured by François Pinet were widely imitated and counterfeited by unscrupulous entrepreneurs in France and elsewhere. See "The Shoe and Leather Trades Chronicle," *Shoe and Leather Trades Chronicle* 8, no. 96 (January 1, 1881): 33; "Paris Boots Made in Stafford," *Shoe and Leather Trades Chronicle* 8, no. 96 (January

1, 1881): 44; Léo d'Orfer, "Les Contrefaçons d'Articles Français," *Franc Parleur Parisien*, no. 53 (August 5, 1884): 1–2; Argus, "La Contrefaçon Allemande," *Franc Parleur Parisien*, no. 56 (September 20, 1884): 4; no. 57 (October 5, 1884): 4–5; "Les contrefaçons," *Franc Parleur Parisien*, no. 67 (March 5, 1885): 7; "Annonce Judiciaire: Contrefaçon de la Marque des Chaussures Pinet," *Moniteur de la Cordonnerie* 36, no. 13 (July 1, 1885): 5; "Les contrefaçons étrangères," *Franc Parleur Parisien*, no. 106 (October 20, 1886): 7.

92. Michel Pelletier, *Droit Industriel, Brevets d'Invention, Marques de Fabrique* (Paris: Baudry et Cie, Libriares-Éditeurs, 1893); "Principales Marques de Fabrique de la Corporation et des Industries qui s'y Rattachent," *Moniteur de la Cordonnerie* 39, no. 23 (December 1, 1888): 16.

93. Paolo Cherchi Usai, "The Institute for Incoherent Cinematography," in Paolo Cherchi Usai, ed., *A Trip to the Movies: Georges Méliès, Filmmaker and Magician (1861–1938)* (Rochester, N.Y.: George Eastman House, 1991), 25.

94. Mannoni and Malthête, eds., *Méliès, magie et cinéma*, 228. See also 272.

95. The first of these trademarked and copyrighted sales materials appear to be the supplements issued between the 1903 and 1905 editions of Méliès' American catalogues. *Geo. Méliès of Paris: Cinematographic-Films, Life Moving Pictures, Comical, Magical, Mystical Views, Trick-Films, Actualities, etc.*, Supplements nos. 1, 2, and 3 (New York: Geo. Méliès, 1904).

96. *Complete Catalogue of Genuine and Original "Star" Films* (1903), 7; *Complete Catalogue of Genuine and Original "Star" Films* (1905), 3.

97. John Barnes speculates that it had specific origins in late nineteenth-century print culture in "Méliès court après *Les Étoiles*," *Cinémathèque Méliès*, no. 15 (1989): 27–28.

98. Pelletier, *Droit Industriel*, 163–165.

99. Pelletier, *Droit Industriel*, 165–166.

100. Paolo Cherchi Usai, *Silent Cinema: A Guide to Study, Research and Curatorship* (London: British Film Institute, 2019), 38.

101. Richard Abel, *The Red Rooster Scare: Making Cinema American, 1900–1910* (Berkeley: University of California Press), 15–16.

102. Georges Méliès, "Reply to Questionary" (1930), in Solomon, ed., *Fantastic Voyages of the Cinematic Imagination*, 233.

103. Marie-Hélène Lehérissey-Méliès, with Anne-Marie Quévrain, "Deux Films Retrouves au Marche aux Puces: le mystère s'intensifie. . . .," *Cinémathèque Méliès*, no. 15 (1989): 21–26.

104. Malthête-Méliès Quévrain, and Malthête, Avertissement to *Essai de Reconstitution du Catalogue Français de la Star-Film*, 6; Paolo Cherchi Usai, *Georges Méliès*, rev ed. (Milan: Editrice Il Castoro, 2009), 102–103.

105. Letter [from Méliès] to Carl Vincent, January 12, 1937, reprinted in Malthête, ed., "Correspondance de Georges Méliès," 456.

106. A photograph that shows Méliès drawing in the second of the two kiosks was published in Maurice Bessy and [Giuseppe Maria] Lo Duca, *Georges Méliès, mage* (Paris: Prisma, 1945), 156.

107. Typescript summary of letter from Méliès to [Eugène] Lauste, March 23, 1930, reproduced in Eileen Bowser, ed., *The Merritt Crawford Papers* (Lanham, Md.: University Publications of America, 1986), microfilm, reel 3. See also letter from G. Méliès to Paul Gilson, August 9, 1929; letter from G. Méliès to Paul Gilson, August 16, 1929; letter from G. Méliès to Jean-Baptiste Denny, September 18, 1934, reprinted in Malthête, ed., "Correspondance de Georges Méliès," 369, 373, 438. Compare Malthête and Mannoni, *L'Œuvre de Georges Méliès*, 44.

108. Manuscript letter from G. Méliès to [Merritt] Crawford, December 8, 1930; manuscript letter from G. Méliès to [Merritt] Crawford, December 25, 1930, reproduced in Bowser, ed., *The Merritt Crawford Papers*, reel 3.

109. Madeleine Malthête-Méliès, "Jehanne d'Alcy, la prèmiere Star du monde," part 2, *Cinémathèque Méliès*, no. 23 (1993): 32.

110. Quoted in "Transcripts of the Roundtable on Georges Méliès Held at the Cinémathèque Française (Paris, June 17, 1944)," in Cherchi Usai, ed., *A Trip to the Movies*, 145.

111. Uncredited typescript translation of letter from G. Méliès to [Merritt] Crawford, February 5, 1931, reproduced in Bowser, ed., *The Merritt Crawford Papers*, reel 3.

112. William S. Lieberman, *Seurat to Matisse: Drawing in France* (New York: Museum of Modern Art, 1974), 9.

113. Malthête, *Méliès, images et illusions*, 99; Malthête and Mannoni, *L'Œuvre de Georges Méliès*, 20, 117–118, 120.

Chapter 4

1. Georges Méliès, *La vie et l'œuvre d'un pionnier du cinéma*, ed. Jean-Pierre Sirois-Trahan (Paris: Éditions du Sonneur, 2012), 31.

2. According to Stéphanie Méliès, Voisin was a "close friend of Pinet," adding, Pinet was the "father-in-law of Leredu." Mme. [Stéphanie] Méliès, quoted in "Georges Méliès: Réunion du 17 février 1945," 12, Fonds Commission de Recherche Historique, Cinémathèque Française, CRH20-B1, http://www.cineressources.net/consultationPdf/web/a000/037.pdf.

3. Madeleine Malthête-Méliès, *Georges Méliès, L'Enchanteur* (Grandvilliers, France: La Tour Verte, 2011), 172. Legris leads the triumphal procession in the twenty-sixth tableau of *Voyage dans la Lune*.

4. A. Eriat [pseud., Arthur Taire], "Revue Théâtrale," *Franc Parleur Parisien*, no. 196 (February 10, 1890): 40; no. 197 (February 20, 1890): 48; no. 199 (March 10, 1890): 64.

5. Joe Culpepper, email communication to the author, September 4, 2016.

6. The best and most comprehensive biography of Robert-Houdin, which details his relationship to the history of magic and chronicles his successors, is Christian Fechner, *The Magic of Robert-Houdin, "An Artist's Life": Biographical Essay*, ed. Todd Karr, trans. Stacey Dagron (Boulogne, France: Editions F. C. F., 2002), vols. 1–2. On the Théâtre

Robert-Houdin, see esp. Christian Fechner, "Le Théâtre Robert-Houdin, de Jean Eugène Robert-Houdin à Georges Méliès," in Laurent Mannoni and Jacques Malthête, eds., *Méliès, magie et cinéma* (Paris: Paris-Musées, 2002), 72–115; Matthew Solomon, *Disappearing Tricks: Silent Film, Houdini, and the New Magic of the Twentieth Century* (Urbana: University of Illinois Press, 2010), 40–59; and Frédéric Tabet, *Le cinématographe des magiciens, 1896–1906, un cycle magique* (Rennes: Presses Universitaires de Rennes, 2018), 81–92.

7. Daniel Grojnowski, *Aux commencements du rire moderne: L'esprit fumiste* (Paris: Librairie José Corti, 1997); Alain Vaillant and Roselyne de Villeneuve, eds., *Le Rire Moderne* (Paris: Presses Universitaires de Paris Ouest, 2013).

8. Grojnowski, *Aux commencements du rire moderne*, 15. See also Daniel Grojnowski and Denys Riout, *Les Arts Incohérents et le rire dans les arts plastiques* (Paris: Éditions Corti, 2015); Daniel Grojnowski and Bernard Serrazin, eds., *L'Esprit fumiste et les rires fin de siècle* (Paris: José Corti, 1990).

9. Malthête-Méliès and Deslandes both used this phrase to describe Méliès' work, but neither discussed its connection to comedy. Compare Malthête-Méliès, *Georges Méliès*, 311–327; Jacques Deslandes, *Le boulevard du cinéma à l'époque de Georges Méliès* (Paris: Editions du Cerf, 1963), 20.

10. *Phono-Ciné-Gazette*, no. 22 (February 15, 1906): 79.

11. Fechner, *The Magic of Robert-Houdin*, 1:159, 239. Fechner notes a similar sense of humor in Robert-Houdin's published writings.

12. Fechner, *The Magic of Robert-Houdin*, 1:159.

13. G. Méliès, "Le Dessèchement Cabalistique," *Passez Muscade*, no. 50 (1929): 567.

14. Fechner, *The Magic of Robert-Houdin*, 1:414.

15. Méliès, "Le Dessèchement Cabalistique," 567.

16. Méliès, "Le Dessèchement Cabalistique," 568–572. Here, many lines of dialogue are followed by parenthetical stage directions indicating laughter.

17. André Méliès, "Mémoires d'André Méliès," ed. Marie-Hélène Lehérissey-Méliès, *Cinémathèque Méliès*, no. 18 (1991): 42.

18. Daniel Grojnowski, "Les Arts incohérents: De la blague à l'instauration," *Retour d'y voir*, nos. 3–4 (2010): 99–100. Jules Roques called Lévy "grand master of the order" in "Comment on devient incohérent," *Le Courrier français* (March 12, 1885): 2, while Émile Goudeau paternalistically dubbed Lévy "king" and "emperor" of the Incohérents in *Dix ans de bohème* (Paris: Librairie Illustrée, 1888), 189–190.

19. Maggie Hennefeld, *Specters of Slapstick and Silent Film Comediennes* (New York: Columbia University Press, 2018), 4–5.

20. Hennefeld, *Specters of Slapstick*, 124.

21. *Le Courrier français* (April 4, 1886): 1. By 1893, *Le Courrier français*, which had formerly been the "official and officious" organ of the Incohérents, had turned on them. Editor Jules Roques now decried their commercialism and published several disparaging anti-Semitic caricatures of Lévy. Catherine Charpin, *Les Arts Incohérents (1882–1893)* (Paris: Éditions Syros Alternatives, 1990), 43; Grojnowski and Riout, *Les Arts Incohérents*, 110,

120; Luce Abélès, "Naissance des Arts incohérents: Une conjoncture favorable," in Luce Abélès and Catherine Charpin, *Arts Incohérents, Académie du Dérisoire*, Les dossiers du Musée d'Orsay, no. 46 (Paris: Editions de la Réunion des musées nationaux, 1992), 34–35.

22. Mikhail Bakhtin, *Rabelais and His World*, trans. Hélène Iswolsky (1965; Bloomington: Indiana University Press, 1994), 38.

23. Bakhtin, *Rabelais and His World*, 5–6. Bakhtin adds, "No dogma, no authoritarianism, no narrow-minded seriousness can coexist with Rabelaisian images; these images are opposed to all that is finished and polished, to all pomposity, to every ready-made solution in the sphere of thought and world outlook" (3).

24. Grojnowski and Riout, *Les Arts Incohérents*, 115.

25. Grojnowski and Riout, *Les Arts Incohérents*, 149.

26. Méliès, *La vie et l'œuvre d'un pionnier du cinéma*, 31–32; letters from Méliès to Paul Gilson, August 9, 1929, August 16, 1929, reprinted in Jacques Malthête, ed., "Correspondance de Georges Méliès (1904–1937)," in André Gaudreault and Laurent Le Forestier, with Stéphane Tralongo, eds., *Méliès, carrefour des attractions, suivi de correspondance de Georges Méliès (1904–1937)* (Rennes: Presses Universitaires de Rennes, 2014), 368, 370. Fechner claims Méliès performed pseudonymously without naming the pseudonym in "Le Théâtre Robert-Houdin," 92–93. Stéphanie Méliès, however, claimed that Méliès "never performed at the Musée Grévin nor the Galerie Vivienne." Quoted in "Georges Méliès: Réunion du 17 février 1945," 11. See also "Quels tours d'illusion le jeune Georges Méliès faisait-il en public?" *Cinémathèque Méliès Lettre d'Information*, no. 52 (January 2019): 3.

27. "Divers," *Officiel-Artiste* 6, no. 47 (December 2, 1886): 7; P. D., "Inauguration du Théâtre de la Galerie Vivienne," *Journal des Artistes* (December 5, 1886): 406.

28. A. de Jestières, "Semaine Théatrale," *Journal des Artistes* (March 13, 1887): 79; Paul Liones, "Semaine Théatrale," *Journal des Artistes* (April 10, 1887): 111.

29. Méliès, *La vie et l'œuvre d'un pionnier du cinéma*, 32. Years later, Galipaux appeared in Méliès' film *Le Raid Paris—Monte-Carlo en automobile*.

30. Mary Gluck, *Popular Bohemia: Modernism and Urban Culture in Nineteenth-Century Paris* (Cambridge, Mass.: Harvard University Press, 2005), 128–130. See also Coquelin *cadet* [Ernest Coquelin], *Le Monologue moderne* (Paris: Paul Ollendorff, 1881).

31. Malthête-Méliès, *Georges Méliès*, 97.

32. Letter from Méliès to Paul Gilson, August 16, 1929, reprinted in Malthête, ed., "Correspondance de Georges Méliès (1904–1937)," 370.

33. Magnier, "Banquet de la Chambre Syndicale de la Chaussure en Gros de Paris," *Moniteur de la Cordonnerie* 38, no. 5 (March 1, 1887): 4.

34. Magnier, "Banquet de la Chambre Syndicale de la Chaussure en Gros de Paris," 4. Compare "Compte Rendu du Banquet de la Chambre Syndicale de la Chaussure en Gros de Paris," *Franc Parleur Parisien*, no. 114 (February 20, 1887): 28. See also "Informations Signalées par Nos Membres," *Cinémathèque Méliès Lettre d'Information*, no. 45 (July 2016): 5; and Laurent Mannoni, *Georges Méliès, la magie du cinéma* (Paris: Cinémathèque Française, 2020), 34–35.

35. "Le Banquet de la Chambre Syndicale de la Chaussure en Gros de Paris," *Franc Parleur Parisien*, no. 138 (February 20, 1888): 26–27.

36. E[douard-Joseph] Raynaly, *Les Propos d'un Escamoteur: Étude Critique et Humoristique* (Paris: C. Noblet, 1894), 85–86. See, for example, Karl Baedeker, *Paris and Environs with Routes from London to Paris*, 9th ed. (London: Dulau & Co., 1888), 32; 10th ed. (London: Dulau & Co., 1891), 31; 11th ed. (London: Dulau & Co., 1894), 31; and 12th ed. (London: Dulau & Co., 1896), 32. Writer Louis-Ferdinand Céline and filmmaker Sergei Eisenstein were among the child spectators who later wrote about their childhood visits to the Théâtre Robert-Houdin during Méliès' tenure as director.

37. Elsewhere, I have described this singular mode of magic as "incoherent illusionism." See my review of *Georges Méliès: First Wizard of Cinema (1896–1913)* and *Georges Méliès: Encore (1896–1911)*, *Moving Image* 12, no. 2 (2012): 188, and my "L'illusionnisme incohérent," trans. Florent Fajole, in Frank Kessler, Jean-Marc Larrue, and Giusy Pisano, eds., *Machines, magie, médias* (Villeneuve, France: Presses Universitaires du Septentrion, 2018), 127–137.

38. Gilles et de Phlanel, *Farces et facéties de la prestidigitation* (Paris: E. Voisin, n.d.). The author of this book is identified as Méliès in Christian Fechner, *Bibliographie de la Prestidigitation Française et des Artes Annexes* (Paris: Editions F. C. F., 1994), 232.

39. Gilles et de Phlanel, *Florine, ou la Clef d'Or: Féerie en Trois Actes Tirée des Contes Merveilleux de J. Porchat* (Paris: Watilliaux, Éditeur, n.d.); Gilles et de Phlanel, *Les Méfaits de l'Ami Grognard: Comédie en Trois Actes* (Paris: Watilliaux, Éditeur, n. d.). Other plays in Watilliaux's "Théâtre des Enfants" series were also pseudonymously authored, including *Le Mariage d'Arlequin: Comédie en un acte*, by Pierre O... ("Pierrot"), *Le Talisman de Rosette: Féerie en 5 tableaux*, by O. de Seltz ("Eau de Seltz" [Seltzer Water]), *Les Malices de Polichinelle: Parade*, by E. Pinard et A. Ricauvert ("Épinards et Haricots Verts" [Spinach and Green Beans]), *Au clair de la lune: Comédie*, by Pierre Souli ("Pierre Sous Lit" [Pierre under the Bed]). A later bibliography of puppet theater credits all six entries to Pierre O. Compare Paul Jeanne, *Bibliographie des marionnettes* (Paris: E. Lefebvre, 1926), 40.

40. In *Les Méfaits de l'Ami Grognard*, the elasticity motif is linked to specific Paris material referents: a balloon purchased from the Louvre department store and an elephant at the Jardin d'Acclimation.

41. Fechner, "Le Théâtre Robert-Houdin," 102–105.

42. See esp. Paul Hammond, *Marvellous Méliès* (London: Gordon Fraser, 1974), 19–20; David Robinson, *Georges Méliès, Father of Film Fantasy* (London: Museum of the Moving Image, 1993), 6–7. By contrast, Malthête-Méliès notes that Méliès went to the Egyptian Hall in 1884 but asserts no specific relation to Méliès' later productions. Malthête-Méliès, *Georges Méliès*, 63–67.

43. Deslandes, *Le boulevard du cinéma*, 33–49. See also Jacques Malthête, *Méliès, images et illusions* (Paris: Exporégie, 1996), 30–46; Jacques Causyn, "Georges Méliès, illusionniste," *Les Amis de Georges Méliès*, nos. 3–12 (1983–1988); and Jacques Causyn, "Georges Méliès, illusionniste et le théâtre Robert-Houdin," *Cinémathèque Méliès*, nos. 13–30 (1988–1997).

44. Jacques Deslandes, "Trucographie de Georges Méliès (1861–1938)," *Bulletin de la Société Archéologique, Historique et Artistique Le Vieux Papier*, no. 198 (January 1962): 169–180. Compare Hammond, *Marvellous Méliès*, 132–133.

45. Letter from Méliès to Drioux, February 16, 1928, reprinted in Malthête, ed., "Correspondance de Georges Méliès (1904–1937)," 347.

46. *La Rédaction* [Auguste Drioux], "Georges Méliès," *Passez Muscade*, no. 40 (1927): 486–487.

47. Geo. Méliès, "Le Théâtre Robert-Houdin (1845–1925)," *Passez Muscade*, no. 42 (1928): 504; G. Méliès, "Les 'Éloquentes Dissertations' de Folletto," *Passez Muscade*, no. 51 (1929): 524–527; "La Reine des Arts," *Passez Muscade*, numéro spécial (1929): 12–13. See also E. Raynaly, "L'Art Magique" (1916), *Passez Muscade*, no. 46 (1928): 536–537.

48. G. Méliès, "Le Décapité Récalcitrant," *Passez Muscade*, no. 47 (1928): 541–546; no. 48 (1928): 549–554. On the combination of comedy and the fantastic in Méliès' larger body of cinematic work, see Enrico Giacovelli, *La bottega delle illusioni: Georges Méliès e il cinema comico e fantastic francese (1896–1914)* (Milan: Edizioni Bietti, 2015).

49. Méliès, "Le Décapité Récalcitrant," *Passez Muscade*, no. 47 (1928): 542; Jacques Garnier, *Bénévol, le Maître de Mystère* (Orléans: by the author, 1969), 90–104; *Collection Christian Fechner: Magie et illusionnisme* (Paris: H. Gros—G. Delettrez, 2004), 108–109.

50. On the anti-spiritualism of "Le Décapité Récalcitrant," see my *Disappearing Tricks*, 14–15. Comparable mockery of spiritualism can also be found in French caricature journals. See, for example, Douville, "Feuilles au vent," *Le Grelot*, no. 964 (September 29, 1889).

51. Diane Arnaud finds this motif in many periods and geographic regions of film culture in *Changements de têtes de Georges Méliès à David Lynch* (Aix-en-Provence, France: Éditions Rouge Profond, 2012). See also A.-M. de Bélina, *Nos peintres dessinés par eux-mêmes: Notes humoristiques et esquisses biographiques* (Paris: E. Bernard et Cie, Imprimeurs-Éditeurs, 1883), 31, and Jacques Malthête "Quand Méliès n'en faisait qu'à sa tête," *1895*, no. 27 (1999): 21–32.

52. *Revue Illustrée* (March 5, 1887). On Jan van Beers, Incohérent, see J. A. H. "M. L'Incohérent," *Oxford Magazine* (March 4, 1885): 136–137.

53. Nicholas Sammond, *Birth of an Industry: Blackface Minstrelsy and the Rise of American Animation* (Durham, N.C.: Duke University Press, 2015), 212. Relevantly, Sammond argues, "the fantastic and resistant form of the blackface minstrel was an embodied corollary to the plasmatic substance" of drawing.

54. See also Méliès' drawing of a minstrel and the drawing he made in connection with *L'Omnibus des toqués ou Blancs et Noirs* in Jacques Malthête and Laurent Mannoni, *L'Œuvre de Georges Méliès* (Paris: Éditions de la Martinière, Cinémathèque Française, 2008), 65, 120.

55. Fechner, *The Magic of Robert-Houdin*, 295; Christian Fechner, *La Magie de Robert-Houdin: "Secrets des Soirées Fantastiques,"* vol. 3 (Boulogne, France: Editions F. C. F., 2005), 269.

56. Malthête-Méliès identifies the two card players in the Méliès version as Leborgne, whom Méliès met during his military service, and Roberval, a friend from secondary school, and says the film was shot by Lucien Reulos. She also identifies the game they are playing as manille, which is played with a 32-card deck. In the Méliès version, the server is a woman rather than a man. Malthête-Méliès, *Georges Méliès*, 180–181; Madeleine Malthête-Méliès, "Questions Diverses," *Cinémathèque Méliès*, no. 31 (1997): 16; Jacques Mény, "Premier Film, Tourné par Méliès, Retrouve en Juin," *Cinémathèque Méliès*, no. 31 (1997): 19; Eugénie Rozzi, "Quelques Souvenirs sur Une Jeune Actrice," *Cinémathèque Méliès*, no. 14 (1989): 25–26.

57. Michelle Aubert and Jean-Claude Seguin, *La Production cinématographique des frères Lumière* (Paris: Bibliothèque du Film, 1996), 210–211. In the Lumière version, the person directly facing the camera is Alphonse Winckler, the father-in-law of Auguste Lumière and Louis Lumière.

58. Henri Bergson, *Laughter: An Essay on the Meaning of the Comic*, trans. Cloudesley Brereton and Fred Rothwell (London: Macmillan, 1913), 9–10.

59. Bergson, *Laughter*, 10.

60. *Complete Catalogue of Genuine and Original "Star Films" (Moving Pictures)* (New York: Geo. Méliès, 1908), 87.

61. Madeleine Malthête-Méliès, Anne-Marie Quévrain, and Jacques Malthête, *Essai de Reconstitution d'une Catalogue Français de la Star-Film, Suivi d'une Analyse Catalographique des Film de Georges Méliès Recensés en France* (Bois d'Arcy, France: Services des Archives du Film du Centre National de la Cinématographie, 1981), 232.

62. See my review of *Georges Méliès: First Wizard of Cinema (1896–1913)* and *Georges Méliès: Encore (1896–1911)*, *Moving Image* 12, no. 2 (2012): 188.

63. Méliès, *La Vie et l'œuvre d'un pionnier du cinéma*, 46.

64. Charles Bertram, *Isn't It Wonderful? A History of Magic and Mystery* (London: Swan Sonnenschein and Co., 1896), 127.

65. Charles Musser, *Edison Motion Pictures: An Annotated Filmography, 1890–1900* (Pordenone, Italy: Le Giornate del Cinema Muto; Washington: Smithsonian Institution Press, 1997), 467. See also Musser, *The Emergence of Cinema: The American Screen to 1907* (New York: Charles Scribner's Sons, 1990), 231, 271–272.

66. See my *Disappearing Tricks*, 33–35.

67. On this film, this illusion, and the trope of the vanishing woman, see esp. Lucy Fischer, "The Lady Vanishes: Women, Magic and the Movies," *Film Quarterly* 33, no. 1 (1979): 30–40; Karen Beckman, *Vanishing Women: Magic, Film, and Feminism* (Durham, N.C.: Duke University Press, 2003); and Katharina Rein, "'The Vanishing Lady,' the Railway, and Illusions of Movement," in Katharina Rein, ed., *Illusion in Cultural Practice: Productive Deceptions* (London: Routledge, 2021), 87–103. See also Pierre Jenn, *Georges Méliès, cinéaste* (Paris: Éditions Albatros, 1984), 26–27; Réjane Hamus-Vallée, "La sauce et le poisson: Pour une esthétique de l'effet méliésien," in Gaudreault and Le Forestier, with Tralongo, eds., *Méliès, carrefour des attractions*, 97–106; and Tabet, *Le cinématographe des magiciens*, 117–130.

68. Jasper Maskelyne, *White Magic: Story of Maskelynes* (London: Stanley Paul & Co., 1936), 73; Beckman, *Vanishing Women*, 205n10.

69. In some stage versions of "The Vanishing Lady," the woman came onstage carrying a handkerchief and only the handkerchief remained on the chair after she vanished. In Méliès' version, d'Alcy enters carrying a fan, which remains in her hands throughout the time she is onscreen.

70. Bertram, *Isn't It Wonderful?*, 127–128.

71. Professor Hoffmann [pseud.], *More Magic* (London: George Routledge and Sons, 1890), 455. Hoffmann's account of "The Vanishing Lady" spans pp. 448–456; he notes on pp. 455–456 that Hartz, among others, did not include vanishing the veil in his presentation of the illusion.

72. "Royalty's Magician: A Chat with Mr. Charles Bertram," *New Penny Magazine* 5, no. 61 (1899), reproduced in *The Wizard Exposed: Magic Tricks, Interviews, and Experiences* (Glenwood, Ill.: David Meyer Magic Books, 1987), 98.

73. Hoffmann, *More Magic*, 453. See also 209–210.

74. See illustrations in Albert A. Hopkins, ed., *Magic: Stage Illusions and Scientific Diversions, Including Trick Photography* (New York: Munn and Co., 1897), 42–43. Compare *La Nature* (July 18, 1891): 176.

75. Bertram, *Isn't It Wonderful?*, 127.

76. Bertram, *Isn't It Wonderful?*, 126.

77. Priska Morrissey, "La garde-robe de Georges Méliès: Origines et usages des costumes de vues cinématographiques," in Gaudreault and Le Forestier, with Tralongo, eds., *Méliès, carrefour des attractions*, 177–188.

78. Cinema employed slightly thicker celluloid film than still photography that could be more readily perforated and was less likely to tear as it was pulled through the sprockets of a motion picture camera as well as celluloid film coated with the slower emulsion appropriate for striking positive prints from a negative. Unlike forms of still photography, cinema employed the same base in both its negative and positive phases.

79. In 1870, the process for creating celluloid, one of the first artificial plastics, was patented. Originally a trademarked name, celluloid was industrially produced on a relatively large scale during the 1870s and 1880s, when it was often used as a durable and relatively inexpensive substitute for ivory in the manufacture of small articles. Robert Friedel, *Pioneer Plastic: The Making and Selling of Celluloid* (Madison: University of Wisconsin Press, 1983). See also my "The Medium Is the Magic: Trick Films and the Imagination of Celluloid," in *Alexandra Navratil: This Formless Thing* (Winterthur, Switz.: Kunstmuseum Winterthur; Amsterdam: SMBA Amsterdam, Roma Publications, 2013), 85–100; and Pansy Duncan, "Celluloid™: Cecil M. Hepworth, Trick Film, and the Material Prehistory of the Plastic Image," *Film History* 31, no. 4 (2019): 92–112.

80. Michael Stephen Smith, *The Emergence of Modern Business Enterprise in France, 1800–1930* (Cambridge, Mass.: Harvard University Press, 2006), 219–236.

81. Laurent Mannoni, "1896, Les premiers appareils cinématographiques de Georges Méliès," in Mannoni and Malthête, eds., *Méliès, magie et cinéma*, 123; Maurice Noverre, "L'œuvre de Georges Méliès: Etude rétrospective sur la prèmiere entreprise industrielle

de cinématographie théâtrale (1896–1914)," *Nouvel Art Cinématographique*, 2d ser., no. 4 (October 1929): 61–62.

82. Paolo Cherchi Usai, *Silent Cinema: A Guide to Study, Research and Curatorship* (London: British Film Institute, 2019), 122.

83. Joshua Yumibe, *Moving Color: Early Film, Mass Culture, Modernism* (New Brunswick, N.J.: Rutgers University Press, 2012), 46–48.

84. Jacques Malthête, "Un feu d'artifice improvisé: Les effets pyrotechniques chez Méliès." *1895*, no. 39 (2003): 61–72; André Méliès, "Suite de la publication des Mémoires," ed. Marie-Hélène Lehérissey-Méliès, *Cinémathèque Méliès*, no. 17 (1990): 24.

85. Quoted in "Transcripts of the Roundtable on Georges Méliès Held at the Cinémathèque Française (Paris, June 17, 1944)," in Paolo Cherchi Usai, ed., *A Trip to the Movies: Georges Méliès, Filmmaker and Magician (1861–1938)* (Rochester, N.Y.: George Eastman House, 1991), 149.

86. Solomon, *Disappearing Tricks*, 30–31.

87. Quoted in "Transcripts of the Roundtable on Georges Méliès," 151. Lallement also recalled the effect of the Bazar de la Charité fire in "Georges Méliès: Réunion du 17 février 1945," 14–15.

88. André Méliès, "Mémoires d'André Méliès," ed. Marie-Hélène Lehérissey-Méliès, *Cinémathèque Méliès*, no. 19 (1991): 25. See also Mannoni, *Georges Méliès, la magie du cinéma*, 130.

89. Malthête, "La vie et l'œuvre de Georges Méliès," 22; André Méliès, "Mémoires d'André Méliès," *Cinémathèque Méliès*, no. 19 (1991): 23.

90. Laurent Mannoni, "1896, Les premiers appareils cinématographiques de Georges Méliès," in Mannoni and Malthête, eds., *Méliès, magie et cinéma*, 117–133.

91. Colin N. Bennett, *The Handbook of Kinematography: The History, Theory, and Practice of Motion Photography and Projection*, 2d ed. (1911; London: Kinematograph Weekly, 1913), 217, my emphasis.

92. Bennett, *The Handbook of Kinematography*, 220–222.

93. See, for example, the frame enlargement from a print of *Voyage dans la Lune* reproduced in Solomon, ed., *Fantastic Voyages of the Cinematic Imagination: Georges Méliès's Trip to the Moon* (Albany, N.Y.: SUNY Press, 2011), 7.

94. Edward Chauncey Worden, *Nitrocellulose Industry: A Compendium of the History, Chemistry, Manufacture, Commercial Application and Analysis of Nitrates, Acetates and Xanthates of Cellulose as Applied to the Peaceful Arts*, vol. 1 (New York: D. Van Nostrand Co., 1911), 1.

Chapter 5

1. Georges Méliès, *La Vie et l'œuvre d'un pionnier du cinéma*, ed. Jean-Pierre Sirois-Trahan (Paris: Du Sonneur, 2012), 34. Méliès' memoirs were originally published in 1938 in an uncredited Italian translation. The quoted phrase appears in Italian as "la nuova professione di cineasta" in "Un documento eccezionale: Le Memorie di Georges Méliès," *Cinema* [Milan], no. 40 (February 25, 1938): 120. First published

in the original French as "la profession nouvelle de cinéaste" in Georges Méliès, "Mes Mémoires," in Maurice Bessy and [Giusuppe Maria] Lo Duca, *Méliès, mage* (Paris: Prisma, 1945), 145.

2. André Gaudreault, *Film and Attraction: From Kinematography to Cinema*, trans. Timothy Barnard (Urbana: University of Illinois Press, 2011), 71, 74.

3. Jean Giraud, *Le Lexique français du cinéma des origines à 1930* (Paris: Centre National de la Recherche Scientifique, 1952), 65–66; compare 141–142.

4. Giraud, *Le Lexique français du cinéma*, 49; Geo. Méliès, "Les Vues Cinématographiques," *Annuaire général et international de la Photographie*, vol. 16, ed. Roger Aubry (Paris: Plon, 1907), 389.

5. Georges Méliès, "Kinematographic Views," trans. Stuart Liebman and Timothy Barnard, in Gaudreault, *Film and Attraction*, 141.

6. Letter from Georges Méliès to Maurice Noverre, July 1928, reprinted in Jacques Malthête, ed., "Correspondance de Georges Méliès (1904–1937)," in André Gaudreault and Laurent Le Forestier, with Stéphane Tralongo, eds., *Méliès, carrefour des attractions, suivi de correspondance de Georges Méliès (1904–1937)* (Rennes: Presses Universitaires de Rennes, 2014), 349.

7. Jane M. Gaines, review of *Les Pionnières du cinéma*, *Journal of Film Preservation*, no. 99 (2018): 164.

8. Gaudreault, *Film and Attraction*, 74.

9. Gaudreault, *Film and Attraction*, 75.

10. Richard Abel, *The Red Rooster Scare: Making Cinema American, 1900–1910* (Berkeley: University of California Press, 2000), 16.

11. Peter Wollen, *Signs and Meaning in the Cinema*, rev. ed. (Bloomington: Indiana University Press, 1972), 104.

12. *L'Homme-orchestre* was titled *The One-Man Band* in Méliès' American catalogues, where it was described as follows: "The object is to produce a band of seven individual musicians, each playing a different instrument, from one man. This is done in a startling manner, all seven musicians being exact likenesses of one another, and their grimaces and contortions while mastering the music is most amusing to witness." *Complete Catalogue of Genuine and Original "Star Films" (Moving Pictures)* (New York: Geo. Méliès, 1903), 19. John Frazer explains the complexity involved in making this film, "Seven repeated exposures were required as well as perfect timing of the activities of the musicians. Absolute precision in matching body position was necessary. The camera had to be cranked at a constant rate of speed." Frazer, *Artificially Arranged Scenes: The Films of Georges Méliès* (Boston: G. K. Hall, 1979), 82.

13. Matthew Solomon, *Disappearing Tricks: Silent Film, Houdini, and the New Magic of the Twentieth Century* (Urbana: University of Illinois Press), 149n41; André Méliès, "Suite de la publication des Mémoires et notes d'André Méliès," ed. Marie-Hélène Lehérissey-Méliès, *Cinémathèque Méliès*, no. 16 (1990): 15–16. See also "M. Grivolas," *L'Illusionniste*, no. 67 (July 1907): 293–294.

14. Jacques Malthête, "La vie et l'œuvre de Georges Méliès," 26. Malthête notes that Méliès incorporated "L'Étoile" as a "Société générale de cinématographie" in 1897–1898,

but describes its existence as "apparently very fleeting." Malthête, ed., "Correspondance de Georges Méliès," 349fn98, 349fn99. See also Laurent Mannoni, *Georges Méliès, la magie du cinéma* (Paris: Cinémathèque Française, 2020), 130.

15. Madeleine Malthête-Méliès, *Georges Méliès, L'Enchanteur* (Grandvilliers, France: La Tour Verte, 2011), 215. See also letter from Méliès to Noverre, July 1928, in Malthête, ed., "Correspondance de Georges Méliès," 349.

16. *Complete Catalogue of Genuine and Original "Star Films"* (1903), 5–6.

17. Manuscript letter from G. Méliès to [Merritt] Crawford, December 8, 1930, emphasis in original, reproduced in Eileen Bowser, ed., *The Merritt Crawford Papers* (Lanham, Md.: University Publications of America, 1986), microfilm, reel 3. Thus, Gaston Méliès was responsible for remitting regular payments to Méliès in Paris, and a cache of surviving receipts is evidence of some of these payments. Jacques Malthête, "Les ventes de la *G. Méliès Manufacturing Company* en 1912–1914," *Cinémathèque Méliès*, no. 26 (1995): 32–41. See also letter from G. Méliès to Paul Méliès, August 28, 1913, reprinted in Jacques Malthête, "Les Collaborateurs de Georges Méliès: 1—Tainguy," *Cinémathèque Méliès*, no. 29 (1996): 28.

18. Letter from Méliès to Noverre, July 1928, reprinted in Malthête, ed., "Correspondance de Georges Méliès," 349–350.

19. Uncredited typescript translation of letter from G. Méliès to [Eugène] Lauste, January 23, 1930, reproduced in Bowser, ed., *The Merritt Crawford Papers*, reel 3.

20. Alberto Cavalcanti, Foreword to Frazer, *Artificially Arranged Scenes*, xv.

21. Georges Méliès, "En marge de l'histoire du cinématographe," *Ciné-Journal*, no. 883 (July 30, 1926): 7, 9; no. 884 (August 6, 1926): 9, 11; no. 885 (August 13, 1926): 9, 11; no. 887 (August 27, 1926): 22–23; no. 888 (September 3, 1926): 9, 11–12; no. 889 (September 10, 1926): 7, 9; no. 890 (September 17, 1926): 2, 4; Georges Méliès, "L'Importance du scénario," *Cinéa et ciné pour tous réunis*, n. s., no. 24 (April 1932): 23, 25.

22. Letter from G. Méliès to May de Lavergne [Marie-Joséphine Kien], April 4, 1937, reprinted in Malthête, ed., "Correspondance de Georges Méliès," 478; manuscript letter reproduced and transcribed in *Cinémathèque Méliès*, no. 14 (1989): 34–35. Compare letter from G. Méliès to Carl Vincent, January 16, 1937, reprinted in Malthête, ed., "Correspondance de Georges Méliès," 458. During the 1930s, when Méliès and Stéphanie Méliès were retired in Orly, they reportedly went to the movies every week. Two places were reserved for them for every Sunday evening show at the Orly cinema, and they sometimes expressed their opinions about the films they saw there, according to Mimi Dassonville-Corson, "Témoinage Orlysien," *Cinémathèque Méliès*, no. 16 (1990): 30.

23. Letter from Méliès to Noverre, July 1928, reprinted in Malthête, ed., "Correspondance de Georges Méliès," 349–350.

24. Solomon, *Disappearing Tricks*, 123–124.

25. Uncredited typescript translation of letter from G. Méliès to [Eugène] Lauste, January 26, 1931, reproduced in Bowser, ed., *The Merritt Crawford Papers*, reel 3. In this letter, Méliès wrote, "In this regard one of our prominent reporters has just returned from Hollywood where he made a personal survey for the Parisian daily, 'Le Journal.' He came back to Paris yesterday and 'Le Journal' have published his interviews and

findings. I am sending you a clipping from yesterday's paper." This clipping appears to have been Maurice Dekobra, "Au Royaume des Stars: La machine aux scénarios," *Le Journal* (January 25, 1931): 1–2.

26. Manuscript letter from G. Méliès to [Merritt] Crawford, December 31, 1930, reproduced in Bowser, ed., *The Merritt Crawford Papers*, reel 3.

27. Letter from Méliès to Lauste, January 26, 1931.

28. Letter from Méliès to Crawford, December 31, 1930.

29. Uncredited typescript translation of letter from G. Méliès to [Eugène] Lauste, February 5, 1931, reproduced in Bowser, ed., *The Merritt Crawford Papers*, reel 3.

30. Letter from Méliès to Crawford, December 31, 1930.

31. Letter from Georges Méliès to Auguste Drioux, June 18, 1934, reprinted in Malthête, ed., "Correspondance de Georges Méliès," 435.

32. Richard Abel, *The Ciné Goes to Town: French Cinema, 1896–1914*, rev. ed. (1994; Berkeley: University of California Press, 1998), 10–18.

33. Manuscript letter from G. Méliès to [Merritt] Crawford, December 8, 1930, reproduced in Bowser, ed., *The Merritt Crawford Papers*, reel 3. In an earlier letter, Méliès took a swipe at "the Gaumont, Lumière, and Pathé 'club.'" Manuscript letter from G. Méliès to [Merritt] Crawford, November 17, 1930, reproduced in Bowser, ed., *The Merritt Crawford Papers*, reel 3.

34. François Caron proposes that a number of "new métiers" appeared in France during the Second Industrial Revolution, although his synoptic account of the two industrial revolutions in France has relatively little to say about cinema, mainly noting the emerging film industry's dependence on ample supplies of celluloid. Caron, *Les deux révolutions industrielles du XXe siècle* (Paris: Albin Michel, 1997), 38–40, 131.

35. Letter from G. Méliès to Auguste Drioux, March 3, 1936, reprinted in Malthête, ed., "Correspondance de Georges Méliès," 447.

36. Laurent Creton, "Figures de l'entrepreneur, filières d'innovation et genèse de l'industrie cinématographique: Lumière, Pathé et Méliès," in Jacques Malthête and Michel Marie, eds., *Georges Méliès, l'illusionniste fin de siècle*? (Paris: Presses de la Sorbonne Nouvelle, 1997), 136–137.

37. This exchange is reported in several places, including Mannoni, *Georges Méliès, la magie du cinéma*, 266; Roland Cosandey, "Georges Méliès as *L'Inescamotable Escamoteur*: A Study in Recognition," in Paolo Cherchi Usai, ed., *A Trip to the Movies: Georges Méliès, Filmmaker and Magician (1861–1938)* (Rochester, N.Y.: George Eastman House, 1991), 65; and Georges Sadoul, *Les pionniers du cinéma, 1897–1909*, rev. ed., ed. Bernard Eisenschitz (1948; Paris: Editions Denoël, 1978), 293, where it is reportedly directed at Léon Gaumont.

38. Jacques Malthête, "La vie et l'œuvre de Georges Méliès: Petit précis spatiotemporal," in Jacques Malthête and Laurent Mannoni, eds., *Méliès, magie et cinéma* (Paris: Paris-Musées, 2002), 27; Eileen Bowser, *The Transformation of Cinema, 1907–1915* (New York: Charles Scribner's Sons, 1990), 26.

39. Quoted in "Georges Méliès: Réunion du 17 février 1945," 23, Fonds Commission de Recherche Historique, Cinémathèque Française, CRH20-B1, http://www.cineressources.net/consultationPdf/web/a000/037.pdf.

40. Creton, "Figures de l'entrepreneur," 151.

41. Méliès, "Kinematographic Views," 138, 140.

42. Maurice Noverre, "L'œuvre de Georges Méliès: Etude rétrospective sur la prèmiere entreprise industrielle de cinématographie théâtrale (1896–1914)," *Nouvel Art Cinématographique*, 2d ser., no. 4 (October 1929): 59.

43. Caron, *Les deux révolutions industrielles*, 38.

44. Malthête, "Les Collaborateurs de Georges Méliès: 1—Tainguy," 27–33.

45. For example, François Lallement worked in the Passage de l'Opéra laboratory and Jules-Eugène Legris performed magic at the Théâtre Robert-Houdin, but appear onscreen dressed in uniforms, respectively, in the seventh and twenty-sixth tableaus of *Voyage dans la Lune*. One of Méliès' collaborators, Maurice Astaix, recalled, "for the big productions [. . .] everybody went to Montreuil with their costumes." Quoted in "Transcripts of the Roundtable on Georges Méliès Held at the Cinémathèque Française (Paris, June 17, 1944)," in Cherchi Usai, ed., *A Trip to the Movies*, 155.

46. Méliès, "Kinematographic Views," 142; typescript letter from G. Méliès to [Merritt] Crawford, February 5, 1931, reproduced in Bowser, ed., *The Merritt Crawford Papers*, reel 3.

47. André Méliès, "La féerie familière," in Georges Sadoul, *Georges Méliès* (Paris: Seghers, 1961), 146. See also André Méliès, "Suite de la publication des Mémoires et notes d'André Méliès," ed. Marie-Hélène Lehérissey-Méliès, *Cinémathèque Méliès*, no. 14 (1989): 18–20.

48. André Méliès, "Suite de la publication des Mémoires et notes d'André Méliès," *Cinémathèque Méliès*, no. 16 (1990): 13.

49. André Méliès, "Suite de la publication des Mémoires et notes d'André Méliès," ed. Marie-Hélène Lehérissey-Méliès, *Cinémathèque Méliès*, no. 17 (1990): 17.

50. Jacques Malthête, "Georgette Méliès," trans. Aurore Spiers, in Jane Gaines, Radha Vatsal, and Monica Dall'Asta, eds., *Women Film Pioneers* (New York: Columbia University Libraries, 2016), https://wfpp.columbia.edu/pioneer/georgette-melies/.

51. Uncredited typescript translation of letter from G. Méliès to [Eugène] Lauste, November 29, 1930, reproduced in Bowser, ed., *The Merritt Crawford Papers*, reel 3.

52. Madeleine Malthête-Méliès, Anne-Marie Quévrain, and Jacques Malthête, *Essai de Reconstitution d'une Catalogue Français de la Star-Film, Suivi d'une Analyse Catalographique des Film de Georges Méliès Recensés en France* (Bois d'Arcy, France: Services des Archives du Film du Centre National de la Cinématographie, 1981), 234, 324, 338; André Méliès, "Suite de la publication des Mémoires et notes d'André Méliès," *Cinémathèque Méliès*, no. 17 (1990): 25.

53. Quoted in "Transcripts of the Roundtable on Georges Méliès," 151.

54. Quoted in "Transcripts of the Roundtable on Georges Méliès," 151, 155.

55. Letter from G. Méliès to Carl Vincent, January 16, 1937, reprinted in Malthête, ed., "Correspondance de Georges Méliès," 458.

56. André Ratouis, *Travail Garanti: Chambre Syndicale Corporative Unique, Institution Professionelle Démocratique et Sociale* (Paris: Clermont [Oise], 1880), 30, paraphrasing a February 8, 1866, gathering.

57. Bénard, "L'Enseignement Professionnel," *Franc Parleur Parisien*, no. 127 (September 5, 1887): 129; no. 128 (September 20, 1887): 137.

58. Méliès, "Kinematographic Views," 141.

59. J.[acques] Malthête, "Petite chronique historique des deux premières décennies du spectacle cinématographique: Un petit tour parmi les trucs," *Cinémathèque Méliès*, no. 4 (1983): 21–27; J.[acques] Malthête, "Petite chronique historique des deux premières décennies du spectacle cinématographique: Le monsieur de l'orchestre," *Cinémathèque Méliès*, no. 5 (1984): 6–13; Jacques Malthête, *Méliès, images et illusions* (Paris: Exporégie, 1996), 53–63; Jacques Malthête, "Les deux studios de Georges Méliès," in Malthête and Mannoni, eds., *Méliès, magie et cinéma*, 160–169.

60. André Méliès, "Suite de la publication des Mémoires et notes d'André Méliès," *Cinémathèque Méliès*, no. 14 (1989): 15–16.

61. Malthête, "Les deux studios de Georges Méliès," 135–159. See also Malthête, *Méliès, images et illusions*, 53–63.

62. This Montreuil office was seldom used, according to André Méliès, who reported that Méliès preferred using his office in the Passage de l'Opéra, where he often cut films. André Méliès, "Mémoires et notes d'André Méliès (suite)," ed. Marie-Hélène Lehérissey-Méliès, *Cinémathèque Méliès*, no. 18 (1991): 35.

63. Méliès, "Kinematographic Views," 136.

64. Jacques Malthête, Introduction to Méliès, "Kinematographic Views," 133–136; Roland Cosandey and Jacques Malthête, "Les Vues cinématographiques de Georges Méliès (1907): Le texte et ses parages," *Miscellanées Méliès*, no. 2 (2018): 17–25; Anne-Marie Quévrain, "Artificially Arranged Scenes: À propos des 'Vues Cinématographiques,'" *Cinémathèque Méliès*, no. 17 (1990): 12–17.

65. Roland Cosandey, "Georges Méliès as *L'Inescamotable Escamoteur*: A Study in Recognition," in Cherchi Usai, ed., *A Trip to the Movies*, 99n6.

66. Paolo Cherchi Usai, "The Institute for Incoherent Cinematography: An Introduction," in Cherchi Usai, ed., *A Trip to the Movies*, 25.

67. Méliès, "Kinematographic Views," 150.

68. Méliès, "Kinematographic Views," 142, 147.

69. André Méliès, "Suite de la publication des Mémoires et notes d'André Méliès," *Cinémathèque Méliès*, no. 17 (1990): 17. Compare Méliès, "Les Vues Cinématographiques," 373–377. On the difficulties of identifying Méliès' multiple collaborators, see Paolo Cherchi Usai, *Georges Méliès*, rev. ed. (Milan: Editrice Il Castoro, 2009), 103–104.

70. Paolo Cherchi Usai, *Silent Cinema: A Guide to Study, Research and Curatorship* (London: British Film Institute, 2019), 96.

71. Malthête, "Les deux studios de Georges Méliès," 155. See also Marie-Sophie Corcy, Jacques Malthête, Laurent Mannoni, Jean-Jacques Meusy, *Les Premières Années de la société L. Gaumont et Cie: Correspondance Commerciale de Léon Gaumont, 1895–1899* (Paris: Association française de recherche sur l'histoire du cinéma, 1999), 218.

72. Malthête, "La vie et l'œuvre de Georges Méliès," 24, 27; André Méliès, "Suite de la publication des Mémoires et notes d'André Méliès," *Cinémathèque Méliès*, no. 17 (1990): 21; Julien Dupuy, *Georges Méliès: À la conquête du cinématographe* (Paris: Studio Canal, 2011), 79.

73. Jacques Malthête, "L'appentis sorcier de Montreuil-sous-Bois," in Gaudreault and Le Forestier, with Tralongo, eds., *Méliès, carrefour des attractions*, 145–155.

74. Madeleine Malthête-Méliès, Anne-Marie Quévrain, and Jacques Malthête, *Essai de Reconstitution du Catalogue Français de la Star-Film, Suivi d'une Analyse Catalographique des Films de Georges Méliès Recensés en France* (Bois d'Arcy, France: Services des Archives du Film du Centre National de la Cinématographie, 1981), 115; Madeleine Malthête-Méliès, *Analyse Descriptive des Films de Georges Méliès Rassemblés entre 1981 et 1996 par la Cinémathèque Méliès* (Paris: Les Amis de Georges Méliès, 1996), 43–44; Solomon, review of *Georges Méliès*, 189; Frank Beaver, *Dictionary of Film Terms: The Aesthetic Companion to Film Art*, 5th ed. (New York: Peter Lang, 2015), 30.

75. Jacques Malthête, "Des précisions sur la carrière de Méliès!" *Cinémathèque Méliès*, no. 28 (1996): 28–31; letter from G. Méliès to Léon Loiseau, April 3, 1906, reprinted in Malthête, ed., "Correspondance de Georges Méliès," 321.

76. Méliès, "Kinematographic Views," 150.

77. Noverre, "L'œuvre de Georges Méliès: Etude rétrospective sur la prèmiere entreprise industrielle," 70.

78. Noverre, "L'œuvre de Georges Méliès: Etude rétrospective sur la prèmiere entreprise industrielle," 70; André Méliès, "Suite de la publication des Mémoires et notes d'André Méliès," *Cinémathèque Méliès*, no. 17 (1990): 20–21, 24. André Méliès reports that Méliès eventually replaced the double-cinematograph with two separate, independently operated, Pathé cameras and that his sister Georgette Méliès operated the second of the two.

79. Cherchi Usai, *Silent Cinema: A Guide*, 162. The parallax difference in framing produced by two side-by-side cameras allowed recent film presenters with access to parallel versions of the same title to anachronistically present Méliès' *Le Chaudron infernal* and *L'Oracle des Delphes* in stereoscopic 3D. Anne-Marie Quévrain and Jacques Malthête, "Nouvelle surprise, nouvel avatar: Des films de Méliès en 3D!" *Cinémathèque Méliès Lettre d'Information*, no. 28 (March 2010): 10–11.

80. Méliès, "Kinematographic Views," 137.

81. Quoted in "Transcripts of the Roundtable on Georges Méliès," 151.

82. Noverre, "L'œuvre de Georges Méliès: Etude rétrospective sur la prèmiere entreprise industrielle," 69–70; André Méliès, "Suite de la publication des Mémoires et notes d'André Méliès," *Cinémathèque Méliès*, no. 17 (1990): 24.

83. Méliès, "Kinematographic Views," 141–142.

84. Méliès, "Kinematographic Views," 145.

85. Méliès, "Kinematographic Views," 145. Compare Frank Kessler and Sabine Lenk, "L'adresse-Méliès," in Malthête and Marie, eds., *Georges Méliès, l'illusionniste fin de siècle?*, 183–199.

86. Méliès, "Suite de la publication des Mémoires et notes d'André Méliès," *Cinémathèque Méliès*, no. 17 (1990): 24.

87. Méliès, "Kinematographic Views," 145. See also David Mayer, "Acting in Silent Film: Which Legacy of the Theatre?," in Alan Lovell and Peter Krämer, eds., *Screen Acting* (London: Routledge, 1999), 10–30.

88. André Méliès, "Suite de la publication des Mémoires et notes d'André Méliès," *Cinémathèque Méliès*, no. 14 (1989): 21. Photographs of Méliès rehearsing actors were published as illustrations to Méliès, "Les Vues Cinématographiques," 379; and Georges Méliès, "The Silver Lining," *Sight & Sound* (Spring 1938): 9.

89. Méliès, "The Silver Lining," 7.

90. Méliès, "Les Vues Cinématographiques," 390–391; Noverre, "L'œuvre de Georges Méliès: Etude rétrospective sur la première entreprise industrielle," 63.

91. André Méliès, "Suite de la publication des Mémoires et notes d'André Méliès," *Cinémathèque Méliès*, no. 14 (1989): 18; André Méliès, "Suite de la publication des Mémoires et notes d'André Méliès," *Cinémathèque Méliès*, no. 17 (1990): 23; André Méliès, "Mémoires et notes d'André Méliès (suite)," *Cinémathèque Méliès*, no. 18 (1991): 37; André Méliès, "Mémoires et notes d'André Méliès," ed. Marie-Hélène Lehérissey-Méliès, *Cinémathèque Méliès*, no. 20 (1992): 16.

92. Malthête, "La vie et l'œuvre de Georges Méliès," 24; Astaix, quoted in "Transcripts of the Roundtable on Georges Méliès," 151, 153; Lallement, quoted in "Georges Méliès: Réunion du 17 février 1945," 14.

93. Malthête-Méliès, *Georges Méliès, L'Enchanteur*, 312–313. Photographs of Méliès' film developing laboratory were published as illustrations to Noverre, "L'œuvre de Georges Méliès: Etude rétrospective sur la prèmiere entreprise industrielle," 63.

94. Georges Méliès, "Le Théâtre Robert-Houdin (1845–1925)," *Passez Muscade*, no. 43 (1928): 515. Méliès notes that a number of Robert-Houdin's electrical illusions, which required much less electricity, were powered by bichromate batteries. This was the same type of power source used by Robert-Houdin. Christian Fechner, *The Magic of Robert-Houdin, "An Artist's Life": Biographical Essay*, ed. Todd Karr, trans. Stacey Dagron, vol. 1 (Boulogne: Editions F. C. F., 2002), 116, 237.

95. André Méliès, "Mémoires et notes d'André Méliès (suite)," *Cinémathèque Méliès*, no. 18 (1991): 37–38; Malthête-Méliès, *Georges Méliès*, 207–208. On Paulus as an Incohérent, see Catherine Charpin, *Les Arts Incohérents (1882–1893)* (Paris: Éditions Syros Alternatives, 1990), 33. The films were *Paulus chantant: Derrière l'omnibus* [lost], *Paulus chantant: Coquin de Printemps* [lost], and *Paulus chantant: Duelliste marseillais* [lost].

96. Mannoni, *Georges Méliès, la magie du cinéma*, 177; Solomon, *Disappearing Tricks*, 46; Christian Fechner, *The Magic of Robert-Houdin*, 2:25; "Les Prestidigitateurs Célèbres: Hamilton," *L'Illusionniste*, no. 10 (October 1902): 1.

97. Malthête-Méliès, Quévrain, and Malthête, *Essai de Reconstitution du Catalogue Français de la Star-Film*, 9.

98. Malthête, "Les deux studios de Georges Méliès," 152. Compare Méliès, "Les Vues Cinématographiques," 388.

99. André Méliès, "Suite de la publication des Mémoires et notes d'André Méliès," *Cinémathèque Méliès*, no. 14 (1989): 18.

100. François Caron, *Les grandes compagnies de chemin de fer en France, 1823–1937* (Geneva: Droz, 2005); Bernhard Siegert, *Relays: Literature as an Epoch of the Postal System*, trans. Kevin Repp (Stanford, Calif.: Stanford University Press, 1999); Simone M. Müller, *Wiring the World: The Social and Cultural Creation of Global Telegraph Networks* (New York: Columbia University Press, 2006).

101. André Méliès, "Suite de la publication des Mémoires et notes d'André Méliès," *Cinémathèque Méliès*, no. 17 (1990): 19.

102. *Complete Catalogue of Genuine and Original "Star Films"* (1903), 8; *Complete Catalogue of Genuine and Original "Star Films" (Moving Pictures)* (New York: Geo. Méliès, 1905), 1, 4.

103. See my "Negotiating the Bounds of Transnational Cinema with Georges Méliès, 1896–1908," *Early Popular Visual Culture* 14, no. 2 (2016): 155–167.

104. Paul Hammond, *Marvellous Méliès* (London: Gordon Fraser, 1974), 54; Rosa Cardona and Joan M. Minguet, "Méliès en Barcelona y en Madrid: La Expansión de la Fascinación," in Mannoni, *Georges Méliès: La Magia del Cine*, 183–191. See also Luke McKernan, *Charles Urban: Pioneering the Non-Fiction Film in Britain and America, 1897–1925* (Exeter: University of Exeter Press, 2013).

105. Yuri Tsivian, "Méliès in Russia: A Reception Study," in Cherchi Usai, ed., *A Trip to the Movies*, 113–135.

106. *Complete Catalogue of Genuine and Original "Star Films"* (1903), 8; *Complete Catalogue of Genuine and Original "Star Films"* (1905), 4.

107. Mannoni, *Georges Méliès, la magie du cinéma*, 266–268.

108. Méliès, "En marge de l'histoire du cinématographe," *Ciné-Journal*, no. 885 (August 13, 1926): 11.

109. James Lastra, *Sound Technology and the American Cinema: Perception, Representation, Modernity* (New York: Columbia University Press, 2000), 64–65.

Conclusion

1. Madeleine Malthête-Méliès, *Georges Méliès, L'Enchanteur* (Grandvilliers, France: La Tour Verte, 2011), 40–41. See also Georges Méliès, *La vie et l'œuvre d'un pionnier du cinéma*, ed. Jean-Pierre Sirois-Trahan (Paris: Éditions du Sonneur, 2012), 29–30.

2. André Méliès, "Suite de la publication des Mémoires et notes d'André Méliès," ed. Marie Hélène Lehérissey-Méliès, *Cinémathèque Méliès*, no. 14 (1989): 20.

3. André Méliès, "Suite de la publication des Mémoires et notes d'André Méliès," *Cinémathèque Méliès*, no. 14 (1989): 20. See also Laurent Mannoni, *Georges Méliès, la magie du cinéma* (Paris: Cinémathèque Française, 2020), 86, 88.

4. Méliès' early experiences with the mise-en-scène of a marionette theater were paralleled by another cinéaste who later made his own version of Faust, the German film

director F. W. Murnau, who "was given one of the little puppet theatres" when he was a boy, as his brother recalled, and had "used [it] to dramatize [...] fairy tales for our family audience." Quoted in "Murnau Remembered," in Lotte H. Eisner, *Murnau* (Berkeley: University of California Press, 1973), 14. As a child, Orson Welles also reportedly played with a puppet theater. Maurice Bessy, *Orson Welles: An Investigation into His Films and Philosophy*, trans. Ciba Vaughan (1963; New York: Crown Publishers, 1971), 4.

5. See esp. Erkki Huhtamo, "Twin-Touch-Test-Redux: Media Archaeological Approach to Art, Interactivity, and Tactility," in Oliver Grau, ed., *MediaArtHistories* (Cambridge, Mass.: MIT Press, 2006), 71–101; Erkki Huhtamo, "'Shaken Hands with Statues...': On Art, Interactivity and Tactility," in Christiane Paul, ed., *Second Natures: Faculty Exhibition of the UCLA Design / Media Arts Department* (Los Angeles: Regents of the University of California, 2006), 17–21.

6. Antonia Lant, "Haptical Cinema," *October*, no. 74 (1995): 45–46.

7. Advertisement, *Leeds Times* (December 27, 1884).

8. Meredith A. Bak, *Playful Visions: Optical Toys and the Emergence of Children's Media Culture* (Cambridge, Mass.: MIT Press, 2020), 21.

9. Charles Musser, "Toward a History of Screen Practice," *Quarterly Review of Film Studies* 9, no. 1 (1984): 59–69; Charles Musser, *The Emergence of Cinema: American Cinema to 1907* (New York: Charles Scribner's Sons, 1990), 15–54. See also Laurent Mannoni, *The Great Art of Light and Shadow: Archaeology of the Cinema*, trans. Richard Crangle (Exeter: University of Exeter Press, 2000); Olive Cook, *Movement in Two Dimensions: A Study of the Animated and Projected Pictures Which Preceded the Invention of Cinematography* (London: Hutchinson & Co., 1963); and Erkki Huhtamo, "Screen Tests: Why Do We Need an Archaeology of the Screen?" *Cinema Journal* 51, no. 2 (2012): 144–148.

10. S. M. Eisenstein, *Beyond the Stars: The Memoirs of Sergei Eisenstein*, ed. Richard Taylor, trans. William Powell (London: British Film Institute, 1995), 9, 290–291, 800n8. See also my "Visible and Invisible Hands: Chomón's Claymation and Object Animations," in Réjane Vallée, Jacques Malthête, and Stéphanie Salmon, eds., *Les Mille et Un Visages de Segundo de Chomón: Truqueur, Coloriste, Cinématographiste... et Pionnier du Cinématographe* (Villeneuve d'Ascq, France: Presses Universitaires du Septentrion; Paris: Fondation Jérôme Seydoux-Pathé, 2019), 102.

11. John Frazer, *Artificially Arranged Scenes: The Films of Georges Méliès* (Boston: G. K. Hall, 1979), 174–175.

12. Eisenstein, *Notes for a General History of Cinema*, 151, capitalization, emphasis removed.

13. Jacques Malthête, "Structure du théâtre Robert-Houdin sous la direction de Georges Méliès," in Jean-Luc Muller, ed., *Autour de Robert-Houdin* (Paris: Éditions Georges Proust, 2019), 209–232. See also Georges Méliès, "Le Théâtre Robert-Houdin (1845–1925)," *Passez Muscade*, no. 41 (1928): 495–497; no. 42 (1928): 503–505; no. 43 (1928): 513–516; no. 44 (1928): 519–521. Before Méliès became director, these shows included Lemercier de Neuville's Pupazzi and Dicksonn's Fantoches Artistiques. Conversation with Didier Moreau, August 22, 2016; Christian Fechner, "Le Théâtre Robert-Houdin, de Jean Eugène Robert-Houdin à Georges Méliès," in Laurent Mannoni and Jacques Malthête, eds., *Méliès,*

magie et cinéma (Paris: Paris-Musées, 2002), 91. See also Lemercier de Neuville, *Souvenirs d'un Montreur de Marionnettes* (Paris: Maurice Bauche Éditeur, 1911), 316.

14. Geo. Méliès, "Le Théâtre Robert-Houdin (1845–1925)," *Passez Muscade*, no. 42 (1928): 503.

15. John Gaughan, with Jim Steinmeyer, *Antonio Diavolo: A Souvenir of His Performance: Concerning the History and Restoration of Robert-Houdin's Celebrated Trapeze Automaton* (1986; n.p.: by the authors, 1999), 9. See also Christian Fechner, *La Magie de Robert-Houdin: "Secrets des Soirées Fantastiques,"* vol. 3 (Boulogne: Editions F. C. F., 2005), 380–383, and Adolphe Blind, *Les Automates Truqués* (Geneva: Édition Ch. Eggimann; Paris: Éditions Bossard, 1927), 42–46.

16. Geo. Méliès, "Le Théâtre Robert-Houdin," 503.

17. Fechner, *La Magie de Robert-Houdin*, 3:202–207, 332–345, 380–383, 404–409. On the former, see also my "Trick Automatons as Media Archaeology: *Antonio Diavolo,"* *Early Popular Visual Culture* 18, no. 4 (2020): 448–460.

18. Christian Bailly, with Sharon Bailly, *Automata: The Golden Age, 1848–1914* (London: Sotheby's, 1987); Christian Bailly and Sharon Bailly, *Automata at bagatelle* (Paris: Association des Amis des Automates, poupées et Jouets Anciens, 1993), 20–21.

19. Pathé produced a number of films during this period that ostensibly involved automatons, including *Enfants terribles.*

20. *Complete Catalogue of Genuine and Original "Star Films" (Moving Pictures)* (New York: Geo. Méliès, 1908), 106.

21. Méliès, *La vie et l'œuvre d'un pionnier du cinéma*, 29.

22. René Perrout, *Tresors des Images d'Epinal* (1910–1912; Paris: Editions Jean-Pierre Gyss, 1985), 215–216.

23. Fechner, "Le Théâtre Robert-Houdin," 89–90; Paul Hammond, *Marvellous Méliès* (London: Gordon Fraser, 1974), 15.

24. For examples dating from the second half of the nineteenth century, see *Collection Christian Fechner: Magie et illusionnisme* (Paris: H. Gros—G. Delettrez, 2004), 70–76, and *The Christian Fechner Collection of American and European Magic*, part 3 (New York: Swann Galleries, 2007), 177–187.

25. *The Christian Fechner Collection*, part 3, 181.

26. Bak, *Playful Visions*, 15.

27. Fechner, "Le Théâtre Robert-Houdin," 91–93; Fechner, *The Magic of Robert-Houdin, "An Artist's Life": Biographical Essay*, ed. Todd Karr, trans. Stacey Dagron, vol. 1 (Boulogne: Editions F. C. F., 2002), 299–305. Voisin's 1895 catalogue advertised an illusion credited to Méliès. Jacques Deslandes, *Le boulevard du cinéma à l'époque de Georges Méliès* (Paris: Editions du Cerf, 1963), 44fn1.

28. "G. Méliès," *L'Illusionniste*, no. 21 (September 1903): 169.

29. *Appareils de Prestidigitation & Trucs Pour Théâtres De Fabrication française et irréprochable mis en vente par Caroly*, no. 4 (Paris: Académie de Magie, c.1911).

30. "Nouveautés de la Maison Caroly," *L'Illusionniste*, no. 84 (December 1908): 127.

31. Bernard Lonjon, *Émile Reynaud, Le veritable inventeur du cinéma* (Polignac: Éditions du Roure, 2007), 94–96.

32. Méliès, *La vie et l'œuvre d'un pionnier du cinéma*, 31–32.

33. Maurice Noverre, *La Vérité sur l'invention de la projection animée: Émile Reynaud, sa vie et ses travaux*, ed. Sébastian Roffat (1926; Paris: L'Harmattan, 2013). See also Maurice Noverre, "La vérité sur les premières projections publiques de séries chronophotographiques," *Nouvel Art Cinématographique*, 2d ser., no. 5 (January 1930): 47–50.

34. David Robinson, "Incunabula of Animation," *Griffithiana*, no. 38/39 (1990): 217.

35. Robinson, "Incunabula of Animation," 217.

36. *Complete Catalogue of Genuine and Original "Star Films"* (1905), 36.

37. Madeleine Malthête-Méliès, Anne-Marie Quévrain, and Jacques Malthête, *Essai de Reconstitution du Catalogue Français de la Star-Film, Suivi d'une Analyse Catalographique des Films de Georges Méliès Recensés en France* (Bois d'Arcy, France: Services des Archives du Film du Centre National de la Cinématographie, 1981), 164.

38. Quotations from *Complete Catalogue of Genuine and Original "Star Films"* (1905), 36.

39. Quotations from *Complete Catalogue of Genuine and Original "Star Films"* (1905), 36.

40. Frazer, *Artificially Arranged Scenes*, 129–130.

41. An 1897 directory of French toymakers included around a dozen different firms that advertised magic lanterns. A. Clavel, *Annuaire des Jouets: Annuaire Officiel des Jouets & Jeux, des Bazars, Bimbeloterie, Articles de Paris et des Industries Annexes* (Paris: Chambre Syndicale des Fabricants de Jouets et Jeux, 1897), 19, 21–22, 27, 30–31, 46, 66, 92–93, 114.

42. Clavel, *Annuaire des Jouets*, 27, 47. In the American catalogue description this was described as a "monster." *Complete Catalogue of Genuine and Original "Star Films"* (1905), 36.

43. Georges Méliès, "En marge de l'histoire du cinématographe," *Ciné-Journal*, no. 883 (July 30, 1926): 9.

44. Thierry Lecointe, with Pascal Fouché, *Des fragments de films Méliès disparus ressuscités par des flip books (1896–1901)* (New Barnet: John Libbey Publishing, 2020), 161–262.

45. Marie-Hélène Lehérissey, email communication to the author, January 16, 2021.

46. Turgan, "L'Exposition Universelle: Les Jouets," *Univers Illustré* (November 9, 1878): 703; *Annuaire-Almanach du Commerce et de l'Industrie* (Paris: Didot-Bottin, 1888), 1480.

47. "Quelques Jeux du Même Éditeur," appended to *En Afrique: Nouveau Jeu de Voyages* (Paris: Watilliaux, 1897), 1–13.

48. "Brevets d'Invention," *Bulletin des lois de la République française*, no. 1500 (Paris: Imprimerie Nationale, 1893) 441; "Catalogue Complet des Brevets Français délivrés au 31 octobre 1891," *Revue Industrielle* (November 7, 1891): 451; "Quelques Jeux du Même Éditeur," 14–18, 20–21.

49. G[uillaume]-Michel Coissac, *Histoire du Cinématographe, de ses origines à nos jours* (Paris: Éditions du "Cinéopse," 1925), 593; "Brevets d'Invention," *Photo-Gazette* 9, no. 4 (February 25, 1899): ix.

50. *Annuaire du Commerce et de l'Industrie Photographiques* (Paris: Aux Bureau de la Photo-Revue, 1902), 161. See also Lecointe, with Fouché, *Des fragments de films Méliès disparus*, 53n3.

51. "Le voyage a Pékin par air, par fer, par terre et par mer: jeu nouveau" [catalogue entry], Pennsylvania State University Libraries, https://catalog.libraries.psu.edu/catalog/17038590.

52. Georges Méliès, "Kinematographic Views," trans. Stuart Liebman and Timothy Barnard, in André Gaudreault, *Film and Attraction: From Kinematography to Cinema* (Urbana: University of Illinois Press, 2011), 139. See esp. Jacques Rittaud-Hutinet, *Le Cinéma des origines: Les frères Lumière et ses operateurs* (Paris: Champ Vallon, 1985); Bernard Chardère, *Le roman des Lumière* (Paris: Éditions Gallimard, 1995), 386–439; Jacques Aumont, "Lumière Revisited," trans. Ben Brewster, *Film History* 8, no. 4 (1996): 416–430; Jacques Malthête, "Gaston Méliès aux États-Unis," in *Le Cinéma Français Muet dans le Monde: Influences réciproques* (Toulouse: Cinémathèque de Toulouse, Institut Jean Vigo, 1988), 175–179; Jacques Malthête, ed., *Le Voyage autour du monde de la G. Méliès Manufacturing Company (juillet 1912–mai 1913)* (Paris: Association "Les Amis de Georges Méliès," 1988); Malthête-Méliès, *Georges Méliès*, 385–391; and Anne-Marie Quévrain, "Pourquoi Gaston Méliès," *Cinémathèque Méliès*, no. 14 (1989): 9–12; *Cinémathèque Méliès*, no. 15 (1989): 31–36. See also the documentary film *Gaston Méliès and His Wandering Star Film Company* (Raphaël Millet, 2015).

53. Edouard Fournier, *Histoire des jouets et des jeux d'enfants* (Paris: E. Dentu, Éditeur, 1889), 2.

54. Henry René d'Allemagne, *Histoire des jouets* (Paris: Libriairie Hachette & Cie, 1902), 7. See also Mary Hillier, *Dolls and Doll-makers* (London: Weidenfeld and Nicolson, 1968), 43; Léo Claretie, *Les Jouets: Histoire–Fabrication* (Paris: Ancienne Maison Quantin Librairies–Imprimeries Réuines, 1893), iii.

55. Claretie, *Les Jouets*, ii–iii.

56. Claretie, *Les Jouets*, iii–iv, 70, quotation in English.

57. Claretie, *Les Jouets*, 89–98. See also "Rapport de la Chambre syndicale de la Literie & des Industries qui s'y Rattachent sur la Queston du Travail dans les Prisons," *Le Jouet* 6, no. 6 (September 1896): 44–48.

58. Brian Selznick, *The Invention of Hugo Cabret* (New York: Scholastic, 2007), 34–35; Brian Selznick, *The Hugo Movie Companion* (New York: Scholastic Press, 2011), 84–87.

59. Colin Williamson, *Hidden in Plain Sight: An Archaeology of Magic and the Cinema* (New Brunswick, N.J.: Rutgers University Press, 2015), 157.

60. Williamson, *Hidden in Plain Sight*, 159.

61. Clavel, *Annuaire des Jouets*, 32.

62. *Guide Remboursable de Paris* (Paris: Guides Nilsson, 1910), 160.

63. According to Malthête-Méliès, d'Alcy was Méliès' mistress for about six years during the 1890s while appearing at the Théâtre Robert-Houdin. Malthête-Méliès, "Jehanne d'Alcy, la prèmiere Star du monde," *Cinémathèque Méliès*, no. 22 (1993): 20–29.

64. Letter from Chemins de Fer de l'État Direction Contentieux Bureau to Manieux, February 13, 1922, Cinémathèque Méliès. See also "Georges Méliès: Réunion du 17 février 1945," 3–4, 6, 9, Fonds Commission de Recherche Historique, Cinémathèque Française, CRH20-B1, http://www.cineressources.net/consultation-Pdf/web/a000/037.pdf.

65. Malthête-Méliès, *Georges Méliès*, 433, 436; "Jehanne d'Alcy, la prèmiere Star du monde," part 2, *Cinémathèque Méliès*, no. 23 (1993): 22, 27–28.

66. Madeleine Malthête-Méliès, "Jehanne d'Alcy," 24–25, 28. See also *Cinémathèque Méliès*, no. 22 (1992): 0.

67. The second kiosk was located in a more remote part of the station and was partly concealed by a pillar. Malthête-Méliès, *Georges Méliès*, 454.

68. Malthête-Méliès, "Jehanne d'Alcy," part 2, 31.

69. Mannoni, *Georges Méliès, la magie du cinéma*, 280–281. For examples of autochrome images, see Bertrand Lavédrine and Jean-Paul Gandolfo, with Christine Capderou and Ronan Guinée, *The Lumière Autochrome: History, Technology, and Preservation*, trans. John McElhone (Los Angeles: Getty Conservation Institute, 2013). Compare the trichrome by Auguste and Louis Lumière, *Les Jouets de Noël 1898*, reproduced in Beaussant Lefèvre, *Livres et Autographes Photographies* (Paris: Drouot, 2016), 70.

70. See, for example, Charles Péan, "La Question des Couleurs," *Jouet Français* 1, no. 3 (July 1888): 21–22; G.S., "Jouets Empoisonnés," *Jouet Français* 5, no. 9 (December 1895): 71–72; A.C., "Jouets Empoisonnés," *Jouet Français* 5, no. 11 (February 1896): 86. At least one firm, Bourgeois Aîné, sold "safe colorants" to French toymakers. Clavel, *Annuaire des Jouets*, 24.

71. Letter from Méliès to Auguste Drioux, March 27, 1929, reprinted in Jacques Malthête, ed., "Correspondance de Georges Méliès (1904–1937)," in André Gaudreault and Laurent Le Forestier, with Stéphane Tralongo, eds., *Méliès, carrefour des attractions, suivi de correspondance de Georges Méliès (1904–1937)* (Rennes: Presses Universitaires de Rennes, 2014), 355.

72. Malthête-Méliès, *Georges Méliès*, 405, 421, 433, 459; Malthête, ed., "Correspondance de Georges Méliès," 407fn281.

73. Manuscript letter from G. Méliès to [Merritt] Crawford, December 8, 1930, reproduced in Eileen Bowser, ed., *The Merritt Crawford Papers* (Lanham, Md.: University Publications of America, 1986), microfilm, reel 3.

74. Mannoni and Malthête, eds., *Méliès, magie et cinéma*, 30; Malthête and Mannoni, *L'Œuvre de Georges Méliès*, 322, 324. See also *Cinémathèque Méliès*, no. 22 (1993): 30, where it is dated 1929.

75. Méliès, *La vie et l'œuvre d'un pionnier du cinéma*, 87. Malthête-Méliès writes that the kiosk was open from 8:30 in the morning until 11 o'clock at night, although her grandfather recalled a slightly longer working day in the kiosk, from 7 in the morning until 10 in the evening.

76. Quotations from André Méliès, "Suite de la publication des Mémoires et notes d'André Méliès," ed. Marie-Hélène Léherissey-Méliès, *Cinémathèque Méliès*, no. 16 (1990): 16; and Maurice Noverre, "L'œuvre de Georges Méliès: Etude retrospective sur le premier « Studio cinématographique » machiné pour la prise de vues théâtrales," *Nouvel Art Cinématographique*, 2d ser., no. 3 (July 1929): 73.

77. Malthête-Méliès, "Jehanne d'Alcy," part 2, 27–28. See also Malthête-Méliès, *Georges Méliès*, 459.

78. Letter from Chemins de Fer de l'État Direction Contentieux Bureau to Manieux, February 17, 1930, Cinémathèque Méliès.

79. Philippe Dagen, "17 oeuvres des Arts incohérents," *Le Monde*, February 3, 2021.

INDEX

Printed and bound by CPI Group (UK) Ltd, Croydon, CR0 4YY

09/06/2025

14686135-0001